YEARNINGS

W9-ACL-167

"This wonderful book does what so many like it fail to do: embrace the magic of day-to-day living, the spirituality that can be found in our questions, our mistakes, our passions, and our doubts. Life is indeed messy, but as Irwin Kula shows us, sorting through it is what transforms us to higher ground, and there is wisdom in how the heart approaches what it yearns."

> —Mitch Albom, author of *For One More Day*, *Tuesdays With Morrie*, and *The Five People You Meet in Heaven*

"Irwin Kula shows us how to live our humanness—the pleasures and the challenges, the messiness and the triumphs—with a profound acceptance of our desires and foibles and a joy that can only come from understanding."

> —Deepak Chopra, author of *Peace Is the Way* and *How to Know God*

"Profound but accessible, challenging but persuasive, rooted in tradition but filled with startling insights, this book will leave you looking at yourself and the world differently. Highly recommended."

> —Harold Kushner, author of *When Bad Things Happen to Good People*

"*Yearnings* is pure silk for the soul, a book that contains that quality of soul wisdom that comes from the heart of the Jewish tradition. This alchemy of soul and heart is destined to make this book a classic."

> —Caroline Myss, author of *Anatomy of the Spirit* and *Sacred Contracts*

"Irwin Kula is a masterful teacher. He is passionate about his message and every page shimmers with excitement as he conveys his inner knowing that 'you can become all that you yearn to manifest'—very readable!"

> —Dr. Wayne W. Dyer, author of *Inspiration* and *The Power of Intention*

"A wonderful guide to love and clarity through the many different joys and sorrows we encounter. These meaningful insights from Jewish wisdom are important to anyone wanting to engage fully with life and are conveyed with a beautiful spirit."

> —Sharon Salzberg, author of *Lovingkindness* and *Faith*

"Once you see the world through Irwin Kula's eyes, you will never see it quite the same way again. *Yearnings* is brimming with Kula's essential, pervasive, and paradoxical insights and moving stories. Reading *Yearnings* is a life-transforming experience."

 —Rabbi Joseph Telushkin, author of *A Code of Jewish Ethics* and
  Jewish Literacy

"Passionate, eloquent, personal, and profound. In an era when popular books by spiritual teachers abound, this gem of a book stands out from the crowd. Readers of all backgrounds (both secular and religious) will find themselves returning to this book again and again as they struggle to deal with life's everyday practical, ethical, and spiritual challenges."

 —Jeremy D. Safran, Ph.D., Professor and Director of Clinical
  Psychology, New School for Social Research

"This sagacious book will be a blessing to all who read its teaching on the value of spiritual yearning."

 —*Spirituality & Health*

"Provocative, engaging, and transforming, *Yearnings* is a shofar blast of a book that will open your eyes and stir you, inspiring you to break free of inertia and move forward in your spiritual evolution."

 —*Jewish Woman*

"Kula identifies seven 'yearnings' . . . describing them with warmth and wit and showing how these yearnings can be not so much fulfilled as adjusted and transformed in the context of a real life. Highly recommended."

 —*Library Journal*

"This book, written for Jews and non-Jews, weaves insight and practices from the Jewish tradition, demonstrating the great legacy of our people's wisdom."

 —*Sh'ma*

YEARNINGS

YEARNINGS

EMBRACING THE SACRED MESSINESS OF LIFE

IRWIN KULA

WITH LINDA LOEWENTHAL

hachette
BOOKS

NEW YORK   BOSTON

Hachette Books
Hachette Book Group
1290 Avenue of the Americas
New York, NY 10104

www.HachetteBookGroup.com

Printed in the United States of America

RRD-H

Originally published by Hyperion.
First Hachette Books trade edition: November 2014

10   9   8   7   6

Hachette Books is a division of Hachette Book Group, Inc.
The Hachette Books name and logo are trademarks of Hachette Book Group, Inc.

The Hachette Speakers Bureau provides a wide range of authors for speaking events. To find
out more, go to www.hachettespeakersbureau.com or call (866) 376-6591.

The publisher is not responsible for websites (or their content) that are not owned
by the publisher.

Design by Karen Minster

The Library of Congress has catalogued the hardcover edition of this book as follows:

Kula, Irwin.
Yearnings : embracing the sacred messiness of life /
by Irwin Kula with Linda Loewenthal.
p. cm.
Includes bibliographical references.
ISBN 1-4013-0192-4
1. Spiritual life—Judiasm.   2. Life—Religious aspects—Judaism.
3. Jewish way of life.   4. Desire—Religious aspects—Judaism.
I. Loewenthal, Linda.   II. Title.
BM723.K83 2006
296.7'2—dc22
2006018823

ISBN 978-1-4013-0913-8 (pbk.)

TO
DANA,
GABRIELLA,
& TALIA,

who teach me
the meaning of life
every day

"Keep two pieces of paper in your pockets at all times.
One that says 'I am a speck of dust.'
And the other, 'The world was created for me.'"

—Rabbi Bunim of P'shiskha

"Where is the thread now?
Off again?
The old trick!
Only I discern
Infinite passion and the pain of
Finite hearts that yearn."

—Robert Browning

CONTENTS

PREFACE

YEARNING. AFTER TWENTY-THREE YEARS AS A RABBI, I can think of no more defining human experience. So many people speak to me about their longing to answer life's deepest questions. Especially in recent years, when world events seem to be more confusing and frightening, people are looking for a center that can hold in what they see as a growing wasteland of conflicts and contradictions. They yearn for peace that comes from unity. They seek enduring truths. They hope for comfort and guidance.

Great wisdom traditions are born of this desire for answers, this urge to make sense out of chaos and discover what really matters in life. What we forget in the rush of modern life—a lapse that I believe intensifies our fear—is that these yearnings are no different today than they were in the times that gave rise to such mystic visionaries as Moses, Buddha, and Jesus. In those times, too, people were challenging traditional ideas and beliefs, and asking new questions. Institutions they had always relied on were changing, and even tumbling down. Old ways of believing, behaving, and belonging that provided meaning and security were dying and new ways had not yet been born. Like us, people were at once fearful and excited, uncertain yet animated about emerging truths and understandings.

Whether it's Buddhism, Christianity, Islam, or Judaism, wisdom traditions are rich with methods and philosophies designed to support and guide us, to help us explore and deepen our understanding of ourselves and the world. These traditions are meant to be lived. Yet so much of their wisdom is buried under centuries of dogma. Often they become a means of claiming the superiority of certain religions, cultures, and ideologies. The need to be right is winning out over the search. Ideas and insights meant to illuminate the human experience, to explore conflicts and dualities, are being used to dampen, dispel, or repress exploration and conversation, sometimes erupting into culture wars or violence.

As the world around us becomes more confusing and frightening, many of us have turned inward to find some kind of solace. The quest for self is the contemporary quest for God. We want to know exactly who we are. We want to find perfect love; to feel enduring happiness and fulfillment; to know that our work will make a difference in the world. And this personal search for purpose, joy, and contentment can be just as noble as the search for grand philosophical truths and global solutions.

This is a psychological age, the era of self-improvement and personal growth, one that offers a unique opportunity to explore and reengage with wisdom traditions. All the contradictions and conflicts that we experience in the world are born deep within our consciousness. When we look into our selves and discover what is radiant and dull, ugly and beautiful, clear and confusing, harsh and gentle, it isn't just ourselves we're discovering; we're unfolding the mysteries of the universe. If we can become aware of these polarities; embrace them, even celebrate them, we are taking a giant step toward what the mystical tradition of Kabbalah calls repairing the world.

Wisdom traditions are meant to be lived.

Americans are sometimes accused of being blindly optimistic and materialistic. We want it all. And this does have its drawbacks. We can become overly driven or consumed by our desires. But, paradoxically, if we don't want it all, we'll never find enough. We'll never come close to reaching our own potential. At the same time, if we forget that we're always wanting and always finding, meaning will continue to elude us, and so will the love and joy we seek.

Jewish wisdom teaches that our yearnings generate life. Desire animates. As the prophet Amos says, "Seek Me and live." Jewish wisdom urges us to go for it, to seek answers to our deepest questions, to search for spiritual and personal fulfillment while knowing we will never finally get there—oh, but the discoveries we'll make along the way! We are meant to live, to search with intention. When we can uncover our deepest longings for intimacy, pleasure, creativity, and self-understanding, life yields illumination and happiness. Far from being a burden, our desires themselves become a path to blessing.

Jewish wisdom offers powerful ideas and tools for living with the anxieties of contemporary life: its ambiguities, its contradictions, its insecurities. I hope it won't sound grandiose to say that I want to help create a new understanding of our contemporary experience by digging deep into this ancient tradition.

Our yearnings generate life.
Our desire animates us.

Through both contemporary and biblical stories, I will explore methods of the sages, showing how we can use this wisdom to examine our own lives. These will not be lessons about overcoming all odds, obeying some external command, or finding some ultimate truth. Rather, they will be teachings that celebrate the inevitable messiness of life, of living with grace in uncertainty. Far from keeping us in line, this wisdom tries to push us off line. Crossing boundaries is the only way to grow. No one knew this better than the biblical authors who wrote about generations of transgressors and adventurers whose yearnings and foibles pushed them beyond their familiar selves; whose journeys took them to the place between meaning and meaninglessness, to the borders of promised lands.

Rather than teach absolute truths, Jewish teachings invite us to dance with dualities and contradictions: Life and Death; Hate and Love; Right and Wrong; Sorrow and Joy. There is no perfect balance nor final solutions; no end to the highs and lows, to the darkness and the light. And thank God, because there's so much richness, so much dimension, in those tensions and anxieties; so many opportunities to deepen our understanding. Building a life is an endless and glorious project.

The practices and insights in this book are based on teachings that have evolved over three thousand years. Generations of mystics and sages have wrestled with profound questions and challenges, the messiness and complexities of the human experience, and they invite us to do the same. There are no scripts to be found in their many texts, no fixed choreography to be followed in the dance of life. Rather, this wisdom is an intricate improvisation, complete with rhythms, melodies, cues, and many dancing partners to accompany us, teach us, and support us.

Jewish wisdom invites us to allow sadness into the circle of joy, to bless our carnal pleasures, to fully express our grief, to both give and receive with generosity. Our most intimate relationships or, in religious language, our covenantal relationships are often the most challenging improvisations: dances of pain and forgiveness, excitement and boredom, hunger and satisfaction.

Life is an endless and glorious project.

Our jobs and careers are the playgrounds for our yearnings for success and accomplishment; where we play out patterns of childhood and our need to make a difference in the world; where we struggle with failure and financial need; where we compete and create partnerships.

These life challenges can be informed by such religious ideas as covenant, holiness, sacrifice, commandment, idolatry, Messiah, and Sabbath. They may seem anachronistic or confining, but when turned inside out offer dynamic, adaptable, even radical methods for broadening our perspective in all areas of life. They become lenses through which to see and celebrate our unending complexity. They facilitate and enrich our infinite unfolding.

Please join me on an excursion into the depths of this ancient tradition and into seven of our most wondrous yearnings. My deepest wish is that these insights drawn from the wells of Jewish wisdom will inform and enrich your own search for meaning; that they will bring both support and delight into your daily lives.

YEARNINGS

YEARNING FOR
TRUTH

HUMBLE ABSOLUTES

"WHEN YOU'VE GOT AN ANSWER, IT'S TIME TO FIND better questions."

My mother said this countless times during my childhood, especially when I'd come home from school, passionate about an idea I'd learned from a teacher I admired. I'd be showing off to my brothers, arguing my point over dinner, and my mother would inevitably present her challenge. My resistance followed just as inevitably: She wasn't a scholar—she should learn from me. But then I would quickly sober under her fierce gaze and raised eyebrow.

"What have other teachers taught? What other questions need to be asked? Maybe there's more." And soon I'd be wandering into my father's study to find out. When I emerged, I invariably had a new insight to report to my mother, an answer that finally would floor her. But this merely led to a whole new round of heated discussions. My mother embodied a central Jewish teaching: Every answer to our important questions leads to a new important question. The truth *can* set us free, but only if we're always in the process of discovering it.

She taught this message in many other ways as well. When my five brothers and I fought, she never wanted to know what "really" happened, who was at fault, who hit first. If one of us would try to blame the other, she'd say, "And you? Are you one hundred percent blameless?" My mother had the uncanny ability to recognize that a single story should never be told as though it's the only one, that truth lived in every telling, and that there was no escape from responsibility for our own decisions. She taught me that precisely when I was sure I was right, this was a signal to look at the other person's feelings and point of view. If I didn't, there was no winning. And when I did, winning no longer seemed to be the point.

Throughout the centuries sages have tried to pry us loose from our certainties so that we can discover still deeper insights and expand our moral universe. They understood that since no two human situations are identical, every answer is by its nature a provisional one. There always will be another moral dilemma tomorrow and another the next day. There are never final answers to life's big questions; only more profound questions. There's something so liberating and expansive about this teaching. The search for truth is not about letting go; it's about going deeper. The goal is not reaching a single realization but living the process of realizing again and again.

> **The search for truth is not about letting go; it's about going deeper. The goal is not reaching a single realization, but living the process of realizing again and again.**

Jewish wisdom encourages us to be sacred skeptics. Many think skepticism is paralyzing, hopeless, cynical; but it's the opposite. Skepticism inspires us to know more. Skepticism can be revelatory. When we both hold and question our truths we become lifelong learners rather than absolute knowers—as well as more interesting and much easier people to be with. Not seduced by certainty, we can be open to the truth.

Yet in all my years as a spiritual counselor I've never met anyone who doesn't want answers, who doesn't hope that at some point in his or her life everything will fall into place. We long for a comfortable landing place, the contentment of completion: in short, the truth of who we are and what we've been. We may pride ourselves in being open-minded, accepting, and flexible but we all maintain beliefs we consider self-evident: ideas and unquestioned presumptions that surface when the going gets tough, when we feel challenged or most vulnerable.

The world at large and American society in particular are polarized by opposing, hard-held answers to controversial issues: abortion and capital punishment; who may or may not marry; even how the world was created, to name just a few. Unfortunately, the wisdom traditions designed to help us deepen our questions—from religion to science, philosophy to psychology—have become disciplines of knowing, for defending absolutes.

We've forgotten that as mere mortals we are meant to search as much as to find. After all, each of us has had only a few decades of what has been a fourteen-billion-year evolution. We are finite creatures. How could we possibly have access to what is infinite: some all-encompassing Truth about the world or even our True selves? The fact is that there is no issue, large or small, that we can understand fully. When we think we've found the final truth we're a little less alive, a little less awake, and the world itself is diminished.

There's a wonderful story that imagines an all-knowing, infinite God, one who would surely have access to the Truth but who actually sees more value in the search. In this story, the God character wakes up on the sixth day of Creation with what may be the most creative idea ever: humankind. Full of wonder and excitement, God can hardly wait to get to work. As so many of us do before we undertake a momentous task or face a risky venture, God first asks for the advice of consultants, in this case the angels. But the angels are ambivalent, undecided, caught between Truth and Love. Truth argues against the idea of humanity, fearing that human beings will lie and kill in their pursuit of Truth. But Love understands that humanity will engage in great acts of altruism and self-sacrifice, and that God's desire is born out of that most powerful of yearnings: the yearning to love.

In the end God decides to go with Love, and in that moment has a realization: Truth on earth cannot be what it is in heaven. In heaven there is Truth; on earth there are truths. Absolute truth cannot exist for any human being. And so Truth is cast out of heaven and down to the earth. There Truth is shattered into pieces, fragments of it everywhere, so many that they are impossible to count. And Adam, the very first human being, is created out of the dust of the earth, out of those very

shards of Truth. From now on there will be only partial, multiple, and
contradictory truths. And human beings will search
forever for truths within themselves and throughout
the entire world. Life will be an ongoing act of creating,
revealing, and discovering. Each person, each culture,
each religion has part of the truth; none has it all.

**In heaven there
is Truth; on earth
there are truths.**

The sages who wrote this story understood, as my mother did, that
we are meant to yearn for truth; to continually search. It's built into our
DNA. At the same time, there are infinite ideas, feelings, and intuitions
swirling around and within us, no matter how we may try to streamline
our lives. We so often feel conflicted, stuck between opposing positions.
This can be unnerving, even frightening. How can we contain the anxiety and confusion? The sages remind us that more expansive and profound truths lie within every conflict awaiting our discovery. When we
meet a paradox, we have the hope of making progress in discovering
truth.

The Talmud, the classic Jewish wisdom text, has been studied for
more than fifteen hundred years. No wonder. It contains four hundred
years of recorded debates about human life and is brimming with paradoxes and insights about how to enrich our lives. There are truths
tumbling onto truths, echoing off each other, allowing the reader to interpret and decide. Among the most intense of the Talmud's arguments
are those between two ancient philosophers and legalists named Hillel
and Shammai.

Each had his own academy and different approach, much like contemporary think tanks such as the Brookings Institute and the Heritage
Foundation; the Chicago School of Economics and the London School of
Economics; the Freudians and the Jungians. Students would study and
discuss issues that ranged from sweeping social policies to everyday life.

Periodically the academies would emerge with decisions, most of
which were in direct opposition to each other: two very different truths.
Then the fun would begin. Hillel and Shammai would have a grand debate. How do we create economic justice? What do couples do when

love fails? How do we make time sacred? What does it mean to be vulnerable in this world? One might think clear decisions would be necessary and appropriate given the weightiness of these matters. But rather than provide answers or a simple list of rules to follow, the Talmud shows us the arguments of these great philosophical schools. It invites us into their sparring matches and reveals the contradictions for us to contemplate.

In the large majority of cases when a decision was reached, the verdict would go according to Hillel. But it wasn't because Hillel was objectively correct. The Talmud says about both teachings "These and these are the words of the living God." So why did the rulings go to Hillel's school? Because of Hillel's ethics of discovery, the spiritual practice of his search, the method of investigation. The school of Hillel always studied and wrestled with Shammai's opinions, often teaching them before its own. Hillel's school understood and valued the partial truth of the other side, and they used Shammai's insights to inform their own, to broaden their perspective, to come up with the most inclusive answer. In other words, every truth has the potential to lead to a wider reality. Every truth offers a deeper understanding of life. Hillel didn't win at the expense of Shammai; he won for the benefit of us all.

The teacher who first taught me about these great debates was a wonderful man named Rabbi Mordechai Glatzer. I was eleven and he seemed ancient to me at the time, a real grandfather type, but in fact he was only middle-aged. He was one of the most traditionally observant Jews in the Jewish day school I attended, and he is the gentlest person I've ever met. I, on the other hand, was a problematic student, to say the least. I would shout out answers, get up and walk out of class when I got bored, and talk to my friends. I got away with constant misbehavior only because I got good grades; otherwise, I have no doubt I would have been expelled, or at least regularly suspended. As punishment I spent half of my fifth grade year sitting in the back of the third grade class doing my lessons, and incredible amounts of time in the hallway or in the principal's office.

But Rabbi Glatzer had a very different approach than my other teachers had. He sat me in a chair at the front of the classroom, right next to his desk. Whenever I would fidget, shout out an answer, or turn around to motion to a friend, he would come over, still teaching, and gently stroke my face and say under his breath, "It's okay, it's okay." He had the softest hands I can remember. And I would immediately calm down. He was the first teacher who accepted me, who could see my intelligence and my lack of self-control and somehow hold them both together. And when he died suddenly from a heart attack toward the end of that year, it was my first devastating loss. I wondered if any heart could love that much for that long without breaking from the effort.

I was grateful to him on so many levels, especially for bringing those two ancient schools, Hillel and Shammai, into my life. The idea that disagreement and friction led to revelation appealed to both my intellect and my rambunctiousness. And the fact that Rabbi Glatzer was so wedded to the most conservative interpretations of the tradition in his own life made it all the more striking that he valued the openness and dissonance of these ancient scholars. Like Hillel, he embodied this thinking. Like my mother, he shaped my thinking forever.

Whenever I disagree with someone, I think of Hillel and Shammai. I try to reframe my perspective through the lens of the other person, allowing my opinion to blend with the different truths of someone else. When I explore divisive issues with my students I ask them to argue the side with which they disagree first; to write an essay from that point of view before writing one from their own. If a student has a strong feminist interpretation, I ask her to argue for the conservative and traditional interpretation, and I ask the student with a conservative position to argue from a feminist position. It's amazing how much better the final essays are from the students who actually do this exercise. When two ideas conflict, it isn't because one is necessarily true and the other false. It's that each represents a different perspective on reality. As physicist Niels Bohr taught: The opposite of a fact is a falsehood but the opposite of a profound truth is very often another profound truth.

Some students are just too afraid, and they resist. A student once said it plainly, "I don't want to be convinced that I'm wrong." He didn't want to compromise his own position because he thought it would weaken him. But there's nothing compromising about arguing for the side you disagree with. Anyone fighting fiercely about an issue can go deeper. Anyone can find a partial truth, no matter how small, in an opposing position. And a wider truth always emerges from the fray. The intrinsic worth of every human being means every idea has some sort of claim on the truth. At the very least, every person has the right to be heard.

But, as my student intuited, there's no doubt that hearing the other side can really change you. If you teach the point of view you disagree with, you will be altered. If you listen, really listen, to your spouse or your child, your boss or your perceived enemy, if you allow their point of view to sit alongside your own, it's incredible how you and the situation can be transformed. You may even see that the ideas you are willing to fight to the death for are the very ones you're most unsure about; the fierceness of your answer a mask for uncertainty. You realize that we never have any independent opinions that are wholly ours, points of view

> **The intrinsic worth of every human being means every idea has some sort of claim on the truth.**

that we came to on our own. We've inherited them from our parents or rebelled against their views; we had a childhood trauma or a fear that has influenced us greatly. Never mind the television we watch or the books we read. Even the way we feel on the day we write the paper or have the argument influences the position we take. Context is everything.

At the same time, we must be careful not to simply say that since everything is partially true, nothing really matters, as if there aren't standards of right or wrong. Yes, in every view there is a partial truth. But not every view is equally true. There are standards of right and wrong, gradations of truth. I've heard so many people use the phrase "This is my truth" or "That's your truth" as a way to defuse conflict and stifle discussion. This relativism is just lazy absolutism. It makes the claim that in effect we each have our own absolute truth, and so anything goes; why fight the fight? This spineless and limp relativism is as frustrating as hostile know-it-all absolutism. Both halt the search for truth.

It's not that we shouldn't have opinions and perceptions, passionate feelings and beliefs. We should argue with and criticize those views we believe to be wrong. No idea or insight should be either automatically accepted or totally dismissed. Even extreme opinions have an important role in society: They probe the middle, ensuring neither moral inflexibility nor flabbiness. When we engage in serious dialogue, within ourselves and with each other, our worlds expand; our truths are refined, and we can incorporate the truths of others, finding new positions and even shared ethical visions.

Martin Buber was a twentieth-century philosopher of religion who taught at a time when other philosophers were declaring that God is dead. Like Hillel, rather than declaring this false and defending his own faith, Buber integrated this new truth into his teaching. He affirmed the validity of even the most extreme doubt and in the process softened the nihilism of his peers. Buber understood that faith is so much richer, so much more meaningful and authentic, if we also can doubt. We need faith. Without it the future seems barren, and progress and innovation would be impossible. But we also need doubt if truth is to continue to unfold.

The expression "Don't lose faith" is a half-truth; sometimes you have to lose it in order to find it more deeply. Buber spoke of "moment gods." My teacher Rabbi Irving "Yitz" Greenberg spoke about "moment faith" and "moment doubt." These days there seem to be the absolute faith people and absolute doubt people. What would the world look like if more of us were "moment faithers" and "moment doubters," if more of us wrestled with the truth? Maybe peace would visit us more often.

• • •

IF I HADN'T GROWN up with the mother I had and the texts I studied, I would never have married my wife of twenty-five years. Relationships are a constant dialectic between faith and doubt; times of great love and profound ambivalence. When we attach to an idea—an idol—of who our lover is or should be, we set ourselves up for a fall. But if we hold the truth of who *we* are and *they* are more lightly, with room to grow and change, it's amazing the arguments and crises we can weather.

Coming from a large, closely knit family, I always knew that I wanted one of my own. So you can imagine my dismay when the woman I was convinced I wanted to marry (from the moment I met her), announced to me in the middle of a romantic, dreamlike weekend on the shore, that she never wanted to have children. I gasped, repressing the urge to literally get up from our cozy beach blanket and run. Who was this woman I thought I loved more deeply than anyone? It hurt more than anything I can remember anyone had ever said to me.

Yet in the depths of my pain and anger, I could hear myself asking again in a more gentle voice, "Yes, who is this woman I love?" In a flash I recalled some of our early conversations when we were first getting to know each other. Dana had told me about her parents' fighting, how it had hurt her as a child. And I also thought of the many times Dana had spoken to me with love and admiration about how her mother, an early feminist, had taught her the value of having a career. She feared being taken off track, engulfed by the demands society places on women even in her generation.

I could feel myself soften. Yes, this was her truth right now. And it made sense given

> Relationships are a constant dialectic between faith and doubt.

the context she had been in and in which she still found herself. After all, my context of being raised in a relatively harmonious, large family surely accounted for my yearning for children. Maybe we both would continue to feel the same way. Or maybe one or both of us would change our minds. Somehow I believed our relationship would create a different context in which another truth would emerge. I married her, and we now have two teenage daughters. If I hadn't listened to Dana, listened beyond her immediate words, I certainly would have left that beach. If I hadn't believed that even the most tightly embraced truths have the potential to change, I would have lost so much.

Over the years, in the new context Dana and I created together, we both began to see another, deeper truth about her upbringing. Despite their differences with each other, which Dana found painful, her parents unconditionally loved their children—they gave of themselves in a way I'd never seen before and which became a model for me. She also began to remember the good times—how her parents, both ballroom dancers, moved so beautifully together and how, no matter what, they'd stayed loyal to each other for more than fifty years.

Jewish wisdom teaches that the truth we have access to is temporary; even those truths that seem indisputable or essential. Of course, there are obvious factual truths like two plus two equals four, the sun is shining, or I'm five-foot-eleven. But fact is not synonymous with truth and confusing the two leads to an impoverishment of mind and spirit. There are other truths—our interpretations of facts or events, our stories of who we are and where we are going, our emotional and moral truths. True here means something different than true in a news account or a lab report: It is true to life at its deepest and most complex.

Precisely when you grasp these truths, say "aha," and then relax into them, they will change or shift. I call them "moment truths." It's not that they disappear and a new truth emerges out of nowhere. Rather, each realization leads to a deeper one and then a deeper one after that. It's not that Dana lost the truth she uttered that day on the beach. She really didn't want to have a family situation like the one she grew up in, and she didn't want to sacrifice her career. But both of us needed to listen closely to her pronouncement to see if there was a deeper truth underneath.

Later, a different truth emerged. It turned out Dana did decide to leave her fast-track job in favor of creating her own business so that she could spend more time with her family. She saw that climbing the corporate ladder was no longer what she wanted but that it was also possible to not give up her career. I still remember her exact words to me nine years after that initial conversation, because the phrasing struck me. "The truth is, Irwin, I want more time with the kids." Her current "truth" couldn't have been more different than the one she was so convinced of almost a decade earlier. And once her context changes further, her truth concerning work and family will likely shift again.

When we see our truths as ever-deepening, as beginnings rather than endings, we can hold even our most prized truths more loosely. Absolute truths become humble absolutes. Humility is among the most important spiritual qualities. The only word ever used by the writers of the Hebrew Bible to describe Moses, its unequivocal hero, is the word "humble." Moses confronts the all-powerful Pharaoh; leads the Israelites out of slavery to freedom; carries the Ten Commandments down from Mt. Sinai. He's the only character to experience God face to face. And he was humble about it all.

Truth without humility can easily turn into arrogance or dominance, and inevitably leads to dead ends, both literally and figuratively. The Hebrew word for "truth" is *emet*. If you remove the first letter you have the word *met*, which means "death." In other words, the mystics taught, if you only have one side of the story you've begun a death spiral. When you think about leaders in history and today who think

Humility is among the most important spiritual qualities.

they have the only answer, that they have access to the Truth, it becomes clear how profoundly important humility is. Only by holding our truths humbly, lightly, knowing that they are not absolute, can we avoid arrogance and dead ends in our lives.

All new understandings take time to emerge and blossom. The word "Israel" means "wrestling with God." In other words, discovering again and again the truth, reality, God, whatever we choose to call it stretches and deepens our lives and enlivens and expands our moral universe. New truths may challenge us or make us uncomfortable for a while but they always bring us to the next level of understanding.

After all, there is no final arrival in life, but rather a series of arrivals.

Insights pop up unbidden, extending the horizon of our consciousness and setting us on new paths. This may sound heavy or difficult, and some may find it frustrating, even excruciating: Is there no end to the searching? But it's actually far less painful than clinging to a familiar truth despite changing circumstances and the inevitable fluidity of life. The yearning for Truth and Enlightenment is one of our defining human qualities. We can seek clarity with passion and commitment while knowing we'll never get there.

This book is a collection of humble absolutes. It is meant to help us wrestle with, deconstruct, and re-imagine the truths we hold self-evident. *Emet* is composed of the first, middle, and last letters of the Hebrew alphabet. The very construction of the word itself urges us always to seek a wider, more encompassing truth.

GOD WILL BE WHAT
GOD WILL BE

"OH MY GOD!" THIS IS A PHRASE SO MANY OF US USE, AND it's no accident. These three words capture a core human experience. I find myself saying them when I suddenly feel outside my usual self, when I am shaken out of my ordinary reality or when I feel a sense of harmony, of mystery, of gratitude. I might be watching my children play and be overcome by their beauty. I might have an epiphany about my place in the world that comes out of nowhere. Or I am overwhelmed with gratitude as I make love with my wife. And then there are those moments of horror and tragedy when I experience an overwhelming fearful awe. Watching those two towers collapsing, I found myself saying over and over, "Oh my God. Oh my God. Oh my God." The word God is really just code for an experience felt so intensely, so deeply, that there seems to be no other word to describe it.

Yet the word God so often trips us up. For many of us the notion of a personal God seems anachronistic, something that comforted our parents or grandparents but is irrelevant to us. We've rejected those patriarchal and punitive images we were taught in religious school, in church, or in temple. Others of us are holding on for dear life to a traditional image of an Almighty up in the sky who asserts His will and keeps the score. And still others have internalized the idea; God is within, not outside; God is us. Or perhaps there's no God at all. Everyone has a truth about God or no-God, and typically we're uncomfortable with any other.

"Rabbi, I am a scientist. I must tell you upfront I don't believe in God." These were the words of the Nobel Prize–winning physicist Murray

Gell-Mann when I was introduced to him at a dinner party. It certainly wasn't the first time I'd been greeted this way. And my response is always the same, "That's okay. I don't believe in the God you don't believe in either." What could have been—and is often intended to be—a conversation stopper turned into a lively debate. In order to reject something, one must have an image to reject; quite a paradox. For Gell-Mann, it was the God he was taught about as a child; the voyeuristic Peeping Tom in the heavens who judged his every move. He laughed when I told him that his rejection made him no different from a fundamentalist who's sure the all-judging God in the sky does exist. What makes them the same? They both have the same definition of God. Behind atheism is a powerful religious impulse. God is very much on Gell-Mann's mind.

To deny or affirm; both can be holy. To define God is to express a natural human need to make sense of our existence. To envision no God purges religious conceptions that may be limiting, holding us back. It's never God or no God; it's which God? All descriptions of God are projections— sacred projections. The question is, what images do we use to express the yearning?

It's never God or no God; it's which God?

Gell-Mann, who'd spent his career working with the highly symbolic language of mathematics in an attempt to describe the very origins of the universe and who later that evening regaled us with explanations of string theory, had forgotten that just as string theory is not to be taken literally, neither are our sacred projections. Definitions of God should never be confused with God any more than the description of an orange can capture the taste of an orange.

Gell-Mann was doing what people have done for centuries. We all have an innate desire to imagine something greater than ourselves. That's why every era and culture sees God through the lens of the metaphors and images of the day. When humans lived in caves and relied on wild animals for their survival, they expressed their anxiety and awe through animal gods. During the agrarian age, people created fertility and nature gods. During the age of great city-states when kings ruled from palaces set on high, God became the king of kings in the heavens. But the modern age was inconsonant with that image. When John Glenn brought back his pictures of earth from space, the fixed God in the sky finally was made obsolete—at least for those of us who hadn't yet let go and were willing to. With advances in medical science, humans could create and manipulate life—we were the "masters of the universe." Modern science banished God. In response to this, some have held on to the traditional image of an external Almighty in part as a way to resist the chaos of modernity. And others took their yearning inside, creating a personal divinity, an inner authority.

All images, whether societal or personal, become stultifying if we don't allow them to change and grow as we do. The second of the Ten Commandments urges us not to make a graven image of God. Graven images are not only statues; our conceptions and ideas can become just as concrete. Ironically, religion has broken this commandment again and again by attempting to institutionalize the infinite, by taking what was meant to be a wide open expanse and reducing it to one landscape. Ancient Chinese scriptures say it this way: "When you have names and forms, know that they are provisional. When you have institutions, know where their functions should end. Know when to stop."

The point of the Second Commandment is that any one image is only a partial truth. And a partial truth made absolute puts God in a box of our choosing. Every image of God, even no God, is just a resting place, a moment truth. The Christian hymn "Amazing Grace" says "I once was lost but now I am found," and this is so moving, so true. But all of us know that no one is found forever. Life is a dialectic between being lost and found, found and lost. When we've lost God, it's time to look deeper. When we've found God, it's time to get lost.

As a society we haven't yet imagined the God that captures our collective, contemporary experience. We are trapped between old images and those not yet created. Sometimes I think we shouldn't use the word God for one hundred years. Maybe by then we'll have come up with new metaphors that more fully capture our experience of God and that unite us rather than divide us. Or maybe we'll return to some of the ancient ones.

In fact, many traditions have multiple names for divinity. The *Bhagavad Gita* teaches that God has a million faces. The Muslim tradition has a practice in which one recites and meditates on ninety-nine of the most beautiful names for God. In the Jewish tradition there are hundreds of names: Father, Mother, Lover, Creator, Destroyer, Nurturer, Redeemer, Forgiver, Friend, Life-giver, to name just a few. The name used most often in Jewish texts is also the most mysterious and intimate. It is YHWH, which in English is all consonants and no vowels. In Hebrew it's actually a word with no consonants and all vowels. Either way it's unpronounceable. When you try to say it, you hear the sound of breath, a simple exhale. What is the teaching? The name of God is not meant to be uttered. YHWH is not meant to be known. YHWH is meant to be breathed. In contemporary translations and liturgy, the word YHWH is translated as Lord; quite a stark contrast to the sound of a breath and a telling statement about this traditional projection of God. The name used by the mystics is *Ein Sof*, which means "There Is No End." At this level God is without name. God is a mystery. Or, as I like to say, God is everything in drag.

Maimonides put it this way: "There is nothing higher one can say about God than what God is not." Whatever word, image, or concept we choose, we always need to go beyond it. The name YHWH comes from the same root in Hebrew as the word for becoming. God is always becoming. We will never grasp reality in all its dimensions. And all this not-knowing creates tremendous anxiety, which is exactly why our projections can get the best of us.

Every image of God, even no God, is just a resting place, a moment truth.

The challenge is to remember, even in our moments of turbulence, that God is always just outside of our perception, just ahead of where we are. It is the more expansive truth. As the mystic sage Rabbi Nachman taught, YHWH is an emergent God, evolving and learning along with us. If we remain open to the everything that is God, Reality, Self, or whatever we choose to call it, there is no end to the wonder that awaits us.

Many of us have had moments when our minds and hearts open up to new visions of the world and of ourselves—we fall in love, give birth to a child, discover a groundbreaking idea, make a significant change in our lives. Or maybe we encounter a spiritual truth that was inaccessible to us before. This happened to me in an unusual context for a rabbi: in the pews of a church. For traditional Jews, entering churches is forbidden. I was forty-two years old when I went into one for the first time. I'd passed by the same beautiful old church on my way to work for many years; then early one morning some small voice within me urged me to go in. As I sat in the wooden pew I was engulfed by unfamiliar sights and smells: incense, candles burning, light streaming in through stained glass windows. And then I looked up at the crucifix, a cross with a corpus, the figure of Jesus bleeding from the heart. As I meditated on this central symbol of Christianity for the first time, I was horrified, struck by thoughts about centuries of Christian persecution of Jews. I wanted to run away. My palms were sweating, and I had to hold on to the side of the pew in order to make myself stay. I kept looking and looking, thinking there just had to be something more here than my own tradition's perspective.

It could have been fifteen minutes or forty-five minutes, but I suddenly found myself thinking, "What if my heart was that open? What if I could feel everyone's pain, so much so that my heart exploded?" I understood in a flash the meaning of sacred heart. And I heard the words from a prayer I'd said every day since I was a boy, in a whole new way: "*Karov YHWH L'nishberai Lev,*" God is Close to the Brokenhearted. I didn't convert that day, but my God got an awful lot bigger. And so did I.

When tragedy or trauma interrupts ordinary life, when the fear of loss or its actuality grips us and takes us over, it's amazing how our conceptions of God come into play; and how dramatically they can change. What I've found is that God almost always gets bigger or smaller whether we're overtly spiritual or not. After the initial shock and grief recedes, our vision of reality either becomes wider and open to more and more possibility, or narrower and dominated by fear and bitterness; it rarely stays the same.

A congregant of mine named Ruth was in the midst of one of the most excruciating crises one can imagine. She was the mother of Josh, a sixteen-year-old boy who was dying of cancer. She'd spent every day since the diagnosis praying for a cure, a treatment that would work. A few days before Josh died I was visiting him in the hospital. His father wasn't there because he couldn't bear the pain of watching his son in this state. He was shut down, consumed by depression and rage. But Ruth was sitting right by the hospital bed leaning over every few minutes to moisten her son's lips with a wet cloth.

God is close to the brokenhearted.

Josh had been in this room for more than two months and he had made the room his. There were posters of sports heroes, rock-and-roll celebrities, and supermodels all over the walls. The contrast between the life force of the room and the death of this child was so stark. Josh was sleeping. After a while, Ruth turned to me and asked: "Where is God now?" As the words left her mouth Josh stirred and whispered in the softest yet clearest voice, "Mommy, I am going to die. I love you. No one could have been a better mother to me." Then he went back to sleep. Ruth and I were both speechless with tears.

At the memorial service about a month later, Ruth announced that she was devoting herself to raising money to add a new wing to the hospital that had cared for Josh, one that would be devoted to children with cancer, treating them and researching a cure. She was crying as she stood before us in the midst of profound grief and loss. But there was the same strength and determination I'd witnessed in her as she'd cared for Josh over those many months of his illness. I found myself thinking that Ruth had found where God is. She had found a new place within her broken heart. She'd discovered there was no magical curer for her son in the sky. That image had died with Josh. Now Ruth was to become a curer, not unlike the one she had prayed so hard for. Although she would have done anything not to have learned this truth in this way, her tragedy was going to lead to so much more life.

Something similar happened to Moses in the famous story of the burning bush. For him it wasn't tragedy that awoke him to a new truth, but a deep voice within that seemed to come out of nowhere. Moses was in a great place; he had escaped from Egypt, and was a husband, a father, and a wealthy shepherd of a huge flock. Then one day standing alone on a mountain, his sheep grazing around him, he noticed a "bush aflame that was not consumed." Rather than looking away in fear or continuing on, as many of us would, he stood still and gazed at the bush. And he said, "Here I am." He was fully present. Only when we know where we stand can we know the next step we need to take. Then Moses heard the voice, and it said about the last thing he wanted to hear. It told him to leave everything behind and go back to Egypt to free his fellow Israelites from slavery.

Moses was overwhelmed and wondered, "When the Israelites ask who sent me, what shall I say?" The voice said, "Tell them that I shall be what I shall be. Tell them that's who sent you." Like a Zen koan, God's answer seems to say: "It makes no difference what you call me. I am everything."

Moses had what in the 1960s we called a consciousness-blowing experience. He heard a voice from deep within, and for a moment reality seemed palpable, discernable, and at the same time infinite and impossible. YHWH can also mean "I was. I am. I will be." YHWH is past, present, and future. God is every experience, every place, every person that brought Moses to that time. And now it's up to Moses to decide where he wants to be in his journey.

Unlike Moses, most people evoke a God who tells them exactly what they want to hear—whether God is our intuition, that soft, still voice within that we feel holds some magical truth, or the guy in the heavens who affirms our perception of the world. The biblical teachings tell us that God is sometimes affirming, but more often challenging, even life-changing. After all, the word prayer comes from the same Latin root as the word precarious. What if we understood that God challenges every truth? What if we understood, as Moses did, that God is often that counterintuitive voice, the one that questions, that urges us beyond or deeper than we already are? As my mother always said, "Irwin, God rarely agrees with you. That's how you know it's God."

There's a mystical tradition that at the end of every year the names of God weaken; they wear down from use. By using God's names during the year, we actually deplete the names' ability to connect us to the experience. Like all language, the words we use for God begin to hide as much as they reveal. And so we do a kind of mouth-to-mouth resuscitation for God. Over the High Holidays, Rosh Hashana and Yom Kippur, those names must be re-infused with meaning so that once again they can serve as a connection to all that is. God then can expand to incorporate the new insights revealed in the last year and the hopes for the new year.

The central Jewish meditation is the *Shema*: "Hear Israel, YHWH is our God, God is One." It is meant to be practiced three times a day both as a kind of mantra designed to pull us outside ourselves and as a means to root us where we are. We are meant to recommit to the idea of God as we understand it every single moment, because everything is in flux and everything is God.

I got into a lot of trouble when I appeared on the national television series *Frontline*, as part of a show called "Faith and Doubt at Ground Zero." I said that I experience God as "No Thing." Was this rabbi denouncing and denying the existence of the Divine? But what I asked was simply, "How can there be something outside All-there-is?" I asked if maybe it was time for a new God, a more complex, expansive perception that suits our postmodern age; a time when most of our absolutes, including the primacy of science, have been challenged, even shattered; when definitions of God and no-God lead so often to disconnection and conflict. Perhaps we've reached a time when we can live joyfully in the face of the unknowable. Perhaps we have entered the era of panentheism. Unlike pantheism, the idea that the universe and God are the same, panentheism—another koan—is the intuition that reality doesn't ex-

> The more we embrace a diversity of names for God, the more our minds and hearts will open and expand.

haust God; rather all of reality is inside God. All that is, is All that is. "I will be what I will be."

Toward the end of that dinner with Murray Gell-Mann, as I listened to him describe his career, I found myself thinking that quantum reality, an idea he helped pioneer, in fact pointed toward this new God. Whereas classical physics envisioned a reality in which things were always definitely one way or another, quantum mechanics describes a reality in which things sometimes hover in a haze of being partly one way and partly another. As the physicist Brian Greene says, "It is a reality that remains ambiguous until perceived." In other words, YHWH.

By the time we finished dessert, Gell-Mann surprised me by conceding that perhaps he was in fact doing what the author of Genesis had done. Like so many philosophers before him, he was composing a creation story, in his case for the twenty-first century. One such thinker in that great line of seekers was the twelfth-century Jewish philosopher Maimonides, who re-imagined the spiritual wisdom of his day in light of Aristotelian science. He wrote that unpredictability and spontaneity, what he called miracle, were at the core of existence. The idea of string theory, a cutting-edge field within physics in part inspired by Gell-Mann's work, captures this teaching in mathematical language and expands on it.

String theory is a leap of faith. It's in the realm of the unexplainable. Just as the names for God are metaphor, so, too, is string theory. It posits that there are particles so small that it's impossible to see them. Like violin strings create notes through vibration, these particles unite quantum reality with concrete reality through unperceivable vibrations. This is the so-called unified theory Einstein could never conceive. As Einstein said when referring to ideas about space and time, "There exists a far-reaching uncertainty of interpretation." From the earliest sages to twenty-first-century physicists, there has always been and will always be a yearning to understand all that is; an overpowering desire to grasp reality; to find truth in No Thing. We can, as Greene says, "be filled with incomparable wonderment."

If God is infinite, if reality is unknowable, then who are we? One of the earliest self-definitions is that we are images of God. We are what we imagine God to be. In other words, we're those very metaphors. The more we embrace a diversity of names for God, the more our minds and hearts will open and expand. The very names broaden our self-understanding, our sense of depth and potential. Father, Mother, Lover, Creator, Forgiver, Compassionate One, Destroyer, Curer. We are all of them.

THE SILENT, THIN SELF

"WHAT MAKES YOU UNIQUE?" MY DAUGHTER GABRIELLA was asked this question on a high school entrance application. The essay was due in a couple of days, and it seemed simple enough. Yet she put it off and put it off. When I finally pushed her to complete the essay, she said she couldn't figure out what to write. "Dad, nothing about me is unique." Had Gabriella entered that notorious stage when girls lose their sense of self in the swirl of adolescence? My wife and I were mystified. Gabriella was a developing artist—designing her own clothes—and a talented writer. She was effervescent, loving, and always making new friends. Didn't she see how special she was? Her response blew me away. "Yeah, Dad, but lots of other people are those things. And besides, none of it is all of who I am. I'm everything put together, and not even that. There's always new stuff." Her essay turned out to be a critique of the question, an argument against assuming we are ever complete, entirely knowable. As Gabriella wrote, "What makes me unique is that I am always Gabriella-ing. No one else in the world does that." Each of us is always becoming.

We all share a yearning to know ourselves, to comprehend who we are in the world. We want to find our "true self" and have been taught that if we just look deeply enough we will find it. Of course, we all need a story about who we are, how we came to be, and where we are going. No one can live every moment of one's life as an open question. We need a recognizable identity to get us through the day. But we forget that what we call self is really only a moment truth. There is no single enduring identity. As my mom would caution her sometimes smug sons, "People are always more than you think they are." Shakespeare reminds us that, "We are such stuff as dreams are made on." We need a self-image, but ought not forget that it's just an image; a sense of self. Finding our permanent Self—no matter how much we search—just isn't going to happen. When we think we have this self, it's time to search again.

When we become attached to an identity of any kind—whether it's our profession, our appearance, our talents, or special qualities we take pride in—we've made a partial truth absolute. When you think about it, are any of us really the same people we were a decade ago? Are we even recognizable? It can be mind-blowing when we read an old journal, pull out a dress three sizes smaller or larger, or discover a teenage love letter. And think of all those

> There is no single enduring identity. What we call self is really only a moment truth.

plans we made that never panned out, not only because of unpredictable external events but because we ourselves are unpredictable. As Lewis Carroll's Alice says, "Dear! Dear! How strange everything is today. I wonder if I've changed in the night. Let me think: Was I the same when I got up this morning?"

Gabriella's insight was the same one Moses had while standing at the burning bush: "I will be what I will be." Like God, in that sense, we ourselves are infinite. The Self is a projection, just as God is. This is what we mean in saying we humans are created in the image of God. The images we have of ourselves are really attempts to streamline complexity, to make a neat story out of our many facets. Freud taught that we never will know fully the contents of our minds, of our selves. He called this idea "surplus life." There is a "too-muchness" to our consciousness. In other words, our own psyche eludes our grasp. No wonder the Hebrew word for life is plural: *Hayim* means lives.

When I hear that someone is leading a double life, I think "Just two?"

As cognitive scientists are now discovering, the notion of a single enduring self is just a way to describe how we've temporarily domesticated our inner world. Identity is just a provisional arrangement. Our self is really a container for our multiplicity. It is a resting place, a *makom*; yet another name for God. Nonetheless we yearn for that place to be permanent; to feel an inner coherence and completion; to feel settled down and rooted. We want to overcome the conflicted and contradictory viewpoints that neuroscientists have discovered are always being constructed in our brains without our even knowing it.

The yearning for self is essential to our development but it is of course a quest that can never be fully satisfied. We can never fully grasp the infinite—God's or our own. There's very little difference between the secular belief that we can know who we are and the religious fundamentalists' belief that we can know who God is. Both lead to arrogance and what Christopher Lasch called a culture of narcissism. Could it be that all the striving, the pushing, the climbing, the acquiring, is rooted in this yearning to know that which can never be known? Rather than trying to define who we are, what if we sought an ever-deepening understanding of how *much* we are? Perhaps that's what deeper yearning is really all about.

"I'VE ALWAYS HAD a mind of my own," a friend of mine said. This was Rhea's usual refrain in response to some trouble she'd stirred up at work. Rhea was direct to a fault; a rabble-rouser of sorts. She'd tell colleagues in no uncertain terms how misguided they were and exactly how they should do it next time. She always wanted to run the show and she relished rocking the boat. Needless to say, she alienated a lot of people, especially those who reported to her. "I always fight the good fight, even if it's just me screaming into the wind," was her favorite response when someone complained about her style. "I don't care what other people think," she'd insist. I became concerned that things had gone too far when she told me there was a virtual walkout at a meeting after one of her more extreme outbursts.

When Rhea visited me a few months later, I noticed a dramatic change in her. When I asked her how things were at work, I expected the usual litany of complaints and dramatic stories of her triumphs. Instead she told me how she'd taken a few days off and wasn't sure where her projects stood. When I asked her about an issue I knew she'd felt very strongly about, she said she'd let it go and let her deputy decide. "What happened to the lady with a mind of her own?" I teased. She replied, "You know, Irwin, I just don't have the fight in me these days." A wistful expression crossed her face. I wondered if this metamorphosis had something to do with the death of her mother, who'd died after a long illness.

"Yes, but actually, it was the report card," she said. She told me how she'd been cleaning out her mother's basement. One morning amidst crinkling collages and magic-marker decorated loose-leaf notebooks she came across her kindergarten report card. "Who the hell grades a five-year-old?" she said, and I was relieved to hear her spirit returning. Apparently, under every category on that yellowed card there was some kind of reference to her lack of initiative, her unexplained fearfulness. Her teachers even referred to her as a "follower" and a "wallflower." Her one strength was her gentleness with the younger kids in her class.

This middle-aged woman had excavated a different—and surprising, to her—facet of her identity.

The death of a parent often leaves us more exposed and vulnerable— and sometimes more open to change. And then even an old report card can shatter our self-perceptions. I had no doubt that Rhea would find her spark once again; perhaps she'd discover a gentler, more observant rabble-rouser, one who felt a little less alone. My hope was that she'd give this new self-perception a chance to develop and expand.

I told Rhea a story about one of the most fascinating Biblical personalities: the prophet Elijah. Though on a grander scale, his story wasn't so different from hers. And it has so much to teach us about our own unravellings, those times when we feel lost and alone, when we encounter a new self that might not be so welcome.

Elijah's dramatic struggle to discover a new self redefines the phrase "identity crisis." He had been on a supremely holy mission, and he, too, felt he was screaming into the wind. A passionate, uncompromising, and yet profoundly lonely man, Elijah was filled with zeal for his God. He was determined to convince the people of Israel to cease worshipping the pagan god Baal and return their devotion to their Israelite God. It's the job of prophets to wake people up from their slumbers and set them back on course. But Elijah took this to an extreme. He presented an awesome magic show for the people, even producing fire on a water-drenched altar. Emboldened and still enraged, he then slaughtered the pagan priests. But neither his impressive "miracle" nor his powerful show of force made any difference.

Rather, in response to his murderous acts, Elijah was chased from the city. And so with his life threatened, having failed completely in his mission, Elijah went out into the wilderness where mystical figures often go in search of a new truth. The Hebrew word for wilderness is *midbar*, which literally means "word place." *Midbar* is an in-between space; a wild, unpredictable place where we can encounter parts of us that we don't yet know or haven't allowed to emerge. *Midbar* is our inner landscape. And, like Rhea's mother's basement, it is where we can experience and begin to integrate new selves.

Elijah remained in the wilderness for forty days and forty nights—the period of time in which so many Biblical transformations take place. Noah was on the ark for forty days and forty nights and this was also the amount of time Moses spent on Mt. Sinai. Any significant change takes a while; all new truths need gestation time. Elijah hid in a desert cave at Mt. Horeb, the same mountain where Moses experienced the burning bush and

All new truths need gestation time.

another name for Mt. Sinai. This mountain cave, a sort of inner heights, is the place within ourselves where we can see a new vista, a place to envision our still future self, where we can hear the faint echo of the not-yet-me.

While asleep in the cave, Elijah heard the question, "Why are you here, Elijah?" Depressed and forlorn, his answer was simple: "I am the zealous one, the only one left." But Elijah misunderstood. He wasn't being asked "Who are you?" The question "Why are you here?" is a gentle, inviting question. Where are you, Elijah, in the process of your becoming?

The answer he discovered was no longer to be found in the great winds, the splitting mountains, shattering rocks, and blazing fire—metaphors for the forces that were familiar to him. Elijah the zealous, alienated prophet no longer exhausted who Elijah was. Emerging from the cave, what Elijah heard was a "silent, thin voice." This phrase is more often translated as "a soft, still voice." A whisper is quite audible; its very softness commands attention. But a "silent, thin voice"? What a paradox! How can a voice be silent? But as so many religious traditions teach, when our minds are quiet we can hear things we otherwise would have missed. We encounter ourselves in our silence.

Elijah entered that silence. His self-image softened and his perspective shifted. He chose a disciple and successor who would continue his teachings. Elijah the preacher had become Elijah the teacher.

And yet the fiery prophet didn't totally disappear, as becomes evident at his death. Unique among the Biblical characters, Elijah "does not die." Instead, a fiery chariot and horses appear and he ascends to heaven in a whirlwind. Elijah remained full of zeal; his passion had been essential to who he was in the world. The thunderous zealot and the gentle teacher were one and the same person. Elijah had integrated his different, contradictory selves. Isn't this the way all of us wish to die, with a final deep acceptance and understanding of all that we are?

The story of Moses and the burning bush is also a teaching about how new selves are born. The "bush that burned but would not be consumed" is a symbol of the self that is always transforming but is never extinguished. Maimonides saw the story as a dream in which Moses encountered long repressed aspects of who he'd always been. From the flames, Moses heard many voices: the voice of his father calling him back to Egypt; the

We can never fully grasp the infinite.

voices of the enslaved Israelites pleading for help. And then he heard a voice that said, "I was, I am, and I will be." His different selves were coming together in a moment of realization, taking a new form. The Shepherd of sheep would become a Shepherd of his people.

Like most other Biblical characters who encounter God, Moses was a middle-aged man, settled into a simple, satisfying life; a wife, kids, a good job. And yet—as is familiar to most of us—he felt something was missing, that perhaps he had a larger purpose in life. The thought both frightened and compelled him. Opening ourselves up to the unknown, allowing ourselves to become unmoored, and withstanding the turbulence that accompanies this realization are perhaps the greatest human challenges. Hearing the silence can be tremendously frightening.

Perhaps this is why Moses was in the end compassionate when the Israelites later retreated from their own encounter with God at the site of that very same mountain. While Moses was on top of Mt. Sinai receiving the Ten Commandments, the people below experienced smoke, fire, thunder, the blare of a horn, and they "fell back and stood at a distance." But Mendl of Rymanoff, an eighteenth-century mystic, explained that it wasn't the thunder that frightened the people. "What had they heard at Sinai? The first letter of the first word of the Ten Commandments." The first sentence begins, "I am your God." The first letter of the pronoun "I" is the Hebrew letter *alef*, which is silent. The people heard the silent, still voice; a silence so vast that they simply had to back away. "It was so quiet," another sage taught, "that one could hear the flapping of a bird's wings miles away." What can you hear in the silence? You can hear everything: the everything that is God; the everything that is "I."

Another interpretation takes special note of the phrase "God spoke in a voice . . ." The sages were puzzled. They asked, "In a voice? What voice?" They speculated that it was the sound of six hundred thousand voices, a voice appropriate for every single one of the people standing there. "A maidservant heard it as a maidservant's voice. A suckling child heard it as a suckling child's voice. A warrior heard it as a warrior's voice." The voice of God was their own. In other words, they experienced the enormity of who they were at that moment. And it was nothing less than awesome. They glimpsed their own inexhaustible selves.

We all have our Sinai experiences. Those times—sometimes lasting a lot longer than forty days and forty nights—when there's a crisis or crossroads in our lives. This can result from the death of a loved one, a breach in a relationship, or a loss of a job. Sometimes, this ache just appears, a growing yearning for something more or something else. We become frightened and try to fill the silence and quell the troubling voices. We feel overwhelmed, destabilized and unmoored. These junctures are sacred. For it is precisely when we become strangers to ourselves, and then love the stranger as our self, that we have the greatest potential for self, or "selves," discovery.

I saw this process of self-discovery unfold dramatically in a friend who was undergoing what we commonly call a midlife crisis. Since her mid-twenties she'd been a caring wife, a devoted rabbi, driven, confident, someone with a seemingly clear sense of her role in the world. She'd been one of the first women ordained in her denomination. I often wondered how she kept up the pace, overseeing a thriving and growing congregation while traveling the country to give talks and workshops. Then again, busyness is an effective way to protect one's self, or selves, from hearing other disturbing voices.

On one of these trips, during a particularly dry spell in her marriage, she ran into an old flame. This was her Sinai experience. "As I sat across the table from him, I felt a sense of wonder and desire. I could feel myself opening up in a way I hadn't in more than a decade, as if awakening from a deep sleep." She told me how her body tingled and boundaries began to melt. She felt overwhelmed. As she spoke to me, her voice became softer and softer and there was an unmistakable longing in her eyes. "For that entire weekend, I was head over heels. It was as if I was someone else. The minute I got on the plane to return home, I would have given anything to take back those three days." She told me all this during yet another long plane ride to yet another conference several weeks later. Maybe it was my shocked expression, or the effect of her third glass of wine, but she began to cry. I barely recognized her as her makeup ran to reveal dark circles under her eyes. "I thought I knew myself," she kept saying. But clearly the self she'd thought she knew so well was crumbling.

My friend had kept her lustful self, her restless self, her needy self so tightly under wraps that they'd erupted. She's been a radical pioneer in her work, challenging gender roles, and a "good girl" at home and in her marriage. She had become the subdued, organized, self-controlled wife she believed her husband needed. Now this professional, successful, and dutiful wife was suffocating under the constraints she herself had created. Her feelings of resentment were so unexpected and so powerful that she felt she had no choice but to act on them. As we talked, my friend said something so revealing, "Where was my self-control? What possessed me to actually do it?" She looked shocked when I said, "Out came the 'bad girl.' "

Sitting across the table from her old lover, she'd entered the *midbar*. She had encountered an unfamiliar aspect of herself. My friend hadn't lost control of herself. She hadn't realized there is no essential self, no core self to lose control of. We are, in fact, the relationship between our ever-emerging selves. This is why identities are tension-filled, contradictory, and inconsistent. Sometimes we can only experience this complexity when our carefully constructed self is interrupted, even shattered. In that moment of boundarylessness my friend felt the same yearning the ancients felt for what they referred to as God. She was overwhelmed with the anxiety of not knowing that so often accompanies or follows the ecstasy of discovery, and in response she reached out for her old lover.

> We are the relationship between our ever-emerging selves.

Just as we all have our Sinai experiences we all have our golden calf experiences as well. Only forty days after encountering God in the thunder and lightning and quaking of Mt. Sinai, the Israelites commit a horrifying act of idolatry. While they waited for Moses to return from the top of the mountain with the Ten Commandments and the wisdom that would guide them in the next steps of their journey, they, too, sought an object for their awe—release for the anxiety that inevitably followed their encounter with God, with All that is. And so the Israelites begged Aaron, Moses's brother, to create for them an image of God. Perhaps out of compassion, perhaps to allay his own fears, Aaron agreed and told them to give him their gold rings, from which he created a "molten calf" and an altar before it, proclaiming the next day to be a "festival of the Lord." The festival was marked by wild dancing, a kind of ecstatic devotion and gratitude, perhaps not unlike the rapture of lovemaking. So soon after committing to one God, the Israelites worshipped another. Monotheism in theology is monogamy in the bedroom. Idolatry is adultery by another name.

The story of the golden calf is one of the most powerful and instructive biblical teachings. This notorious tale is traditionally seen as an example of how people can never seem to live up to the God character's expectations; how weak and impulsive we are; how incapable of squelching or resisting our desires. But perhaps we understand these expectations too narrowly. Are we really supposed to be obedient children, denying the full range of our selves? Should we always repress the unpredictable, the unbounded, bewitching, and at times dark and anarchic parts of who we are?

The Ishbitzer Rebbe, an important mystical thinker in the nineteenth century, offers a surprising interpretation of the golden calf story. He saw the people's sin not as an impulse toward idolatry but as an expression of a holy desire, the passion to experience ecstasy and the overflow of life. The Ishbitzer understood that the Israelites' response was a natural outgrowth of their encounter with God. Having tasted the infinite, they craved an anchor for their devotion, so that they could connect even more deeply, reach even higher stages. Think of the lyrics to George Harrison's famous song, "My Sweet Lord," where he says he really wants to know God, really wants to be with God. Rather than simply being an affront to God, the golden calf was actually born out of an overpowering yearning for the Divine: to know and express every aspect of our selves.

Notice, too, that the second of the Ten Commandments Moses brings down from the mountain urges us not to "make for yourself a graven image." It tells us not to make "any likeness of what is in the heavens above, or on the earth below, or in the waters under the earth below or in the waters under the earth. You shall not bow down to them or serve them." In other words, this commandment warns against reducing "all that is" to one idea. If the Israelites had been able to dwell in the silence, they might have had no need for a golden calf.

Similarly, if my rabbi friend had heard the "silent, thin voice," she might not have felt a need to act on her feelings, no matter how urgently she experienced them. Rather she simply might have noticed them, even reveled in the mystery of her unfolding selves. She could have welcomed the new self, the moment truth that emerged from that silence. What if she could have experienced the chafing and discomfort as invitations to expand and explore this other submerged self?

My friend's emerging, erotic self was a signal for her to broaden her self understanding and her marriage, as well. She was surprised when I asked her, "Did you ever think that there might be a 'bad boy' lurking in your husband? Why don't you ask him to come out and play?" I hoped that she might find a place in her own home, in the bedroom, too, for the new self that knocked so loudly on the door. When we are driven to act out, to do what we perceive as wrong, we have an opportunity to open the door wider, invite in that unfamiliar self and hear what it has to say. Temptation is so often a wake-up call.

With this understanding, we can better appreciate Moses's realization, "I was, I am, and I will be" or Gabriella's more simple, "there's always more stuff." We might hear the same question Elijah heard in the wilderness: "Why are you here?" "Where am I?" the question at the crux of most of our crises in life. To be sure, it is difficult to shake off this desperate need to end self-doubt and know exactly who we are. Even months later my friend was still attached to her previous notions of her old, well-defined self. She was still at sea, unable to understand how she could have broken the mold she'd so carefully created. It was clear that she was beating herself up with the same drive with which she'd done everything else in her life. She spoke about her fear that her marriage would end. But I wondered how much of her pain was about this very loss of self. And I wondered how she would save her marriage if she wouldn't confront this loss. If only, like Elijah, she found her *midbar* and returned into her cave. If only she gave herself those forty days and forty nights so that she could reemerge a more integrated, more accepting and giving wife and rabbi.

Here is the central insight: The more we allow our selves to unfold, the less likely we are to unravel. When we hold our identities lightly, knowing that they are temporary constructions, humble absolutes, the crises and crossroads in our lives tend to be less shattering. We've all experienced our angry-self lashing out from nowhere; our helpless-self erupting in tears when we didn't even know we were upset; our betraying-self sabotaging a relationship; our sensual-self coming alive at a sunset; and our spiritual-self melting away our self-established boundaries. When we can embrace these "not me" moments, our more interesting "me" becomes truly alive.

It doesn't always take forty days and forty nights to shift our perspective—mini Sinai experiences await us even in the most mundane of circumstances. The silent, thin voice can be a few seconds of silence, a moment of hesitation before we act. Thich Nhat Hanh, a Buddhist sage, asks us to take an extra breath before answering the phone. I've learned to take a breath before I open the front door after a hard workday. I ask myself, "Irwin, are you home?" When we ask a question, it forces us to pause, to step outside the habitual conversation in our heads and invite in a new voice. Other selves are poised to emerge at our beckoning. Self-realization or, I should say, selves-realization, is always available to us.

· · ·

MY FRIEND RHEA and I had a lot of conversations in the weeks after she told me her report card story. One morning she told me another story about being in a different kind of *midbar*, in this case the Manhattan subway. Like many pushy New Yorkers, she always stood in the same place on the platform, where the door would open to her favorite seat in the front car; she almost always got in before the others waiting beside her. When she was lucky, the seat was empty and she'd get it, and the day got off to a good start.

> **The more we allow ourselves to unfold, the less likely we are to unravel.**

That morning a young man was standing in "her" spot on the platform. To make matters worse, he rushed in before her, making a beeline for "her" seat. She stood right in front of him, fuming for most of the forty-five minute ride; a young man acting that way; what happened to the gentleman offering an older woman a seat? "I tried to be easygoing and let it go. But I almost tripped him on his way out of the train."

Then something unusual happened. When he left and she took the seat, rather than feeling relieved, she felt uncomfortable. As she described it, she asked herself, "Who the hell do I think I am?" Rather than digging into the newspaper—her morning ritual—she looked around the car. "Was there someone else who deserved the seat more than she did?" When she saw a pregnant woman, she sprang up to offer her seat.

Rhea, the fierce, pushy lady always demanding her space, didn't disappear during that ride, just as Elijah's fiery nature didn't go anywhere. Those qualities served her in many aspects of her life. Pushy people are often agents of change in the world. But something in her wanted to explore what it would mean to not take up space for a few minutes, to make room for a different, gentler self, one that might enrich her morning rides and maybe the rest of the world as well.

YEARNING FOR
MEANING

SACRED MESSINESS

"WHAT DOES IT ALL MEAN?" LILY'S FATHER HAD ASKED
her some variation of this question ever since she could remember. "It
was his fault that I spent my early adulthood looking for the answer,"
she joked. Lily was a serious Buddhist practitioner who spent several
weeks a year in silent retreat.

Usually the question came as she and her father stood in the kitchen
cleaning up together after dinner, always an elaborate, meticulous task,
as was everything her father did. She remembered that he had an expression on his face that was at once playful and dead serious. His
yearning was palpable. And she wanted so much to come up with the
answer; what did it all mean? A girl suddenly in the position of reassuring the parent; he looking for the innocent wisdom of a child for a simple, sweet truth; something to soothe his profound anxiety born of a
difficult life.

Perhaps he wanted to witness Lily unfolding before his eyes, amidst
the sound of running water and the soothing rhythm of dishes being
sponged and then dried. Or perhaps the neatening up night after night,
the endless messes being made right, awakened in him a longing to find
meaning in the smallest of things, to have it fill him up. But Lily didn't
feel any of those things. Instead she felt an emptiness sweep through
her, a sadness at how much she didn't yet know and maybe never
would. It seemed like a million answers swirled through her head, what
she'd learned in school that week or read in a novel; some adage she saw
in graffiti on a subway wall. But she also experienced it as a kind of

invitation: to become the kind of person who wasn't afraid to look deeper, beneath the surface of things.

Usually she just said "love," but she knew she didn't really know what it meant. He'd ask her to elaborate, and they'd talk a while longer, eventually turning back toward the tasks remaining, the dishes still on the table, the grease lingering on the stove. But that was the beginning of a lifelong search for my friend. Paradoxically, her dad's yearning for the simple wisdom of a child led Lily down a winding path of continuous discovery. When she sat in silence, she said she sometimes felt a glimmer of what she'd longed for during those evenings, and she wanted to reach out to her father, now dead, touch his hand, and smile reassuringly into his searching eyes.

Don't we all want life to make sense? To find some underlying purpose to the continuous ups and downs, the fear and joy, the accomplishments and disappointments? Like Lily's dad, we want to know "what it all means," as if there were some ultimate wisdom that could ease our striving and uncertainty. The sages encourage us to study life for clues and act as if that understanding were possible. Jewish wisdom sanctions the yearning, even ennobles it, at the same time teaching that there is no meaning: only a kind of dance between meaning and ambiguity; understanding and misunderstanding; faith and doubt; essence and no-essence. And the more joyous the dance, the richer and more holy the life.

We may accept all this intellectually, even think it's obvious. But how many of us see our daily challenges—a disagreement with a loved one, a deadline, even a traffic jam—as holy? Never mind major disappointments or crises; those eruptions of chaos. We relish order, neatness, resolution. We forget that life has no straight lines or easy paths. The process of becoming is circuitous, to say the least. Yet so many of us expend endless energy wishing and trying to make it otherwise. We long for those happy times of satisfaction, even celebration, of feeling like all is well, balanced, and fulfilling. During these times we can look back on our lives, even the

The process of becoming is circuitous. Life has no straight lines or easy paths.

tough times, and see all that led us here as somehow necessary and right. Life does have a purpose after all.

And we can't help but be surprised when those happy times don't last. We believe families are supposed to get along. Jobs are not supposed to be lost. Faces are not supposed to get wrinkles. We judge people when they don't "have it together," especially ourselves. In short, most of us think life is supposed to work out the way we hope it will or even expect it to. We secretly want the kitchen to finally be clean. And yet if the kitchen was always clean, there would be no meals.

I experienced this in the simplest of ways and quite literally when my wife reached the point of despair about the state of our younger daughter's room. No matter how many times Dana had spoken to Talia, tried to convince her that this was no way to live, her room always looked the same, with some variation on how much stuff was gathered on the floor or on the unmade bed. That particular day, it seemed like all of Talia's things were everywhere but where they were supposed to be. I could feel frustration rising in me as I glanced at the hair brush on the windowsill, clothing inside out in the corner, her diary left lying open on her floor, earrings scattered on the dresser. Then I heard myself say, "It's just like Talia: always overflowing." And I realized I was smiling. "Her cup runneth over," I said to my wife, quoting the Twenty-third Psalm.

We stood there looking at the mess, our arms around each other, our anger transformed into wonder at the "muchness" that was our daughter. Suddenly, each thing had meaning—the dress she'd worn at her first dance that last weekend, the earrings I'd bought her for her thirteenth birthday. And she'd left her diary open; how trusting, I thought. When I allowed myself to relax into the teenage messiness, I could see that each thing had a special significance. Perhaps Talia didn't want these things put away neatly, but left out, exposed as if to say "Here I am." For the first time I understood why Talia always said, "It's not a mess to me."

I found myself marveling, as I often do, at what my children have to teach me. What would happen if I slowed down and relaxed into my own messes rather than always rushing to clean them up? What if I stopped trying to solve every problem the minute it came my way, to make what seems wrong right? And how much more rich and meaningful would life be if we all learned to gently sort through our tangled lives? Perhaps our messes are the treasure boxes of our souls. Or it might be more useful to envision a treasure basket not neatly ordered or closed on top, but open and overflowing, meant to be sifted through over and over again. If we lived as though this were true, imagine how much more compassionate we would be with everyone we encounter, including ourselves.

It's a rare and wonderful experience when the vicissitudes of daily life actually expand our awareness, bringing to life something we may have believed but not yet fully embodied. When we enter into the grit of life, the stuff we may resist or want to make go away, it's amazing the gold we discover. Maybe the point isn't, as the popular saying goes, "Keep it simple, stupid," but rather "Keep it complicated, stupid." Maybe we should "sweat the small stuff" as often as we can.

WHEN I ASK an audience to define the word "holy," inevitably I hear words like "pious," "serene," "complete," "untouchable," and "beyond or above the everyday." Someone who is holy has arrived and is meant to be worshipped or looked up to. The word holiday, clearly derived from holy, is used to describe a day set apart from all others. A holy place—like the Wall in Jerusalem, Plymouth Rock, or the location of Buddha's footprint—is a site where we go to seek an experience beyond the ordinary, one that is normally inaccessible to us.

But the sages taught that holiness is available to us in every moment, in every place. We often miss these moments because they can be subtle and get lost in the routine of life, or we may repress them because holy encounters sometimes can be unsettling, at times terrifying. Majestic and awesome one day, ordinary and sweet on another, only to be messy, complex, even chaotic on yet another. Holiness isn't a state to be reached; it's an ongoing act of creativity like the origins of the universe.

In Hebrew the opposite of holy is *chol*, which is translated not as "profane" but as "empty"; in other words, "not yet filled." The word for holy in Hebrew is *kedusha*. A more accurate translation of *kedusha* is "life intensity." To be holy is to be intensely dynamic, ever-changing, and ever-realizing. The Biblical command "You Shall Be Holy" is an invitation to celebrate what philosopher Mark Taylor calls "a maze of grace that is the world." Live as richly and passionately as possible; that's as close to meaning as you will get.

And the messes are the point. Joy and sorrow, good and evil, greatness and triviality, hope and anxiety, the ideal and the actual: The ability to live with these seeming contradictions and the ambivalence and tension they create is what gives rise to wisdom. Our most chaotic periods can be catalysts for understanding. Even our daily frustrations and desires, when we bring them to the surface and wrestle with them, can imbue our lives with meaning. And our moments of wonder and awe, of sheer delight can be so much greater when we've celebrated the multiplicity of life. When things work out as we hoped, when things feel orderly and right; these, too, are holy moments.

The first time I felt this in my bones was a few minutes after my younger daughter, Talia, was born. It was the evening of Rosh Hashana, the Jewish New Year celebrating the creation of the cosmos. It was a month before Dana's due date, and we had been having a festive meal with family and friends at our apartment. As everyone ate and enjoyed the meal Dana had prepared, she began to have mild contractions. She thought nothing of it until they became increasingly stronger. Her eyes grew wide with both fear and joy as they met mine across the table. In that moment the dining room pulsated with energy, excitement, and anxiety. She was going to give birth that night.

> The ability to live with seeming contradictions—and the ambivalence and tension these contradictions create—is what gives rise to wisdom. The messes are the point.

As we walked to the hospital a few blocks away, doing her Lamaze breathing, the streets of Manhattan were transformed; every street light shone more brightly; every car sweeping by seemed to move in slow motion. Five hours after dinner, Dana gave birth to our beautiful Talia. It felt like a dream as Dana held our new baby just minutes after she emerged. Tears flowed down our cheeks. We felt joy and gratitude mixed with exhaustion and the final release of Dana's pain; blood and body fluids were everywhere, and there was that perfect child.

Then I had a thought that knocked the wind out of me. Just about one year earlier Dana had suffered a miscarriage. If she hadn't, Talia would not be in this world. In that moment I was filled with both sadness and peace. I felt the terror of that memory and the gratitude of this moment at the same time. In a flash I understood the Jewish practice of saying blessings when something good *and* when something bad happens. I saw how both good and bad are intricately knitted into the fabric of life. It wasn't that the birth of Talia made the miscarriage okay or that "it happened for a reason." It was the messiness and angst of not knowing the relationship between those two events or the outcome of any event. It was the realization that chaos and coherence are indistinguishable and awe-full.

Beginnings are almost always messy, although we often wish it were otherwise. We'd rather not experience the loss of a pregnancy, the pain and anxiety of childbirth, the digressive first draft, the bumpy first day on the job, the emptiness that is the precursor to almost any creative moment. As natural and understandable as this is, the desire for order distances us from the very meaning we yearn for. The biblical authors invite us to see both the order and chaos of the most amazing creative act of all: the story of the creation of the world. They gave us two stories of creation, two versions of how the world was born. The first version acknowledges the yearning for order, stability, and simplicity. Things seem to swim along marvelously, unfolding as God hopes and expects them to. This is the Genesis creation story most of us are familiar with. Here God is filling the void in the most orderly of ways.

"When God began to create heaven and earth—the earth being un-formed and void, with darkness over the surface of the deep and a wind from God sweeping over the water—God said, 'Let there be light' and there was light. . . . And there was evening and there was morning; a first day." There are six days that follow in the story, each day a new manifestation of life: from the earth and sea to the creation of hu-mankind, "in the image of God . . . male and female God created them." Just like that. And to top it all off, the first week ends with one day of rest, of peace and relaxation for the Creator.

But there is another, very different creation story that is embedded in the Book of Job. This version reminds us in no uncertain terms of the intensity and chaos just under the surface. At the very least, the biblical writings teach, life is a dialectic between order and chaos, harmony and conflict. Life hangs in the balance.

Job is perhaps the messiest biblical story of all: a seemingly perfect life, a man blessed in every way with good fortune who is utterly ru-ined, it seems, for no reason at all. He suffers poverty, illness, and the death of loved ones. It all seems senseless and totally unfair, and Job un-derstandably cries out. There are more than thirty chapters of conversa-tion between Job and his friends, who try to justify what has happened to Job. They even accuse him of having done something worthy of this punishment. They were desperate to find a reason, to make meaning out of something which just might be meaningless. But this actually only served to keep them from the pain of the reality that, quite simply, shit happens. Satan, Mara, Shiva, Accidents, Cancer Cells, Depression—all are ways of talking about roadblocks in our path, what frustrates us and keeps us from living our dreams.

And then there's a voice from the whirlwind that reminds the bereft Job how God created all that is. Job's friends are rebuked for trying to make sense of life at Job's expense, causing him so much more pain. Don't we all do that? In our efforts to find a "reason" for the unreason-able, to justify the unjustifiable, we blame or insinuate or deflect. Un-like Genesis, which is told by an omniscient narrator, Job's story is told in the first person voice of the Creator, the voice of "I." This is how God sees it; or really how we all, at times, experience life. Creation isn't something that happened neatly in the past. Rather, it is ongoing and excruciatingly difficult.

The language here is as beautifully poetic as it is fierce: "Where were you when I laid the earth's foundations? . . . Who closed the sea behind doors when it gushed forth out of the womb . . . when I made breakers . . . and set up its bar and doors? . . . Have you ever commanded the day to break, assigned dawn to its place so that it seizes the corners of the earth and shakes the wicked out of it? Have you seen the gates of deep darkness?" Later God asks Job, "Can you draw out Leviathan by a fishhook?" Chaos is always threatening to break through: The doors are kept closed by force of will; all of Creation is incredibly, intricately fragile. The world is not safe, not stable, but always in flux. As a teacher of mine once put it, "Creation is the story of the confinement and channeling of chaos rather than its elimination."

In this second story, God, like us, has a deep desire for order. But there is also a keen awareness of and respect for chaos. The Genesis creation story represents our deepest hope, and Job reflects our most honest experience of reality. The infinite beauty of creation is inseparable from its destructiveness.

The biblical authors don't favor one version of creation over the other. They understand that creativity alternates between chaos and order. They are in fact inseparable: an ongoing process of ordering and chaos-ing. Yet so often we confuse our yearning for meaning and understanding with a desire for stability and simplicity—and as a result meaning eludes us. It can be so liberating and enlivening to embrace the very stuff we most fear, that which can disrupt, even destroy. Life isn't neat. Meaning can be found in the sacred messiness: when we can experience, even just for fleeting moments, the fragility of creation and the necessity of chaos.

The sages invite us again and again into the soup of creativity. They remind us that even when things seem to be going swimmingly, there's no way it's going to last, not even for more than one chapter, not even for God. Right after the beautiful, simple act of creation in Genesis, that blissful, productive first week where humankind is created in the image of God, we get the Garden of Eden story. Here God forms humankind "from the dust of the earth," already getting a little messy. Then there's Eden—Shangri-La and Walden Pond rolled into one—a seemingly perfect world. It's a paradise where everything is provided, and all seems well. Or not.

> When we confuse our yearning for meaning and understanding with a desire for stability and simplicity, meaning eludes us.

The biblical author doesn't seem to want it to be for long: A tree is placed at the very center of the garden. It's the tree of knowledge of Good and Bad, and it's strictly off limits; a daily reminder that even in paradise we don't have it all. The garden is a metaphor for our consciousness—we all yearn for what we think we cannot or should not have. We all live with absence in the middle of our gardens. The mark of humanity, what made Adam and Eve worthy of being the very first people, was their powerful yearnings for more. And yet desires and urges have a way of "ruining everything," of interrupting paradise, of messing up what we thought on the surface was perfect the way it was.

The first story of humankind marks a very dramatic shattering of a very neatly ordered world. Most of us know the story, although we may not have read it through the prism of our own lives. Just imagine you're Eve hanging out with Adam in the Garden of Eden. You've enjoyed every minute, tasting all the delicious fruits, frolicking in the waterfalls, and sleeping under gentle breezes. There's not a question or concern in your mind, only the sweetness and pleasures of the body. Then one day you wake up ready for a new day and you realize you've wandered everywhere you can go in the garden; you've seen and experienced its wonders. And you feel a little restless, bored. There's a dull ache inside you; there has to be something more.

Then you remember The Tree, and you feel a thrill run up your spine. It's the only mystery remaining, the only fruit you haven't tasted.

And this one might be the best one of all—why else would it be forbidden? Why else would you want it so much? There's a voice growing louder inside you that tells you that if you eat you'll be wise and knowing, and the world will be new again. You wander over to the tree, and you see that there's no fence around it; the fruit in all its lusciousness is there for the taking. You're overpowered with desire; what had been a tickle now subsumes you. When you taste the fruit, you can't believe how alive you feel, how amazing it tastes, and you give some to Adam. You want him to join you, to accompany you to that new place, wherever it is, no matter what the consequences.

And we all know the consequences.

Adam and Eve must leave the garden. Their desires messed up paradise and gave birth to the world. Now freedom and yearning will define humanity for the rest of eternity. And the rest of the story unfolds in all its sacred messiness, all its holy dysfunction, all its dynamic intensity. Would we have it any other way?

Throughout the texts, the biblical authors create situation after situation in which human beings are thrust into the goop of life. The most unsettling and confusing emotions—envy, anger, and fear—drive the story forward. There's story after story of people like Eve messing up; wounded, unconscious people who nevertheless accomplish great things, at times precisely because of their mistakes and weaknesses. Not even the God character seems to be able to make sense of it all. Imagine that; God can't quite get it together. Like all of us, God is becoming—learning, deepening, and expanding.

The Bible, a text so many people over so many centuries have deemed sacred, has at the outset the story of generations of a family in all their pain and insanity. There is no Eureka moment where the grand order of the universe is finally revealed, where life becomes simple and neat. Quite the opposite. There's no novel or soap opera that even comes close to matching the drama and dysfunction of these families: betrayal, favoritism, exile, and murder. And when the Israelites finally arrive, the Promised Land, too, is a mess; the country becomes divided and the great King David, builder of Jerusalem and author of the Psalms, commits adultery and murder both.

For every moment of courage, for every time of great healing, there is a moment of weakness, of hurt or disappointment: The balance is always there. This is exactly what makes the Bible holy. It invites us to find ever-expanding meaning in both the messy and neat; the triumphs and disappointments; the weaving and the unraveling. It's up to us to see the holiness in all this drama; to bring it to life with our own reading and our own living.

The biblical authors did their best to wake us up. They understood that so much more can be learned from disarray, from upset, than from placidity and safety. There are so many unsettling events, chapter after chapter of surprises that buck the status quo at every turn. In Genesis, the theme of the younger sibling surpassing the elder is one we see again and again. At the time it was written—and even today—the eldest son was greatly favored, inheriting the property and wealth of the family and the status of the father. How provocative to have the patriarchs and matriarchs, the very founders of a great people, jockeying for position with God and within their families! How subversive to have the younger child, often as the result of deception, parental favoritism, or even murder, be the favored child.

The story of the first dysfunctional family begins with Cain and Abel. They are the children of Adam and Eve now far from the garden. The younger is Abel, the keeper of the sheep; Cain, the eldest, is the "tiller of the soil." He's trying hard to create a garden: a substitute paradise to please his parents; to fulfill their longings and ease their regrets. When Cain brings an offering from the fruit of the soil, Abel follows with an offering of the first of his flock. What a copycat. And the first of flock, no less. Cain must have thought, "Is he trying to pretend he's the first son; trying to take my place?" God "paid heed" to Abel's offering but not to Cain's; though how Cain knew this is a mystery. Hence the beginning of sibling rivalry.

At this moment of rejection by God, Cain's face fell. God's response seems to be sympathetic to Cain. God tells him if Cain does the right thing, there is uplift. In other words, when you can know your envy and your anger and still be your brother's keeper, it's a high. Then Cain is warned with the famous line, "But if you do not do right, sin crouches at the door." This is the first use of the word "sin" in the Bible. In Hebrew, sin means missing the mark, getting it wrong. What did Cain get wrong? He had imagined, as so many of us do, that reality was designed to meet his needs. And now he had a choice. How would he react to the inevitable unfairness and perceived inequities of life?

Cain may in fact have tried to follow God's advice. The next line says: "Cain said to his brother Abel . . ." We never know what Cain says. Instead Cain kills Abel, acting on, rather than examining, his rage. Cain avoids the messiness, the intensity and pain of investigating his own feelings; he chooses to see his anger as an end rather than a beginning. And in the process Cain kills his only brother. When asked where his brother is, Cain answers, "Am I my brother's keeper?" There really are only two questions we need to answer in our lives: the first two questions of the biblical story, "Where are you?" and "Am I my brother's keeper?" When we're fully conscious, the answer to the first is "Here I am." The answer to the second is always "Yes."

What if Cain could have expressed his envy to Abel? Cain might have asked him, "Did you do something different than I did?" Cain might have looked inside himself to see if his offering was all it could have been. And maybe Abel would have responded to his older brother, "What makes you think your offering wasn't accepted?" If this conversation had happened, maybe Cain would even have seen that he was the favored son. In Hebrew Cain means "acquire or gain," and Abel means "futility." Cain goes on to become the founder of cities. He makes it into the future. And Abel disappears. The paradox is we're the children of Cain.

Perhaps because I'm one of six brothers, I'm very familiar with sibling rivalry. Like Cain, I am the eldest, and often had feelings of envy at how my younger brothers, one after the other, seemed to be coddled more than me. Often along with the privileges, the oldest carries a heavier burden: more expectations, more independence, and the memory, if only faint, of what it felt like to be the only one. I was out of the house at the age of fourteen, working my way through boarding school. This is something I'm both proud of and admit I still sometimes resent. These feelings are still very much alive in me, and I marvel at how often my role as eldest plays out in both my personal and my work life.

Brad is a close colleague of mine, someone I've mentored. I've always wanted him to succeed, to grow, to take on more of the work of running the organization that I lead. In the spirit of this effort, I encouraged Brad to go to an annual conference that, typically, I would have attended. We were both thrilled: he to have the opportunity, I to have the much-needed break from traveling. Then one day he came into my office to tell me that His Holiness the Dalai Lama would be coming to the conference and that our organization had been granted the rare honor of spending some time alone with him. I felt the sting of envy. Brad would get the honor, not I. In biblical language, Brad's offering would be accepted, and I wouldn't even have the chance to give mine. Like Cain, I was the eldest here, higher in the hierarchy, and I could exert my power if I chose to.

> Messy emotions can give rise to generation after generation of wisdom.

Brad must have seen how my face fell at this news. He said, "Irwin, do you want to go?" Perhaps it was because of the generosity of Brad's offer. Perhaps it was because I recognized my envy for what it was: a momentary reaction to an opportunity lost. Or perhaps it was because I heard the same voice Cain did: If you do "right" there is "uplift." Whatever the reason, I insisted he go. In this case the uplift would be not just Brad's but mine as well; I would rise to a greater place within myself, coming closer to being the true mentor I always wanted to be.

As uncomfortable as it was, my envy ended up making our relationship more meaningful, more so than if I had effortlessly encouraged him to go. As he walked out of my office, he smiled knowingly and said, "Thanks, big brother." He knew he'd helped me get somewhere I needed to go. And I found myself thinking about the centuries-old concept called *kinaat sofrim*, translated as "a burning envy among the scribes." This idea originated from the great debates among the ancient sages. Their jealousy of each other—which could often become rather fierce—almost always led to deeper and deeper insights, to more and more wisdom. These men understood the higher purpose of envy—they coveted their fellow scholars' depth of understanding, and as a result they would reach further into the text, often coming up with something even more revelatory: sacred envy—an envy that leads to new possibilities, new truths; messy emotions that give rise to generation after generation of wisdom.

Throughout the centuries, sages have asked the same question Lily's father asked. What does it all mean? Perhaps the only difference is that they knew there is no innocent, simple answer. There's only the search itself: the meaning-making and unmaking; the mistakes and healing; the dirty dishes washed only to be used again; life intensity unfolding everywhere. Once we know this, there is nothing to fear. We are free to dive into the messes, to get nice and dirty, and to experience the transformative power of sorting it all through.

TURNING IT OVER

ALL SACRED TEXTS CONTAIN WITHIN THEM INNATE complexities and profound teachings designed to challenge and awaken us; that's what makes them holy. But this hasn't stopped many orthodoxies, whether religious conservative or liberal secular, from finding literal, safe, and comforting ways to read these holy books. These may be the tried and true teachings some of us learned in Sunday school, lessons about morality and goodness, punishment and reward. They may never have rung true, perhaps bored us to tears, but they were still somehow reassuring, mirroring our desire to have life be normal and familiar. Or maybe we were taught the dismissive read, a way of explaining away or reducing these teachings to archaic tales that have no real meaning in contemporary life. How tempting to make such provocative, sometimes disturbing, stories obsolete.

But the ancient sages understood that spiritual texts weren't meant to confirm our values or sense of the world. They were designed to shake us up and help us discover more of who we are. There's an expression, "Turn it over one hundred times, and on the one-hundred-and-first time you'll understand." It's used by Rabbinic sages to describe the experience of studying and interpreting, turning over every sacred story—reading, discussing, and reading again. When you think you understand a teaching, when you have an interpretation of a story or character that feels comfortable or right, it's time to start over at the beginning.

> Turn it over one hundred times, and on the one-hundred-and-first time you'll understand.

The sages and mystics celebrated the yearning to "figure it out," to discover the essence of any text, including the text called life. This is why study is one of the most important spiritual practices in many traditions, from the Jesuits to Bakti Yoga, Tibetan Buddhism to Judaism. As one of my teachers said, "When I pray, I speak to God. When I study, God speaks to me." The goal is not to prove some divinely ordained truth but to discover exquisite ambiguities and mysteries about ourselves and the world; to find as many humble absolutes as possible. Wisdom isn't about knowing; it's an understanding that meaning is inexhaustible.

As another teacher once told me, "Think of any interpretation of Torah as a road through the countryside. If you don't stray from it, you have no reason to suspect the existence of anything you can't see as you walk along it." When we push ourselves to look more deeply, we discover unexpected insights below the surface.

Our interpretations and our stories, like bad psychotherapy, can keep us on safe, well-worn, predictable paths—but if we turn them over to find new reads we can go into the forest where the richness is. The sages urge us to seek out and celebrate those places where tensions are evoked, where we feel uncomfortable, where very little seems right. The mystical biblical text called the Zohar says that each of us is a sacred scroll. The Bible, the Koran, and the Sutras are all us and we are them. Like their teachings, we are unfinished, unclear, unfolding. We are meant to engage rather than squelch our own mysteriousness. Jewish wisdom teaches us to turn over our own lives; to reach out beyond the familiar to experience awe.

Sometimes it's the most spiritual or intellectual among us, those of us who pride ourselves in being the most probing, clear, or open-minded, who actually are the most self-protective and bound in by our perceptions.

As enlivening and enriching as this is, it can also be tremendously frightening.

All of us interpret, for the most part, without even knowing. We all read reality through the lens of our fears, desires, assumptions, and judgments. Of course, we need our interpretations: They serve as filters to domesticate the uncanny and provide stability and order. But every time we settle on one perception, every time we stop turning over a story, we limit our understanding and miss a deeper insight. In other words, we stunt meaning.

I first became aware of the limitations of my own interpretations as a young rabbi. I was counseling a member of the congregation I was particularly fond of who had been diagnosed with lung cancer. He was asking the questions we all inevitably raise when we feel desperate or devastated: Why me? How will I get through this? I wanted so badly to be gentle and sensitive, to help Harvey put his illness in perspective, to better understand its widest possible meaning.

I explained that both spiritual and secular traditions in all their wonderful pluralism offer different theories about why we get sick, why tragedy strikes. There's a traditional "religious" explanation—which I downplayed because of its harshness—that illness is a kind of punishment for some sin. I talked about the scientific perception that illness is due only to biophysical factors; to genes and the environment. I described the mystical explanation that illness and suffering are inescapable parts of life that can only be transcended in a different world or level of awareness. Then I offered the one that worked the best for me: the existential explanation that illness is itself without meaning, but we give it our own meaning. We find the lesson, the truth that will most inform our spiritual growth.

I will never forget his response. "Do you see what you're doing?" he said, not without a kind of edgy anger. "I'm not an object that warrants a theory to be explained. None of this comes out of concern or sadness. You're so scared of getting cancer yourself that it's you who needs the theories—they help you, not me." Of course, he was right. All my interpreting was a way of protecting myself. Each of these explanations was profound and true—after all, they'd emerged and been transmitted through generations for a reason—but the only authentic response to Harvey's news was an expression of love and shared vulnerability: "Here I am. I care about you. It's scary." Harvey changed my life—and my feelings about illness. I would always love the interpretation game, but I would never play it the same way.

When we can look underneath our perceptions for the feeling, fear, or desire that inevitably led us there, a more profound teaching inevitably emerges. When we don't, we remain in a fantasy land of our own design, one that often has fortified boundaries keeping us from the rest of life. When we turn it over, even the most mundane encounters can become infused with meaning.

This was the case during what started as a casual conversation with a well-dressed, athletic-looking man on a bench at an ice cream shop in Cape Cod. After talking about the weather and the ice cream, he asked me what I did for a living. Usually I receive a polite nod or a smile, maybe an averted gaze. But when I told him I was a rabbi, he immediately launched into a diatribe about how he'd rejected Judaism, the religion he was raised with, how hypocritical it was, and how useless the whole concept of spirituality was for him. Part of me just wanted to walk away: Who needs that kind of anger and bitterness on vacation? Another part of me wanted to fire back a cutting response, but I controlled myself.

The fact that I was having such a visceral reaction meant something was going on within me: He clearly was hitting some of my own doubts. How often had I expressed outrage about religion today; how it's nothing but an attempt to transmit spiritual mystery to people who haven't experienced it by people who haven't experienced it, either? But, I thought, it was one thing for an expert to criticize and another thing hearing it from some arrogant guy on the beach. Whenever there's a strong emotion—anger, fear, anxiety—it's almost always a defense against an eruption of the too-muchness of life. That's when we tend to hold on to our interpretations or judgments, literally, for dear life. And, of course, the uncomfortable place is always the place to go; it's where self-realization happens. Both he and I needed to go there.

I wondered if maybe this man had something to teach me. I asked him what he did for a living. He told me he was the head of one of the leading fertility centers at a major hospital on the East Coast. I was impressed and wondered if he saw a deeper purpose to his work. He looked perplexed and annoyed by the question. But I persisted. "Just tell me what it feels like to do what you do." He surprised me by shaking his head and saying, "You'd never understand."

Now I was hearing spiritual language, a hint at the ineffable. "Try me," I said, to which he replied with a strange calmness, his eyes looking directly into mine, "A person comes into my office thinking they have death inside them, and when I'm lucky (a secular word for "blessed"), when they leave, they have life." I was floored. From death to life: He had articulated one of the orienting metaphors of every spiritual tradition.

I took a chance and asked him if he could possibly experience even a faint connection between what he was doing and an intuition about one of the deepest human yearnings, so deep that it is no less than "God's" first blessing: "Be fruitful and multiply." I was surprised to see his face soften and tears start to come to his eyes. He hadn't realized until then that his career could be seen as a spiritual practice. By turning it over, looking underneath, he heard himself for perhaps the first time express aloud the depth dimension of his work. He was engaged on a daily basis with something so immediate, so primal: the very thirst for life.

This doctor embodied what I've so often found to be true: The very people who most resist organized religion often are the most intensely alive and engaged in the complexity of life. Although they may not see themselves as holy, they are. Religion, which was originally designed to help deepen and ignite our experience, simply doesn't fulfill its promise as it is most often practiced. When we're willing to "turn it over" it's possible to see our passionate rejection as an overpowering yearning to be part of something

> When we're willing to "turn it over," it's possible to see our passionate rejection as an overpowering yearning to be part of something larger than ourselves, as a distinctly spiritual longing.

larger than ourselves, as a distinctly spiritual longing. There's no telling what the doctor will do with this insight, but for the time being he found himself in the very tradition he had rebuked.

Sometimes I encourage people to use the actual biblical stories as catalysts for investigation; rubbing their experiences up against those of the characters in order to discover new insights about themselves. These stories provide countless opportunities to see human foibles and life's twists and turns in light of the lives of some of the most memorable characters in literary history. And they help us feel less alone.

When I read and teach these stories I encounter more of who I am. It's not that I lose myself in the characters; rather it's that I find the characters in myself. The stories become mirrors. And this can be startling and disturbing at times, because I see in a flash how I have multiple selves, some not all that appealing. The murderous rage of Cain, the despair of Noah, the grandiosity of Abraham, the bitterness of Sarah, the unworthiness of Jacob, the insecurity of Moses, the lust of King David; they're all in me. I may not have known these selves, or have denied, dismissed, or ignored them, but there they are, and they await my investigation.

The practice of "turning it over" in traditional language is called *midrash*. *Midrash* is the name for the Jewish practice of interpretation, filling in the gaps in the text, even creating new stories in an effort to discover new truths. The word *midrash* actually means "investigation." There are many thousands of pages of *midrash* from over many centuries; an entire literature; hundreds of interpretations of the very same biblical tales. The ancient sages believed that religious texts called out, "Expand on me. Bring me to life." And the stories, dramatic as they are, are left intentionally vague so that we can find the widest possible context and ever-deepening understanding of each story. Then we can interpret *L'tov*, for "the good."

A few years ago, a wealthy and prominent couple in despair consulted me about what they saw as their only son's abandonment of the Jewish faith. This is a common concern and a very painful one, and for many parents it is a complete misunderstanding of their children. Their son was living what they called an "alternative lifestyle," traveling across the country with his band, sleeping with different women, not observing the practices he had grown up with. "He has no idea where he is going with his life," the father said. When I asked them what made them decide to come to me now, they told me that he had tattooed his body, a practice rejected by traditional Jews. I was curious, so I asked them what the tattoo was and where on his body it was. They said the tattoo was a Star of David etched on his ankle. I started to laugh and then, to my surprise, so did they.

I found myself thinking about the story of Abraham. At the very beginning, Abraham hears a call, "Go to yourself, leave your land, your father's house and go to a land that I will show you . . . and you will be a source of blessing." Most people don't know that, in Hebrew, Abraham is literally told to "go into himself," and it's a far more powerful command when read that way. But what's most striking here is the indeterminacy of the journey. The thirteenth-century sage Nachmonides, known as the Ramban, suggested that Abraham wandered from place to place until he finally discovered *his* place. As the Grateful Dead sing, it takes us all time until we can "pick a place to go, truckin . . ."

But who travels without knowing their destination? The easy answer is the fool, the blindly rebellious son. But isn't the fool just as often the innovator; the defiant child the creator? Aren't they the ones who dare to break through conventions to find a larger truth? The nineteenth-century mystic, the Sefat Emet, re-interpreted Abraham's story this way: "Go to the land that I will show you—where I shall make you visible, where your potential will be realized in unpredictable ways." Like many pioneers, Abraham departs from his parents' tradition: The sages imagine that before he left home, Abraham went to his father's store and smashed the idols—the statues of pagan gods which were sold there. Self-actualization demands destabilization.

When I reminded these parents of the readings of Abraham's story, I could see them squirm, undoubtedly with both recognition and discomfort. They were both traditional people and the children of immigrants; driven and successful, determined to live the American dream. They married early, and she stood by his side as he worked hard to climb the ranks in a prestigious accounting firm—one of the first Jews to break through, an idol-smasher in his own way. It wasn't easy to think that their accomplishments and their faith were somehow being left behind.

I wondered if maybe their son might not be breaking with their tradition after all. I asked them, "Does your son make love with his socks on?" If not, every woman he slept with would see the Star of David and know he was Jewish and cared enough about Judaism to mark his body with its sign. He was stepping away, yes. But perhaps he did so in order to find an expression of his tradition that suited him rather than the traditional one his parents lived—working just as hard, climbing different ladders, smashing different idols.

I also thought of an often overlooked detail in the first story of Abraham. His father, Terach, had actually begun the journey to Canaan with him, making it as far as the town of Haran where Terach settled and died. Perhaps Abraham's vision was linked in some inchoate way to his father's. Wherever our parents settle is the place we must set out from. Their dreams inspire us to dream anew. Continuity often comes in the guise of discontinuity, if one looks deeply enough.

I like to think these insights made an impression on this couple. When I ran into them a few years later, I jokingly asked the mother, "How's your assimilated son?" She looked at me quizzically. Then she told me proudly how he had started a music school with a bunch of his musician friends and it was flourishing. A week later I received a copy of a CD of her son's music with a note that said only, "I think he found himself." The fifth song was a mesmerizing original piece from the Sabbath morning liturgy. Sometimes it's only in retrospect that we understand "the call."

> Look deeply enough and you'll see that continuity often comes in the guise of discontinuity.

I always think of the biblical stories as a kind of Rorschach test; when a character's actions spark within us an emotional reaction of some kind, even just a stirring, it's time to look further. The stories that most upset or unsettle us are always the most important. They're the ones that have the potential to teach us about our self-perceptions, our relationships, and our world.

The Genesis story about Rebecca and her two sons, Jacob and Esau, is one such juicy text. I've never met a woman who didn't judge Rebecca harshly. But one student unearthed new insights into this story that informed her own situation: her husband's claim that she favored their younger daughter. My student knew she treated her kids differently: she pushed the elder daughter, who was independent and driven, to work even harder; and she spent much more time with the younger, who was painfully shy. She felt guilty and anxious about the different feelings and hopes she had for her children. Was she pushing one too hard and keeping the other back? Why did she feel more physically affectionate toward her younger and more intellectually engaged by her elder? Did she love them both the same, as she always told them? As she put it, "Please tell me I'm no Rebecca!"

In the story, Rebecca urges her younger son, Jacob, to trick his brother out of his birthright—a blessing from their father, Isaac, that would have made Esau the heir to the covenant with God. The eldest son always inherited the family estate, and this was no different—but what an estate it was! How on earth could a mother do this?

When my student read the passage describing Rebecca's pregnancy premonition that "two nations are born in your womb . . . And the older shall serve the younger" she had an unexpected insight. Rebecca knew her children better than anyone. And so did my student. "Pretending your kids are equal isn't the point. What's really true is that they're different and unique," she said.

Of course, there are times that we do favor one child, when we seem to give one more than the other. And, as painful as this can be, sometimes not doing so can be even more harmful; sometimes favoring is actually appropriate, even necessary. Although we can hold back our favoring and try to make everything equal, we need to ask ourselves, is this really better for our kids? Perhaps the most important role of a parent is to recognize as best we can who our children are and to love them equally in their uniqueness.

IN MANY CASES, other people in our lives are the text we rub up against, and they often help us discover our selves. I don't think it's an accident that so often when something bothers us or when we feel deeply hurt we tend to turn to other people, whether they're friends, lovers, rabbis, or therapists. One could say that we do so in part because we know we need to turn over our problem, to find a new perspective, and this process is always easier and more powerful when another person is there to console us and, in some cases, confront our hard-held truths. By talking to someone else, we are automatically broadening our context.

I've found that the words I use to describe a given situation often become a kind of text for the other person to read. No one writes the script ahead of time, of course. But how we choose to phrase something is every bit as telling as the words the ancient scribes chose to describe the experiences of the biblical characters. I always tell people to be sure to call the friend who won't indulge you, who won't simply confirm what you already think and feel. The ancient scholars never studied alone; they read the holy texts out loud and voiced their opinions to each other. Even today, students are urged not to study alone, but to study with a *chavruta*, a study friend. That way there's always someone around the table to question, to urge them to turn it over again.

This may have been at some level why a bunch of buddies and I created a men's group. A woman colleague coined it jokingly "The he-man's woman-hating club." And we do talk about the women in our lives an awful lot. We also talk about our dreams and about the frustrations and challenges in our careers. One of the things I love about it is

that we're fearless about calling each other on things, never letting anyone feel like a victim for long. And there's lots of joking and gibing.
Inevitably, I walk away feeling like I've lightened up, like I'm holding
some truth, some judgment, some struggle a little more loosely.

One year the dynamic of the group changed dramatically when one
of the members' children was diagnosed with a fatal genetic disease. It's
unlikely that he'll be alive on his twentieth birthday. In the meantime,
Ben continued to seem like any other kid, exuberant and affectionate;
but Michael always knew the timer was ticking. When he said things like,
"Why Ben?"; when he questioned the meaning of his life; when he raged
and blamed God, there was no comforting him. We all felt pretty useless.
Nothing we usually had done to help each other seemed to apply.

One evening we gathered on the boardwalk near a beach. Michael
updated us on the specialists he'd seen and the research he was helping
to fund. Then abruptly he pounded the sand. "I know it's pointless,
pointless! Why the hell doesn't God do something?" God was clearly a
metaphor for his own guilt and feelings of helplessness. No matter how
much he did he felt it wasn't enough.

I told him that I didn't think it was an accident that he talked about
God more than he ever had before. Michael was like we imagine God to
be—aware of the joy and the pain; of how life would unfold, and how it
would end. It made me realize that omniscience was not all it was cracked
up to be. Unlike the rest of us, Michael knew when one of his children
would die and that he'd be alive to experience the agony and loss.

As I said this, I could feel the energy shift. He shook his head yes
and then no. He told us how just the other day he'd watched Ben playing in the yard with a child his age. We braced ourselves for the sorrow
he would express. Instead he told us that he'd enjoyed every second of
watching his son yell and walk and stumble and laugh. He'd realized in
that moment that life felt utterly full. I'll never forget his words, "I know
it's partly his mortality that makes me love him so acutely, makes me
savor every one of his smiles and every one of his tears. This is the next
step, I guess. I'll smile sometimes, too, even though I cry inside always."

We were all quiet for a few minutes. One of my friends broke the silence and said he imagined a crying and smiling God reaching out to embrace Michael. He turned away from us toward the waves. The five of us walked over and hugged him at the same time; now we were crying, too.

DUALITY DIVING

PICTURE A ROOM LINED WITH SHELVES UPON SHELVES of books, and a long table in the middle of the room with several books laid open, overlapping each other. A group of men is crowded around them, some old and bearded, some barely out of boyhood. They are quietly reading aloud to each other, stopping every once in a while to discuss what they've read. Then all of a sudden they are shouting, pointing their fingers at each other and the words before them. Then they settle down again.

The traditional study halls where these debates take place are called "houses of seeking." It's there that students wrestle with the meaning of sacred texts. At the Yeshiva I attended hundreds of people sat across from each other for ten or twelve hours a day, our voices ebbing and then erupting again well into the evening. We'd discuss and analyze, parsing down each teaching sometimes to individual letters to reveal insights. There was so much emotion and vitality in the room; it was far more than an intellectual exercise. At the end of the day we would be mentally and physically drained, and spiritually energized.

> **Disagreement is a gift. It alerts us to something wonderful waiting to be uncovered, telling us it's time to dive deeper.**

Anyone listening to one of these conversations might be struck by how rarely one point of view prevails over the others. Winning isn't the point, and neither are resolutions or conclusions. What every student hopes is that out of the argument, the seemingly clashing interpretations, will come a broader perspective than any one student could create on his own. Disagreement is a gift. It alerts us to something wonderful waiting to be uncovered, telling us it's time to dive deeper.

Wouldn't life be richer if we saw all of our conflicts from this standpoint? Rather than dividing us, arguments would be about finding connection. Rather than one side coming out on top, the goal would be to find the relationship between points of view. When we look closely enough, all insights are actually dependent on and inseparable from each other. Sages from all traditions teach that there actually is no such thing as a single, stand-alone idea. There's an intricate web of insights that we are always weaving. When we clash with someone else, when we become stuck in our own perceptions, it's because we've overlooked the threads. We see boundaries and obstacles instead.

Even if we believe intellectually that everything is interconnected and interdependent, most of us still see hierarchies and pendulums everywhere. We're always swinging between seemingly exclusive and obvious opposites. I'll name just a few. As you read them see whether you naturally regard each one as equivalent or related, or tend to judge one and have a preference for the other. Order-Chaos; Clarity-Confusion; Spiritual-Carnal; Master-Slave; Sanity-Madness; Meaning-Absurdity; Anxiety-Serenity; Moral-Immoral. It's amazing how often we carve up our experiences into dualities—practically every moment if we're really honest with ourselves.

At the same time, we want so badly to believe and experience the world as one. We yearn for unity and harmony; a place where polarities magically dissolve. But we'll never get there; no such place exists. The mystical understanding of Oneness is not that there are no dualities, it's that they all flow from the same source. Opposites need not be opposing nor need they disappear—but they can coexist.

One of the clearest statements of this is from Isaiah, who says, "I form the light and create darkness. I make peace and create evil. I, the Lord, do all things." In less overtly religious language, the Taoist philosopher Lao Tzu wrote, "Is there a difference between yes and no? Must I fear what others fear? What nonsense! Having and not having rise together. Difficult and easy complement each other. Long and short contrast each other. High and low rest on each other. Front and back follow each other."

For the sages, argument and debate were sacred conversations and holy practices precisely because they unearthed dualities. The sages knew that when we divide up our world, we inevitably feel separate and alienated from others and even from ourselves. But they also knew that most of us are not mystics, and that it's an innate human quality to judge and polarize. They actually encourage us to uncover our judgments; to both confront and embrace them. They teach us to hold opposing ideas together, to live inside the paradoxes. The definition of a paradox is a seeming contradiction that holds the possibility of a new truth.

I've found that when I am in the midst of an argument with a loved one, when I'm mired in some inner conflict, when I encounter an idea or emotion that makes me uncomfortable or judgmental, the wisdom of the rabbinic sages can loosen my hold and allow me to see a new possibility, a wider perspective. I remember the first time my daughter said, "I hate you!" My first impulse was to yell back, "Don't you ever say that to me again. We don't use that word in this house!" But as it was coming out of my mouth I held back and was struck with the realization that of course this little four-year-old girl didn't hate me. Her hate was one of the many emotions bound up in her love for me. Rather than demonizing her reaction, I heard "I love you so much that I really hate you sometimes." My hope was that Gabriella would gradually become more in touch with her hate and consciously integrate it into her love. Then maybe she'd be a little mellower—at least until her teenage years!

Every relationship is a paradox, especially our more passionate ones. We dance between dualities of love and hate on a regular basis. I've often wondered how many fewer divorces there would be if we could absorb this truth. I know so many people who dismiss or distance themselves from their hateful, angry feelings out of guilt or fear—and they're always the ones who love less passionately. They also tend to hate more viciously, because their hate is no longer complemented by love. Or they project their rage and wind up feeling hated themselves.

When we recognize dualities for the paradoxes they really are, our understanding of the world and ourselves knows no bounds. There is an art to this. I call it "duality diving." When I surface my thoughts and feelings—especially to someone else who can challenge me—I can begin to examine them. When I make my internal dialogue external, giving voice to the dualities of right and wrong, strong and weak, whatever it is that particular day, I begin to see a wider perspective.

Inevitably, for everyone there comes a time (or times) when the way we divvy up our life no longer makes sense. The grandest, most operative polarities through which we see ourselves, our relationships, our work, and the world back us into a corner and cause us pain. And then it's time to dive, to widen, to make room for new truths to emerge.

A friend of mine named Ellen came to me one day in great distress about what she saw as her lack of motivation: She was resisting looking for a new job after being out of work for three months. She'd been a high-powered woman—an executive and innovator in the magazine world who'd launched several thriving businesses during her fifteen-year career. When she was forced out of her job

Every relationship is a paradox, especially our more passionate ones.

in a nasty corporate coup, her husband, friends, and colleagues all wondered why she was letting this one bad experience keep her from re-entering the ring.

She was also mystified, describing herself as depressed and lost. She described how those first few weeks she'd wake up in the morning with a familiar burst of adrenaline, as she always had, ready to take on the day; the routine running through her head—shower, grab coffee and paper for the train, make it to the office in time to answer e-mails before that first meeting. Then she'd fall back on the pillow completely disoriented and deflated. There was no place to go. She used to earn almost twice what her husband made. Now she sat in her pajamas watching him march off to work every day. She felt like a failure, like she was wasting her time, letting her family down. Her anxiety was palpable. Then why, I wondered, had she turned down a major position at a new magazine just being launched?

"I don't know. I just couldn't. I've lost my spunk, my drive," she said. She told me she'd always been a risk-taker, full of purpose and ambition. Now she felt passive and lazy, confused and stuck. She certainly was stuck, caught in dualities and judgments of her own making: active-passive, productive-lazy, purposeful-purposeless, ambitious-resigned, clear-confused.

I asked her what she did with her days. She told me about a bus ride she'd taken one afternoon; how strange it felt to sit among old ladies and school kids as the bus slowly wound through her town. She described the sunlight streaming through the windows, the sound of the grumbling motor, the sights she saw as she traveled through neighborhoods she'd never even noticed before. She also spoke with a kind of wonder about hanging out with her neighbor who had just came back from the hospital with twins; walking her son to school; stopping to get a cup of coffee at a nearby café.

"But I feel like I'm just escaping, not accomplishing anything," she said. I suggested that she was actually working pretty hard, struggling with her old definition of success, trying to find a context for these languid, restful days. After being forced out of her job she was now being forced in. Far from being lazy, she was locating the dancing partner of accomplishment that she'd relegated to a corner. It was the perfect time to escape! She might have felt she was failing or withdrawing but she actually was dancing, waltzing, weaving. True, she wasn't producing in the way she was used to; rather, she was harvesting other selves. Accomplishment and escape aren't polar opposites. They go together. When you diminish one, you end up diminishing the other. Of course, she felt confused, uncomfortable; she was learning a totally new dance.

I suggested that in this materialist, capitalist, accomplishment-oriented world, perhaps she was taking the biggest risk of her life, far bigger than those she'd taken on the job. She was allowing herself to feel the

range of human experience. She had the "driven" part down; now it was
time to park for a while and enjoy the scenery—the scenery of her wider

> **Accomplishment and escape
> aren't polar opposites. They
> go together. When you
> diminish one, you end up
> diminishing the other.**

self. The goal wasn't necessarily to find the
perfect balance between doing and being, escape and accomplishment; to become a
completely integrated person. That would be
impossible anyway—and it'd be pretty boring. Rather, the goal was to find a dynamic
equilibrium. It would always be a dance—sometimes a waltz, sometimes a
tango, and sometimes standing by the wall, waiting for the next song.

I asked her to entertain the possibility that withdrawing was actually
a courageous act, that from pausing, from escaping, can come great creativity. Sometimes it's necessary to escape when you are imprisoned. And
maybe her old ethos of success had become just that: a prison. Perhaps
within her duality was a whole new possibility; what she saw as an irreconcilable conflict was really a paradox, and inside was a new truth. I told
her an ancient story of heroism and escape, one that determined the entire course of the Jewish tradition.

In 70 c.e. the Temple in Jerusalem, the holy center, was under siege
by the Romans. The most important rabbi of the time, Rabbi Yohanan
Ben Zakkai, was in Jerusalem when it was surrounded. For many
months he and his compatriots had fought the Roman siege. This, they
thought, was the only true demonstration of faith. Even when things
looked really bad, they resisted with everything they had. Surrender
would mean failure and blasphemy, the end of Judaism. They had no
choice.

But at some point Rabbi Yohanan began to feel otherwise. Did faith
demand fighting to the end, even when it was clear they could lose
everything? Maybe there was another way to be courageous. Instead of
fighting to the bitter end, he decided to try to escape. His fellow Jews—
even his own uncle, one of the leaders of the Zealots—condemned him,
accusing him of being a coward, committing treason, and abandoning
his people.

How Rabbi Yohanan must have felt! What anguish to leave behind his friends and family, to let the Temple go. But he sensed that escape, too, was a way of fighting for what he believed in. His compatriots favored one side of the duality; but resistance is always a dance between retreat and attack, active and passive. Defending oneself and what one values sometimes demands leaving. It can be the ultimate accomplishment and an incredible demonstration of bravery. So the rabbi had his students put him in a coffin and carry him outside the walls of Jerusalem. What an incredible image! That coffin meant the death not just of one form of Judaism, but of a way of looking at the world.

The rabbi redefined courage, finding a new way to fight for one's religious and cultural survival, for one's identity. Duality diving always demands that we allow for the death of one way of organizing reality and the birth of another. This can be so wrenching. And far from being cowardly, it's incredibly risky. In this case escape was quite literally not without its risks. Before letting coffins out of Jerusalem, the Zealots would put swords through them to make sure that no one was abandoning ship. Just before he was to meet his end, Rabbi Yohanan emerged from the coffin and asked the Roman general permission to settle with his students in a small town nearby. Remarkably, his request was granted. The Temple was destroyed and Jerusalem fell to the Romans. But the rabbi started a new school that became the foundation of the next era of Judaism, rabbinic Judaism. He taught that study and prayer, words and intention, would replace the old forms of temple worship. God would no longer be in one place but exist among the people themselves whenever they engaged in acts of loving-kindness.

Of course, there was no guarantee that the rabbi's decision would bear such fruits. Even on his deathbed many years later, he questioned his actions. As he lay thrashing around, clearly in distress, his students asked him if he was afraid of dying. He told them he feared something far greater: that his decision to leave Jerusalem decades before may have been a terrible mistake, one that would forever alter the destiny of his people, maybe not for the better. When we dive into our dualities and break them open, there's always tremendous uncertainty.

The stakes were surely lower for Ellen than they were for the rabbi, but she, too, had no idea what the result would be. Would she be able to help support her family? Would she find meaningful work? Ellen needed to allow her definition of accomplishment to die. It simply wasn't sufficient to meet the challenges of that point in time. Success for Ellen demanded that she view escape, failure, and not getting ahead as a full partner with her previous self-image.

When I saw Ellen a month or so later, she had taken on some consulting work and she was making new connections in her field. She had also begun to write for herself and play with her children every evening. "When I allowed myself that escape, when I saw that it might actually be proactive, that I might be doing something after all, I started having some fun. Now I know I don't have to rush back into the same high-powered situation. Even if I did, I wouldn't do it in the same way." Out of a seemingly irreconcilable duality came new insights. Escape led to the birth of a new understanding of accomplishment.

In our culture, some of the most painful dualities seem to surround issues of success and failure. Whether it's a child's performance in school, a relationship challenge, or a career issue, we tend to see things through the lens of this duality. Success means accomplishment, progress; life is meant to be an upward arc, a seamless line to the top. We're meant to fulfill our utmost potential. When we don't, we've failed in some way. And we better get back up on our feet and do it better next time. Of course, there's great value in ambition; without it society would not continue to evolve. But when we can dive into our dualities around success and failure, ambition and contentment, accomplishment and complacency, we might broaden and enrich our understanding of what it means to achieve.

This was certainly the case for me. A few years ago after reaching the "top" of my organization, I hit bottom. I was burnt out and disillusioned after years of teaching and aggressive fundraising, and I made the abrupt decision to take a sabbatical with the knowledge that I might not return. This was a difficult move for me, although I was incredibly grateful that my organization was willing to give me these months.

During this time, I struggled with my self-image. I had always been the driven one in my family. The eldest of six in a family of modest means, I had begun earning a living when I was a teenager, and it had been nonstop since then. Now, at the age of forty-three, I found myself sitting in my underwear in an armchair in my living room for weeks at a time, doing nothing except for taking an occasional walk. I had no motivation, no desire to accomplish or produce anything, and I felt guilty. I judged myself: "I've lost my ambition. I'm not the successful person I thought I was."

One day on one of my many walks along the Hudson River, I noticed that the water was completely placid, not a ripple anywhere, a very unusual sight for this giant river. I found myself saying out loud, "Just because it's still, does it mean nothing's going on down there?" I pictured currents beneath the surface, fish swimming everywhere. And I began to wonder if that was also true for me, that in fact my dormancy was somehow dynamic, active. Passivity on the surface was connected to constant movement underneath. I was unmoored, flowing with the tide, and I wasn't sure where it would take me. This was rather unnerving, because I sensed it just might change my life. For once being ambitious wasn't about getting to the next tier, the next manifestation of success. It was about going with the flow—my internal flow—and seeing where I'd end up.

The first place that current took me was back to my childhood. I began to think about where all this mania for external success and accomplishment had come from. I wanted to understand why I felt such disdain for slowing down. I needed to examine my own dualities. I began to see that I had always judged my father for his lack of drive, for never realizing his potential. He was so brilliant, so charismatic, such a talented musician and singer. But rather than reaching for the stars, conducting an orchestra or joining the opera, he had remained a cantor serving just a couple of congregations for over forty years. I realized that, perhaps as a result of this judgment, I'd always been motivated by a desire for public success and financial reward. I was wary of ever being complacent, determined to never settle. I always had to do more, get to that next meeting, give that next lecture, get that next donation.

During this time, I was invited to speak at a temple in a town near where I'd grown up. I almost said no. I was supposed to be on sabbatical. More than that, I didn't want to go to Long Island, the place that bound my father and that I'd been so determined to leave. But out of a sense of obligation and probably guilt as well, I went. After the services were over, an elderly lady came up to me. She asked me if I was related to Cantor Kula. When I said yes, she pulled out a manila envelope from her handbag and offered it to me as a gift.

I pulled out an old black-and-white photograph of a young man in his mid-twenties standing next to what looked like a thirteen-year-old baby-faced Bar Mitzvah boy holding a Torah. The young man had pure joy on his face. Suddenly I saw that this was my father. And except for the gray hair he looked exactly the same as he did now. He had the same sparkle in his eye, the same open, gentle smile. The woman told me how more than forty-five years ago my father had taught her son his Bar Mitzvah portion with such care and sincerity. She told me how grateful she'd been. When she saw the announcement for my lecture in the newspaper, she thought maybe I was related and that she just had to come to give me this photo. This woman, now a great-grandmother in her eighties, had kept this photograph for all those years and made a special trip to give it to me.

As I gazed at the photo, I found myself contemplating the contribution my father had made to the lives of this lovely woman and her son. But what struck me the most looking into my dad's glowing young face was that he'd been happy, that he was still happy, and that this alone was enough. I realized just then that I envied and longed for that same feeling of joy, that same sense of success and accomplishment.

What I had always seen as my father's lack of ambition was actually a kind of calm, inner satisfaction with where he was and what he had—a vital and deep connection to his community and a respect for and excellence in his art. I remembered the rabbinic saying: "He who is a hero is the one who can show restraint. He who is wealthy is happy with his lot." Suddenly my father's seeming lack of ambition was so alive and colorful—and incredibly desirable. He was a restrained hero. He was wealthier and more successful than I'd ever imagined.

That night I called my father. I told him about meeting the mother of his former student and how I'd felt as I looked at that wonderful photo. I explained how I'd misjudged him all those years, how wrong I was to think he hadn't lived up to his potential. He had prepared more than two thousand children for Bar Mitzvah and sung at more than a thousand weddings. Not only that, he'd raised six sons, all of whom were friends, and all of whom were accomplished in different ways. He didn't need a concert hall stage. His success had been in the privacy of his office, on the pulpit of the synagogue, and in the intimacy of our home. This realization was both liberating and frightening. My definition of achievement was dramatically altered by one simple encounter, as was my vision of my father. Years later, I'm continuing to search for my own definition of success, but the journey is richer and more joyful than it has ever been.

There are times when duality diving can be an organic internal process, as it was for me with my father. But there are other times when the opposite is true. Our dualities often aren't so easy to locate. We may circle around and around the very same thoughts. We may get depressed. We may spend a lot of time feeling angry at the world for not conforming to our expectations and maybe even get angry at ourselves for feeling this way. When I find myself stuck in a rut, going nowhere, I've found that when I can actually give voice to my judgments and preconceptions, as those scholars did sitting around that table, the paradoxes begin to jump out at me.

Several years ago I realized the power of voicing dualities as I sat in an audience listening to Ram Dass, a wonderful spiritual teacher, who was recovering from a debilitating stroke. He told us that all his spiritual training, all his meditation and study, had not prepared him for the suffering he experienced after the stroke. He was deeply disturbed by feelings of vulnerability and humiliation, by his loss of independence. He needed people's help to move, to eat, to dress, to go to the bathroom. He said he'd gone from the person who years earlier had written a book called *How Can I Help?* to being a "helpee."

He told us of one day as he lay in his bed, disturbing thoughts and feelings swirled in and around him. Suddenly he felt a surge of violent rage, and this frightened him. He berated himself, thinking: "I am Ram Dass. I should have a sense of acceptance and peace." A few minutes later he asked himself, again full of rage, "How could you let this happen? Why can't you be okay with this?" Referring to the title of his groundbreaking book, he remembered saying out loud, "I am supposed to 'be here now!' It's all supposed to be grace. Instead I feel so fierce."

I was struck by the vulnerability he was willing to show us, and all of us in the audience were completely silent. Then he re-enacted what had happened next. He looked from one hand to another and murmured over and over again, "Fierce. Grace. Fierce. Grace." Then he yelled out, "Fierce Grace!" He told us that he'd recognized that he hadn't just had a stroke; he'd been "stroked." And this had given birth to a new kind of grace, and also a new kind of fierceness. He realized grace was not only accepting, refined, peaceful, and loving—the grace of good things. There was also a destructive and ferocious grace. Now, he said, he had "a full view of what grace is all about."

What had seemed irreconcilable to all of us a few minutes before suddenly became integrated. It seemed that as soon as Ram Dass had named the feeling and what he perceived as its opposite, he was moving to a new place. When he held the duality fierce-grace together, a new truth emerged. He had discovered a paradox, and it felt like a revelation to us all. He also told us that this realization deepened his understanding of needing help. "There's independence and dependence. They make a beautiful tapestry." He saw that helpers and helpees dance a wonderful dance; one serves the other. "After all, without helpees, what would helpers have to do?" I remember thinking that Ram Dass's vulnerability now made him incredibly powerful, a potent example for all of us.

When we can name our emotions, as Ram Dass did, they can actually become texts for us to read. This can be a challenge, because emotions often erupt; other times they slowly creep up on us. Either way, they can take over, and it's tough to stand back from them. But when we can, even the most painful eruptions and uncomfortable stirrings become wonderful tools. The more

> **When we name our emotions they can become texts for us to read.**

potent the conflict, the more powerful the insight. For this reason, when I work with people, I'm less concerned with why they feel what they feel; what's important to me is helping them name their emotions in order to find new truths.

One morning a middle-aged woman named Cindy came to me for counsel about her marriage. She told me she hoped I'd help her get to the bottom of her feelings of dissatisfaction and depression and help her "make a decision already." She wondered if there was some wisdom in the Jewish tradition that might help her decide whether she could save her marriage, which had felt more and more empty over the years. Self-help books hadn't worked and neither had marriage counseling. After we'd talked for a while, it became clear that Cindy felt her marriage was over. When I asked why she was still with her husband, she told me she felt like a failure every time she thought about divorce. Failure is a strong word. And I wondered if she might be holding a duality that was keeping her from seeing her situation more clearly. Marriage-success; divorce-failure; this is a duality our culture still fosters, and Cindy had embraced it.

I told Cindy that Jewish wisdom teaches something surprising about divorce, a teaching that Islam also shares. Divorce is a holy activity, just like marriage. This is surprising because Judaism views marriage as among the most holy and important life passages. There is a sacred document called a *ketubah* that every bride and groom sign when they marry, as do the rabbi and two witnesses. It is meant to be binding. Yet there is also a sacred document called a *get*, which is handwritten by a scribe and signed by husband and wife as well as a rabbi and two witnesses; it authorizes a divorce. The *ketubah* invites us to imagine the commitment of marriage is enduring, that we will fulfill our responsibilities to each other. The *get* dissolves those very responsibilities and reminds us that nothing is permanent, which is why the words "till death do us part" are never part of any Jewish wedding ceremony.

Jewish wisdom acknowledges the paradox that the most vital of relationships can end and this, too, can be a holy, intensely alive experience. And yet a divorce is not seen as a total breach—the couple will always be connected in some way, whether consciously or not. I invited Cindy to consider that if the marriage was painful despite all her best efforts, staying married might also be seen as a "failure." And then I asked her, "If both divorce and marriage are sacred, what about your marriage is worth saving?"

Tears came to her eyes, and then she said, "Nothing." She told me how over the last year her husband had been coming home later and later and leaving at the crack of dawn virtually every day. She admired his devotion to his burgeoning law practice, but she felt she didn't know him anymore. And worse, she doubted his love for her and her own love, as well. She also wondered if he was having an affair but had never asked him if this was true.

"Isn't marriage about trust?" she asked me. "If I love him, how can I doubt him this way? It's obvious that our marriage doesn't mean anything anymore." I couldn't counter her, of course; the fabric of her relationship with her husband was something I could never know. Instead, I shared an insight from biblical wisdom, one that's helped me enormously in my own marriage: Faith simply can't exist without doubt. Yes, a marriage is about trust but it is also sometimes about not trusting; about feeling both secure and insecure. If we don't allow ourselves to question, how can we trust? Perhaps Cindy's struggle was actually a sign of her love. Her fears about her husband might actually mean she was taking her marriage seriously; that it mattered.

A teacher of mine once called the Bible the greatest love story ever told. It's the story of the deepening love between God and a people, and it's anything but smooth sailing. Generation after generation, this relationship is a continuing dialectic between doubt and trust, questioning and loyalty. More than a few times, the bond is almost broken, only to be reengaged and strengthened. But the possibility of a permanent breach is always there and this makes the relationship even more vital and real.

The dynamic between God and the people is meant to be a metaphor for what all relationships—especially one as complex and intimate as marriage—are all about. The covenant God makes with the people is in fact very much like a marriage. The *ketubah*, the rabbis say, is the equivalent of the Torah; many *ketubahs* are actually written in calligraphy to look like the ancient scrolls. And both remind us that commitment is not an answer; it's a process. My hope was that Cindy might begin to see her feelings about her marriage in a new light; that she might broaden her concept of love. Even if her husband had had an affair, the marriage might still be worth saving. She would never know if she didn't express her doubts and fears. Only then could there be the possibility that her love would be renewed, or a *get* would be sacred.

I've seen so many people try to work out their relationship problems in isolation, or with a therapist, a spiritual teacher, a friend—anyone except the person they're having difficulties with. Confronting those we love most can be frightening, and often we do so only when the pain becomes acute, or sometimes not even then. This is in part because we believe we can do it on our own, if only we try hard enough; if only we become super-self-aware; if we accept that we're from Venus and they're from Mars.

Our culture has a strong, deeply ingrained belief in the power of the individual. Appreciating each person's uniqueness and rights is so important. But the myth of the self-made man, the solitary pioneer, has taken a new form in contemporary times. It seems that the self has become the ultimate sphere, the place where everything can be worked out and worked through, independent of anyone else. Publishers report that the self-help or self-improvement genre is the fastest growing book category in America. As the comedian George Carlin asks, "If it's really self-help, what do you need the book for?" Personal "coaches" are now replacing therapists, as if life were a game we can win if we only learn the rules.

So many of us put tremendous energy into training our children to be independent, to have self-esteem, to think they can do anything if they put their minds to it. I've often thought that it was the ultimate compliment when a friend or teacher said about my daughter, "She's got a mind of her own." But what are we really teaching our kids? I asked this question of a friend of mine who seemed so upset when his daughter, now a couple of years out of college, asked if she could move back home. He told me how afraid he was that she'd never make it on her own. He saw her return as a kind of failure. He'd invested so much in her education and he'd fully expected her to throw herself into a career or some kind of adventure after she finished school. And all she wanted to do was come home again? Clearly he was quite attached to the idea that independence means strength and dependence is a sign of weakness. And he was clearly struggling with it. "I wish I could welcome her home with open arms. I really do."

Often our dualities cause us some degree of pain, and this is a sign that we need to go deeper. Emotions like guilt, envy, anxiety, and depression often are the alarm bells. In the end, my friend's guilt got the best of him, and he and his wife told their daughter to come home. Over the months, he began to talk warmly of their dinners together, her successes as a freelance journalist, her good and bad choices in boyfriends. He saw that she was creating a life for herself after all, and that the atmosphere his home provided gave her the confidence and freedom to pursue what she really loved. Plus, he had the rare privilege of really being a part of her young-adult life. As Ram Dass said, dependence and independence make such a beautiful tapestry. They make up the web of intimacy.

Sometimes in the doing, our dualities can soften and allow new possibilities to enter. We don't always have to work it all out beforehand. It's often after the fact that we realize we were caught in a duality of our own making. When my buddy told me the story months after his daughter came home, he clearly had discovered the paradox. He realized that his daughter could be both independent and dependent at the same time. He also saw her independence in a new light. He told me with a laugh, "Thank God she was independent enough from me to come home despite my resistance." He came to understand that her dependence on him and his wife allowed for a kind of independence that was much more meaningful than he could have imagined. He was able to allow a new truth to emerge: interdependence. At one point he told me how much he'd come to count on their evening talks and walks to the subway in the mornings. I sensed that he'd become pretty dependent on her. No doubt, when his daughter did decide to leave, my friend would need to dive back into this duality and find yet another new truth.

YEARNING FOR
THE WAY

DANCING WITH
UNCERTAINTY

MOST OF US DEEPLY DESIRE AND CELEBRATE THE FRUITS
of uncertainty without realizing that without the seed, the fruit would
not exist. Discovery, revelation, insight, love, surprise, joy: We would
never have these wonderful human experiences if we didn't allow ourselves to feel unsure, to embark upon journeys without needing to know
where we will end up. Yet in my two decades as a rabbi, no one has ever
come to me for counsel about ways to become less certain, to invite more
questions, to celebrate ambiguity. Not surprisingly, hundreds have
walked into my office encumbered or even paralyzed by uncertainty,
racked with the anxiety of not knowing. They yearn for guidance, a bea-
con that will shine through the messiness and confusion. Almost always
they have a major decision to make, whether about a relationship, a
child, an aging parent, or the direction of their lives. And even if they
don't admit it, they want me to assure them of the outcome they so hope
for. Although I rarely offer that, I can't help but wish for the same thing.

The yearning for certainty—to grasp our future, to shape our des-
tinies—is so powerful and so noble. We yearn to know that things will
work out. We want to be assured that what we do will make our lives
richer and the world a better place. We long for a pathway, at least for a
"road less traveled," as the famous book by M. Scott Peck offered. But
most of the time we create our own path simply by walking even when
we have no clear idea where we are going.

Of course, we all have delicious times of certainty, clarity, confidence, and purpose—more than most of us even recognize. We are

always mastering new skills and reaching goals. Every day is filled with countless easy and seamless decisions. But the uncertain times stand out because they are often so uncomfortable. They create anxiety, fear, and vulnerability. That's why certainty is so seductive. Our culture rewards knowing and makes not-knowing a liability; but about the important things in life, it may well be the opposite. Certainty isn't all it's cracked up to be—it can lead to arrogance, boredom, complacency, and dullness. We all know those certainty gurus, whether religious, political, or those in our own lives. We may envy them their confidence, but we don't want to be in the same room with them for long.

> **Certainty is seductive. Our culture rewards knowing and makes not-knowing a liability; but about the important things in life, the opposite may be true.**

Living the mystery means dancing with certainty and uncertainty, knowing and not-knowing. Parenting is a perfect example of this. It's an unknown journey for anyone who undertakes it; yet there are times of knowing, of mastery along the way. It all starts before the baby's even born—there's so much excitement, fear, and anxiety leading up to that big event. There have been nine months to imagine everything that can go wrong and only so many classes and tests one can take and only so many books one can read.

Then there's the relief of knowing, of that baby in our arms; a sense of clarity and purpose that this is our child and we're going to take care of her. But then we go home and the ride really begins. Just when we get the swing of the baby stuff, we have a toddler, then a school-aged child, then a teenager, and at each stage a whole other learning curve begins. My parents tell me they're still learning how to parent—and they've raised six kids! There's no more humbling experience than parenting. The times of not-knowing far outweigh the certainties. Maybe that's why so many parents I know say having a baby is what made them finally grow up.

The biblical sages understood that the anxiety of not-knowing is the beginning of wisdom. There isn't a single character in the Bible

who understood beforehand the outcome of any journey he or she underwent. What makes these characters so special is not that they are
somehow superhuman, wiser, or more evolved. It's that they don't scale
down their dreams to the size of their fears. They are masters of the
dance between uncertainty and certainty. Every one of them is reluctant
to go on his or her journey; every one of them takes a risk without
knowing how things will work out; every one of them has massive
doubts along the way and needs reassurance that things will be okay;
and none of them fully completes what he set out to do.

Abraham uprooted his family and traveled from Babylonia, the
center of civilization at the time, to a place he knew nothing about. The
indeterminacy of the journey is captured in the words "Go forth to the
land I will show you." The certainty and comforts of Babylonia must
have been pretty appealing; it wasn't until Abraham was seventy-five
that he felt there might be something more. But did even he know
where he was going? Years later he retells the story of his leaving in a
most unusual way: "God made me *wander* from my father's house." I
love his honesty; there's neither bravado nor false humility.

Perhaps out of discomfort with the insecurities and uncertainties of
our own journeys, we read or hear the stories of great characters so differently: We think they hear a loud, clear call to act, to accomplish
grand things—the authoritative voice of God leading every step of the
way. We think they're everything we are not, when really we are all wan-
derers. The mystical text the Zohar tells us that God says to every human being every day "go forth," begin the journey that is yours to make.
What makes us enlightened is that we are not afraid to wander. Doubt
is a prerequisite for any meaningful journey. When we can acknowledge the built-in anxiety rather than maintaining the illusion of certainty, we become humble—which in turn creates a new and more
authentic confidence.

Yet the yearning for certainty is part of being human. Abraham
and Moses longed to know that it all would work out for the best. The
voice of God in these stories at times tells them about the wonderful

things that will happen along the way—Abraham will birth many nations; Moses will lead his people into the Promised Land. This voice is actually a metaphor for their yearning to know ahead of time where their journeys would take them, what the payoff would be. They were wrestling, feeling the push and pull between the realization that they couldn't remain where they were, the certainty that there was more, and the uncertainty about where they were going or how they would get there. They needed to struggle before they could take such enormous risks. In the end they were convinced that they would be headed in the right direction even if they were trailblazing a new path. They embraced the promise but weren't seduced by certainty, or surely they would have given up.

What if we understood that all decisions, even the seeming sure things, are leaps into the unknown? What if we were galvanized, rather than paralyzed, by uncertainty? It could be that our very denial about how unsure we really are in fact causes the most anxiety of all. We mistake ambivalence for weakness, indecisiveness for failing. We try to convince ourselves that the future should be ours to see and that there's actually a discernable and consistent cause and effect to our decisions and actions. Depression, obsessiveness, even paranoia have at

> **Doubt is a prerequisite for any meaningful journey.**

their roots a profound fear of the unknown and usually a wound from the past, a trauma lodged in our unconscious that we're afraid will reoccur. These are extreme reactions to the dread that it could all work out for the worst, that if we're not on the lookout, hypervigilant, or hiding behind the veil of disassociation, disaster awaits us. Extreme anxiety short-circuits life.

Yet if we're really honest with ourselves when we look back on our lives, we can see that all our decisions, large and small, were made from a place of uncertainty and sometimes profound conflict. Rarely have any of us had any idea where our decisions would lead, and other times what we thought would happen turned out quite differently than planned. It's not that life is a crapshoot. It's that vagaries and uncertainties are a part of the human drama. Our journey presents us with catastrophes, traumas, losses, gains, wonders, and miracles. And in the end we must act on faith, not that it will all work out as we want but that our best guess is good enough, that it will somehow lead us to a place of discovery, of new perspective, of a wider self.

A friend of mine had talked for years about starting his own consulting agency after years of hard knocks in the corporate world. He'd been laid off a number of times as companies merged and bosses changed, and even though he was currently employed, he'd had it with the politics, the endless meetings, the whole scene. He'd sweated through many a sleepless night contemplating his next move. He'd created an ambitious business plan for an agency, and at one point had even scoped out office space.

But month after month there was some reason not to go forward. It seemed that whenever our families got together, my wife or I would inevitably ask "So, Adam, hung out the shingle yet?" One evening after several drinks and a fair amount of prodding from me, he confessed that he was utterly terrified. Not only would he not be earning an income right away, but he'd be investing his hard-earned savings in his own venture. And the pain of the so-called "failures" that dotted his career to this point gave him pause—major pause. "Success just isn't in my repertoire," he said.

After more than a year of planning, he still felt that if he analyzed the possibilities, going over and over the potential outcomes in his head, he somehow could ensure the outcome he so desperately hoped for: a thriving business and a renewed sense of confidence in himself. Just maybe, he would find a way to protect himself from the failure he feared, from repeating the traumas of his previous work experiences. He wanted to know ahead of time that he would be successful. As a result, he kept coming up with more questions that needed answering before he could make his decision.

> **All of us have permission to act without knowing. Whether we acknowledge it or not, we are always doing so anyway.**

I remember feeling a rush of both frustration and compassion as I listened to him that evening, watching his increasingly pained expression as he downed glass after glass of wine. "God created the world from a place of not knowing. Surely you can start a business," I blurted out. And I wasn't kidding.

I told him the Talmudic story about how God created and destroyed ten worlds before this one. Each world was so incredibly disappointing, so different than what had been envisioned; an utter failure in the eyes of its Creator. Uncertainty drove God crazy, too. And yet the Creator kept going, desperately trying to get it "right." When God breathed life into the world we know today, once again there was incredible rage about its imperfection. No matter how we try, there's no way to guarantee that things work out as we intend.

But just as this world, like all the others, was about to be destroyed, God paused, having come to a startling moment truth: Simply because one creates something does not mean one can predict or control it. If the only way we can experience success is to be certain about how our actions will play out, we are doomed to disappointment and anger. God embarked on a journey about which very little could be known in advance; one that would be filled with surprises and learning. What a concept: God wasn't sure but did it anyway. No matter how many blows; how many expectations and hopes were dashed; never knowing what would happen next—God stayed with it. Of course, this story is really about our own need to choose life and wonder over paralyzing rage at and disappointment in ourselves and others.

I encouraged my friend to embrace his own uncertainty and go forward. He didn't need to know the outcome of his venture, but he could find the part of him that wanted to do it, make the preparations knowing the risks, and act from that place. Even if his business turned out to be a "failure" it would inevitably lead him to the next place he needed to be, perhaps eventually leading him back into the corporate world with a whole new breadth of experience behind him. And he could be reassured not by the certainty of the future but by the fact that along the way he would continue to decide; every move was an opportunity to either recommit or change directions.

THE NINETEENTH-CENTURY philosopher Franz Rosenzweig taught that life is a succession of leaps into pathlessness. We take a path, follow it, and then we must leap again. There is never a final decision, a choice to end all choices. Every decision is a partial truth; there's always a road not taken. No matter how many maps we read, no matter how hard we study the roads we or others have taken in the past—although of course we must do all these things—the future is unknown. We move at the moment of decision from path to pathlessness.

Halacha, the Hebrew word for Jewish law, comes from the root "to walk." It literally means "the path," "the way," or even more accurately "pathing"; like the Sanskrit word *pratipadyate*, "one who paths." It's the opposite of a fixed or stable law. There are so many ways to path: cut, follow, climb, run, skip, stroll, circumvent. As long as the path we're on takes us where we want to go, we barely notice it. We take in the sights and smells, enjoying the ride, taking the bumps as they come until they get too big or the path disappears or takes a turn into a darker part of the forest. Or maybe it's too straight and narrow. Then we feel trapped, frightened, or bored, and we have to retrace our steps or find another path, or wander in the wilderness for a while.

The Talmud contains twenty volumes of recorded debates about how to live spiritually, ethically, and morally. It's a series of decisions and re-decisions, paths and leaps: a series of arguments and concessions, sages agreeing and disagreeing with each other for over four hundred years. Many people to whom I teach the Talmud are struck by the fact that 75 percent of all the debates and arguments are left unresolved. No final decision is ever reached. This is unique in sacred literature. By not providing definitive decisions, the sages were teaching us that we ought not to fool ourselves. Not even the most intense debate, investigation, or wrestling will allow us to make decisions with anything less than uncertainty and indeterminacy. And the discussion continues into future generations.

All of us have permission to act without knowing. Whether we acknowledge it or not, we are always doing so anyway. Rather than imprisoning us in a malaise, uncertainty can actually liberate us and make life so much more vivid. As Edmond Jabès writes in *The Book of Yukel*, "Certainty is the region of death; uncertainty is the valley of life. Once we can liberate ourselves from the tyranny of needing to be certain, it becomes possible to take, as William Blake wrote, 'eternal delight' in the undecidable." The "undecidable" is where the action is, where the invitation to play, explore, and dance happens.

Jewish wisdom teaches that nothing is more important than what we do. Being paralyzed by indecision is not an option. It's incumbent upon every human being to contribute to the world, to make a difference. That's why our decisions are so important, why as many angles or paths as possible should be considered. The rabbis compared life to a scale: Every act tips toward more life or more death. This is not just poetic or some medieval truth. All of us are an accumulation of our actions. Every moment is a karmic moment. And this gives everything we do more meaning. Decisions are in fact moments of "selving," of cumulative evolution. And not-deciding is as much a decision as changing one's course: It's just pathing by a different rhythm.

There's a wonderful passage in the Talmud describing one of the steps in the process of becoming ordained as a rabbi. Every rabbinical student must make an argument for the purity of a specific food, offering forty-nine reasons justifying his position and forty-nine reasons justifying the position he has not taken. The Talmud had already clarified what foods are pure and what foods are not, so why bother to argue the other side?

Faith can't exist without doubt.

The point is that one cannot understand the reasons for a decision unless one understands the other side. Why forty-nine reasons? Forty-nine, like most numbers presented in wisdom texts, is a metaphor: Seven is a mystical and powerful number, echoing the number of days of Creation.

The implication of seven times seven is that every decision unfolds worlds of possibilities. Every decision creates as many uncertainties as certainties.

The humble absolute that I take from this ancient teaching is that in order for any of us to make a decision about anything important in our lives, it is necessary to fully consider, to take seriously, the option or options we are not inclined to take. Eventually, though, we need to make a decision. We must act in the world. And how much easier can it be to act when we understand that we don't need to strive for 100 percent certainty? Isn't it more authentic to be 51 percent sure instead? Acting from the standpoint of 51 percent can help decisions feel less burdensome, less absolute. Even as we become clearer, we are still engaged in the questions, still aware of our uncertainty. The other 49 percent remains alive in us.

I have observed that three things happen when we act from 51 percent certainty. First, we have a lot more compassion for ourselves. We know our decision could produce an outcome we don't intend, and we accept this ahead of time. Second, if things work out as we'd hoped, we understand that the win may well be temporary. We realize that our decision could end up being a mistake, and at some future point, another choice can be made. There's no need to cling rigidly to a certainty, trying to prove it true. When we don't, it's that much easier to change directions if we choose to do so. Finally, we have much more compassion for others who make different decisions in their lives. We can support them even if we don't agree, simply because we are practiced in holding our own decisions lightly. We can experience the yearning for certainty and yet not let it consume us.

Let's face it, we make thousands of decisions a day, sorting through an infinite amount of information, firing up countless neural pathways, leaping into pathlessness without even knowing it, and usually things just hum along. Until they don't. A dissonance, a disruption, a crisis, a crossroads appears. Then what is unconscious becomes conscious and we tune in to the process that's always going on under the radar. The questions rise to the surface; the stakes suddenly seem high.

My wife, Dana, and I marvel to this day about a decision we made more than a decade ago that at the time seemed so monumental. We faced a decision about whether or not to keep our daughter Talia in kindergarten for an extra year. Talia was the youngest in her class and, although the school officially said she was ready for first grade, her teacher told us that Talia might benefit from staying in kindergarten for an additional year. Our first response was disappointment. How could we "hold her back"?

Not surprisingly, our family and friends assured us that Talia would be fine in first grade. Dana worried how Talia would deal with seeing the classmates she started school with a year ahead of her. How would this affect her self-esteem? The discussing and fretting went on for quite a while until one night close to the day we needed to give the school our decision, Dana and I began laughing at the absurdity of the whole thing.

If we'd gotten pregnant a few months earlier, there wouldn't even be an issue. It all comes down to when you choose to make love! We certainly hadn't obsessed about any of this then. Uncertainty had suited us just fine. Suddenly it seemed silly to use language like "hold back" and "repeat" to describe giving a five-year-old an extra year to play and learn without pressure. What in the world was the hurry? We both began fantasizing about being held back ourselves! Talia returned to kindergarten and she never skipped a beat: To her it was just another year with new friends. She became a leader of her class, and she still is to this day.

One might say that in the end we followed our intuition about what would be right for Talia. But what is intuition really? I'm struck by how often people reverently speak of the so-called "sixth sense." In fact, my consultant friend's wife kept urging him, "For God's sake, just go with your intuition." I wondered if her urgings actually paralyzed my friend. She, too, wanted him to be certain, in another guise. Intuition, it seems, is the modern equivalent of the traditional, authoritative voice of God.

Surprisingly, intuition actually closely resembles the way of the sages rather than some New Age magic. Cognitive scientists have observed how intuition works in the brain—it's literally a creative leap, impossible to track. But a million neurons have been fired in order for that leap to occur. Many thoughts have been had. Many actions have been taken. Many decisions have been made before this one. In other words, intuition is the result of an accumulation of decisions. It is the result of a lineage of thoughts. And what makes it more powerful, still, is that intuition is also the product of those thoughts and feelings we haven't yet even made conscious. Intuition is really a culminating voice, one that speaks of thousands of previous decisions made consciously and unconsciously.

So the ancient sages and contemporary neuroscientists agree. The grand moment of decision we all yearn for may be a necessary illusion, allowing us to take a stand and act in the world. Yet that moment masks what is really an ongoing conversation. When we realize that uncertainty is our natural human state, that ambivalence is our birthright, that we are "selving" just as the biblical authors showed us even the God character was, life becomes even more awesome. We can see that our unfolding is truly remarkable and our decisions and actions are what make that process possible.

A COMMANDING
PRESENCE

"DON'T YOU EVER GET TIRED OF BEING 'THE MEANING OF life guy'?" my daughter Gabriella occasionally asks me with an exasperated roll of her eyes. On a gorgeous summer day in the mountains of Colorado, the answer is most definitely yes. A room full of people sits waiting inside to hear my talk about a grandiose topic—the transformative power of the Ten Commandments—that I'm supposed to give in fifteen minutes. I haven't prepared as I usually do and should be squirreled away somewhere jotting down some notes. Instead I'm hanging out outside talking to a few acquaintances about the little things in life—the delicious dinner we had last night, my lingering jetlag, the size of the crowd.

I'm paying special attention to a well-known philanthropist. I find myself laughing a little too loudly at his jokes. I'd like nothing more than to become a "friend" of this man and for him to contribute to my organization. At the same time, I'm getting more and more annoyed with a woman we both know who keeps interrupting. He already gives money to her institution, and it's thriving as a result; why doesn't she just be quiet? As if that weren't bad enough, when an attractive, much younger woman joins us, I decide to stay outside a few minutes longer. I find myself becoming more and more drawn to her. When she laughs at some joke I make for her benefit, I notice her beautiful smile. When she pushes back her hair, I wonder what it feels like. Sexual thoughts begin to distract me to the point that I almost lose track of our conversation.

But perhaps because of the nature of my talk, and years of practice (and occasional acting out), even as I experience these thoughts and feelings in bold relief, I also am acutely aware of them, excruciatingly so. Rather than resisting, stifling, or silencing them, I am actually consciously raising them. I'm also feeling pretty anxious; there's a tension or dissonance between what I want in the moment and my conscious intention to both acknowledge and contain those same desires.

After a few minutes I feel myself soften. The feelings don't go away, but I begin to hear a more playful voice. Here I am; Irwin the irresponsible, lustful, greedy, envious rabbi supposedly about to offer wisdom about the Ten Commandments. Some meaning of life guy! Then I think, hey, maybe I'll impress the philanthropist and come back to the office with a million bucks. And finally: Look at this gray-haired man in his mid-forties getting a flirtatious laugh out of a woman half his age.

When I finally walk into the building, now ten minutes late, I'm on fire: I feel very much alive. By the time I get to the podium I hear another voice, the voice of the husband. It reminds me that after two decades of marriage, I yearn for my wife whenever I'm away. I am also keenly aware of myself as the teacher, who, for better or worse, has been paid good money to give this talk, money that will in a very real if small way benefit my organization, which needs all the help it can get. More than that, I am here to talk to a roomful of people, some of whom have traveled far to listen. Suddenly, I feel completely present. There's nowhere I'd rather be than on this stage. I like to think I gave a pretty good speech.

Jewish wisdom teaches that our actions, from large to small, are our legacy; it's what we do that counts. There's a saying: "It's not study that is central. It's our actions." Or to put it in more contemporary language, the degree of our enlightenment can be measured by **Our actions are our legacy. It's what we do that counts.** what we do. With spiritual audacity, the sages tell us that God says, "Better that you do what I say than that you believe in me," a paradox if there ever was one.

The sages envisioned a world in which every act would be a *mitzvah*, a word that has come to mean "good deed." Amazingly, I had actually done several *mitzvot* by the time I got to the podium that sunny morning so full of temptation. *Mitzvah* is the Hebrew word for "commandment," or any act deemed to be required by God. But its mystical meaning is "intimacy." A Talmudic poet from the fifth century said there were 613 commandments in the Bible. This was a way of saying that every moment is a commanding moment; there are so many ways (an infinite number, really) to contribute to the world, to connect to ourselves and others.

Commandments are often misunderstood as being external directives, repressive limitations, or old-fashioned lessons in morality. Contemporary religions have portrayed them as instruments of social control. But the biblical commandments, even the Ten Commandments, weren't simply meant to legislate our thoughts or feelings, or even our actions. In fact the Torah never uses the word commandment when describing these ten insights; it refers to them as *devarim*, which means "utterances" or "words." They are a poetic and profound series of intuitions about human behavior.

They make conscious some of our most primal feelings and urges with the understanding that the more we can bring them to the surface, even magnify them, the more likely we are to master them and do good in the world. They are guides—sometimes gentle, sometimes not—that take us deep into our psyches to uncover the desires and yearnings that lurk there. Rather than transcend or try to overcome them, commandments invite us to enter into them fully. What would happen if we opened ourselves up to the power and urgent nature of our longings?

No wonder the Ten Commandments have gained so much prominence. They make conscious some of the most primal human desires, those we are most likely to repress and therefore act out—from the urge to make concrete that which is unknowable (God) to stealing that which is not ours. Most of the time, we act out internal drives and desires we're unaware of—forces we scarcely comprehend. By calling forth these yearnings, the commandments are actually what I call shadow busters or ignorance busters.

Of course, simply following the commandments—not killing, not committing adultery, not stealing—is all well and good. But it's only possible to fulfill a *mitzvah* if one experiences the full range of feelings that run counter to it. If you don't feel anything contrary to the commandment, then it's like an inert chemical; it has no impact or meaning. The commandments are actually catalysts for desires that are always beneath the surface.

How can we acknowledge "I should not" until we experience "I am tempted"? How can we authentically feel "I must do this" if we don't first feel "I don't want to do it"? Whether it's "Rest on the seventh day" or "Honor your father and your mother," we need to first feel the opposing urge: "I don't need to rest. I have to make that deadline no matter what" or "I can't take my mother anymore." The more tempted we are, the more desires we experience, the more meaningful the *mitzvah*. There's no greater mitzvah than to act in the face of temptation.

When we resist a commandment it's often because we experience it as an external pressure. So many people associate commandments with a punishing parent or a nagging spouse; some kind of controlling authority. But the external pressure we feel is really our disguised desire. What we see as oppressive, external rules are merely alienated longings. It's obvious when we think about it: If we didn't have the desire to observe a commandment, we wouldn't feel anxious or pressured. We'd simply go on about our business.

Recently when my wife, Dana, asked me to clean up the study in the morning after one of my late-night working sessions, the books and papers everywhere, I genuinely wanted to do it. It's a reasonable request—my family uses this space during the day for a variety of things, and I like an orderly home as much as she does. The next afternoon, Dana asked me why the room was still a mess. And I lost it—can't she leave me alone for once?! She'd pointed out the very thing I'd hoped to do, but for some reason—probably laziness or childhood baggage—hadn't. The pressure I felt was not from her. It was my own disappointment in myself. I apologized.

The sages understood that our sense of responsibility doesn't always match our actions. We rarely choose to be lustful, lethargic, conceited, greedy, or deluded. None of us wants to do what we believe is wrong. Drives, conventions, habits, and patterns urge us to follow the most familiar course, even if it's inappropriate or destructive. Desires, emotions, thoughts, and compulsions monopolize our consciousness. Sometimes we end up acting in ways we ourselves find incomprehensible. St. Paul lamented, "The good that I would do, that I do not: that which I hate, that do I." The Talmudic sages, like Buddhist teachers, insist that "a person does not do evil except out of ignorance, unless he has taken leave of his mind."

Mitzvah is an artful technology designed to help us loosen the grip of these seemingly alien forces that take us over. The sages knew that when we push them away we make them stronger and more difficult to control. Often they erupt, and then we're really in their grasp. Commandments evoke in us the very urges that we tend to suppress. When we bring them to consciousness, we discover that these tendencies we're not so proud of can sit right next to our more positive patterns, habits, and desires in a kind of harmonious balance. When we acknowledge and integrate our impulses and longings, no matter how "naughty" or destructive, they lose their evil coloring.

There were so many compelling thoughts for me that Colorado morning, so many actions I could have taken or not taken. If I hadn't felt, even enjoyed my middle-aged lust I might have come closer to making a move on that beautiful young woman. As it happened, I did a *mitzvah*; I fulfilled the seventh commandment, which urges us not to commit adultery. We can't fully understand or experience monogamy unless we live a lustful inner life. If we are loath to admit our lustfulness—if we deny, repress, or try to transcend it out of shame or self-consciousness or self-aggrandizement—we'll wind up like Jimmy Swaggart and Jim Bakker. We'll find lustfulness everywhere out there and end up breaking the commandment.

If I hadn't been aware of how much I wanted to get hold of some of that philanthropist's money, or how jealous I was of the woman who already had it, I might have gone back to my office and made the necessary calls. Instead I fulfilled the tenth commandment, do not covet, and the sixth, do not steal (as I was already beginning to strategize about how I could outdo her organization in his eyes). You can't be generous until you know what it means to covet. By surfacing my feelings and becoming fully aware of them, I was able to move on, to do the work of *mitzvah*. I heard all the desires: "I want, I want, I want, I want" and then, a little softer, "I want. Okay, now what?"

Finally I was able to get, really *get* that I was there on that gorgeous day to fulfill the very simple *mitzvah* to teach. It may have seemed obvious that I was going to give the speech in the end. But how engaged or engaging would I have been if I'd gone on automatic, suppressing my need to breathe the fresh air, laugh with friends, have sex, or help the organization I so love?

The biblical poet suggested that there are 613 commandments: 365 (the number of days in the year) plus 248 (the number of bones in the body, according to the science of the day). In other words, we bring all the parts of who we are, "the bad and the good," into every moment, and every moment is a commanding moment. This poetic intuition allowed me to be fully present, to bring my multiple, contradictory, ever-evolving selves to the podium that day.

ALL WISDOM TRADITIONS teach that freedom—from suffering, from hate, from fear, from the material trappings of life—can come only through spiritual practice, whether it's study, prayer, meditation, ritual, or acts of loving kindess. Jewish wisdom is no different. What's surprising to many is that the commandments themselves are a liberation practice.

Those Ten Commandments or "words" were given to the Israelites three months into their desert journey. As they stood at the base of Mt. Sinai soon after being released from slavery in Egypt, it was time for them to come in contact with their inner pharoahs, to begin the real work of attaining freedom. It was time to make life a conscious performance.

The Ten Commandments were "engraved in stone." In Hebrew the word for engraved is *charut*, which comes from the same root as the word for freedom. So it's actually freedom that's inscribed on those tablets! Janis Joplin sang that freedom is another way of saying "nothing left to lose." But isn't it really, "Freedom's just another word for knowing what to do"? In other words, we are free only when we break loose from the physical, emotional, intellectual, and cultural forces that drive us without our even knowing it. Philosopher Isaiah Berlin describes two kinds of freedom. First, there's "freedom from," what he calls negative freedom: breaking free from those unconscious forces that compel us. When we achieve that, we attain positive freedom, "freedom to" do exactly what we know we're supposed to do. There are no longer barriers to being the kind of person we want to be.

The commandments unveil our desires, actually encouraging us to taste hate, greed, envy, lust; to allow them to bloom inside us; to make them fully conscious. In other words, when we can act knowing first what motivates us, and when we can act with intention, then we are free. Of course, we can't always act from a place of freedom; our desires and patterns are bound to get the best of us now and again. We'll never get to the point where we always know what we're supposed to do. But the more aware we are of what drives us, the better shot we have.

> When we can act knowing first what motivates us, and when we can act with intention, then we are free.

For many of us, freedom can be uncomfortable, frightening, and overwhelming. This is another reason why so many people see the commandments as a series of concrete directives. They yearn for a prescription for life, a pathway to "goodness." So they externalize the commandments, telling themselves and others that they better follow them—or else. But the commandments can't tell you what to do; no one and nothing can. We are always free to choose. What the commandments do is help us arrive where we need to be in the moment to make a conscious decision. And the more they hassle us, pressure us, and push us, the more likely we are to make the decision that will serve us well.

I often tell people who take the commandments "literally"—whether they embrace or reject them—to follow the Zen master Baslo's advice: "Do not seek to follow in the footsteps of the wise; rather, seek what they sought." One way to do so is to explore some of the actual *mitzvot* that populate the biblical teachings. When we can *observe* the feelings—the pressure, the annoyance, even the indifference—they create, we can get a taste of freedom.

There are at least two categories of commandment in all wisdom traditions. Most people are familiar with the first, the ethical and moral laws similar to the idea of *kharma* yoga. They are acts of compassion, kindness, and love. Often they seem like simple acts of decency. Within this category are "dos" and "don'ts." The "dos" include visiting the sick, giving to the poor, conducting business honestly, being hospitable to strangers, comforting mourners, and administering justice impartially. We may not really want to do any of these acts because they entail short-term sacrifice of time, money, or emotional discomfort and un-ease. This is precisely the point.

When we resist, we have the opportunity to observe not only the command but ourselves. And just to be sure our consciousness is raised to the fullest, many of these commandments include very specific instructions: precisely how much harvest to give to the poor; how to treat employees; when, how, and with whom you make love; the way to tend to a dead body (considered the highest *mitzvah* because it can never be repaid).

The ethical "don'ts" are perhaps even more familiar. We are not supposed to steal, lie, gossip, use people sexually, provide false information, cheat, take revenge, or commit murder. These are the "of course" commandments; "just common sense" as a student of mine said. I get lots of surprised looks when I point out that any commandment we say "of course" to is one we are in fact not observing. When we dismiss anything out of hand, we are preventing our own growth and expansion; we become less intimate with our impulses and desires.

"Do not murder" invites us to meditate on who we want to murder. Who gets under our skin; who enrages us beyond reason; who cheats us, betrays us? Who are the people about whom we have those delicious, if only fleeting fantasies of murder or revenge, or whom we wish would disappear off the face of the planet? It can be helpful to remember that murderous desires are innate, or in religious language, "God-given"—after all, look at God's track record! In this way they are no different than our most noble ethical impulses. When we open our eyes, when we reflect on the commandment, we begin to see different forms of murder all around us. As I asked my student, "Who are you kidding?" Isn't war the practice of murder? What about poor social programs and health care? On an interpersonal level, the sages taught that humiliation is a form of murder. When we cause the "blood to drain out of someone's face," we have committed soul murder.

These sages challenge us to expand and contract the categories we've created around even the most "obvious" commandments so that we can experience and more genuinely observe them. As a teacher of mine once put it when explaining what can be learned from the Noah story: "If you want to be like God, you have to feel God's murderous rage." It's a learning curve for the "Almighty," too. God has to go all the way in the Noah story—destroying everything but one boatload of all creation—before realizing how wrong it was. If we read this as an internal story, we are obliged to fully feel everything, especially the feelings that frighten us the most.

Interestingly, there are a number of exceptions, some very clear "to dos" under the category of murder in the biblical texts. Some of these commandments are incredibly shocking and disturbing when read at a surface level. But when read at a "surfacing" level, they can be even more intense. One such commandment, one that always gets a rise out of everyone in the room, is the one that tells us to stone a child if he is rebellious. How crazy, how barbaric; who would do that, never mind make it a practice? This is why religion is not only stupid, but dangerous! But practicing or observing this commandment isn't "doing" it. It's letting it "do" you. When we tune in, we may hear ourselves think, "Damn, there's a part of me that really wants to kill that kid."

The rabbis say no one has ever acted on this biblical commandment—of course, there's no way of knowing if this is true—but they don't dismiss it. One might wonder what the purpose of this commandment is if you're not supposed to act on it. This law invites us to think about the times we've felt a kind of uncontrollable rage at a simple infraction, so much so that we've wanted to strike our child, or did. How about when we squelch their spirit, coming down hard on them for some act of disobedience, something as simple as not turning off the TV or not going to bed on time? What about when the baby wakes up for the sixth time in the middle of the night and for a split second we imagine smothering it? What does it even mean when a child rebels; how do we judge and respond to these acts? Most of the time rebelling means someone is doing what we don't want him or her to do; plain and simple. The truth is, all children are going to rebel. The challenge is what do we do when this happens. Allowing our murderous rage to surface is a start. The commandment is meant to amplify our anger and anxiety temporarily. When we let it, it's amazing how rarely we act out our greatest fears.

Then there are those commandments that seem silly or obsolete. There's the one that tells us to return our enemy's ox or ass when it's wandering down the road. But if you meditate on that, what will happen? You may remember how many things you actually do take from perceived enemies: a colleague you feel competitive with who really deserves the credit; that money you owe your ex-wife but don't pay on time.

Those of us who find meaning and guidance in the ethical dos and don'ts are often stumped by the second form of *mitzvah*: the ritual practices. Rituals, too, are integral to every spiritual tradition, and for good reason. They bring us deep into our psyches, beyond common sense. They are designed to speak to the right brain, to access the realm of the imagination. They are pre- or post-verbal; however you choose to look at it. They are nothing less than techniques to facilitate transformation.

At the same time, rituals remind us who we are (or how much we are) and where we came from. They enact, express, and renew our relationships, whether to family, community, culture, cosmos, or God. And they are always a kind of theater. Whether using unusual objects and symbols, language and physical movement, clothing and art, rituals both root us and destabilize us. They confirm the deepest parts of who we are and disrupt our surface selves, inviting us to shed our veils and pretenses, our everyday armor, to renew and deepen our identities and connection to the world. They can weld a community, creating a kind of social magic that solidifies a group. Rituals also can open up new ways of thinking and being in our individual lives.

> **Rituals can be songs of grace and dances of death; they can foment aggression and inspire love; calm the mind and stir things up; enchant the ordinary or transform it.**

Rituals can be songs of grace and dances of death; they can foment aggression and inspire love; calm the mind and stir things up; enchant the ordinary or transform it. The Jewish practice of blowing a shofar on the New Year, the Catholic eucharist, the Hindu mala beads, the Pueblo clowning, the Islamic Great Henna marriage ritual, the Buddhist mandala, the Hopi masked dance—each of these acts invites us to enter an alternative universe. Even if we don't participate in them, witnessing them can send chills down our spine. Many people experienced this after Pope John Paul II died and Pope Benedict XVI was chosen: Catholics and non-Catholics alike sat by their television sets waiting for that white smoke to emerge from the chimney of the Sistine Chapel. When it did, tears came to their eyes even before they knew who the new pope would be.

I'm always amused when I teach about ritual practice and some intellectually sophisticated, highly rational, ethically sensitive person says something like, "This is silly and superfluous. I don't need ritual." "Okay," I ask, "What do you eat on Thanksgiving and who carves the turkey? Do you and your lover have a favorite song? Does your family have designated seats at their dining room tables? Where does the CEO sit in your boardroom?" Imagine a graduation with no pomp and circumstance, no silk cap and gown, where we receive a xeroxed copy of our final transcript in the mail rather than a calligraphied diploma made of parchment. Imagine the death of a loved one with no funeral rites. Imagine saying to your wife or husband, "You know I love you. Who needs a ring?" and then dropping the wedding band into the toilet with a shrug. Even the most cynical people usually get the idea.

What's the difference really between business attire—that dark suit, white shirt, and sober tie you wear to important meetings—and a prayer shawl? A family's favorite expression or a liturgy? The way we set our table and what we put on an altar? In the end it's not a question of ritual or no ritual: it's *what* ritual and the extent to which it defines who we are and where we belong. Of course, there are some rituals that have more meaning than others, that go deeper and wider in our consciousness. But even the seemingly trivial or irrational ones can have an effect on our psyches. There's a ritual not to wear linen and wool at the same time. That's a hard one to explain, but certainly the practice invites us to dress with a consciousness beyond vanity: What is our clothing made of; where does it come from; are we even aware of why we choose the clothing we do? Is it to signify status, or to make us look sexy, thin, or powerful? The extent to which we enter into and participate in any ritual determines the extent to which it will open our minds and hearts.

It takes time and attention to develop a practice, and all rituals are in danger of becoming rote and boring. That's why seeing and participating in another group's rituals can be so exciting and engaging; they're fresh and exotic—and we don't have to work so hard to have an enlivening experience. My experience is that rituals were designed for the spirit, not the mind, and often need only a reinvestment in order to once again become forms of enchantment.

In the fall of 2001 I was asked by the producers of PBS's *Frontline* to be part of a special called "Faith and Doubt at Ground Zero." I had no idea what I was going to do on air. How could anything I said begin to capture or heal this unspeakably tragic experience? When the camera crew arrived, I decided to chant an ancient melody used to read the Book of Lamentations on the day that remembers the destruction of the Temple in Jerusalem. But rather than chanting the traditional Hebrew words to that scripture, I chanted the last words left by people trapped inside the World Trade Center on voicemails and in e-mails to their loved ones just minutes before they died; words that were first printed in *The New York Times*. "Honey, something terrible is happening. I don't think I'm going to make it. I love you. Take care of the children." "Mommy, the building is on fire. There's smoke coming through the walls. I can't breathe. I love you, Mommy. Good-bye." I was struck by how little anger or fear was in these messages. Rather there is simply love; love in the face of death born of hate. The chant, too, evokes this experience. There are many centuries of pain and healing in that melody. The response from viewers was so moving. One woman who lost a friend in the Trade Center sent me an e-mail that said, "It was as if the chant were reaching down inside me and pulling out the pain." Reflecting afterward, I thought it must have been the combination of that ancient chant with the fears and sadness that were so acutely alive for everyone that had made such an impact. This one-thousand-eight-hundred-year-old chant had such power and beauty when imbued with contemporary meaning.

Some rituals surprise and move us, uproot and alter us. Others are meant to root us, affirm our relationships, renew our identity, and tell our story. Holiday celebrations are among the most powerful of these ritual practices. Forget to wish your spouse Happy Anniversary; fail to give your child a present on her birthday; neglect to send a card to your mom on Mother's Day and you will experience something far more intense than the wrath of God! More importantly, you also will miss an opportunity to affirm and celebrate who you are and what your loved ones are to you.

Then there are spiritual or traditional holidays, like Christmas, Easter, Ramadan, and Yom Kippur, that tell a story about our culture, our values, our history. But this ritualized sacred time is not simply about remembering what happened in the past: We re-enact those stories so that they happen to us. Jews have a plethora of holidays. Perhaps this is so because when one lives with the anxiety of uncertainty, there better be a lot of opportunities to pause and take stock; to connect with others that have come before us; to laugh and cry and sing and dance and eat.

Passover is probably the most brilliant ritual/technology in the Jewish wisdom tradition. On this holiday people gather for a meal called a seder and they re-enact the Exodus from Egypt. We experience in our interior life the movement from slavery to freedom. We taste the trauma of slavery in all its bitterness as well as the sweetness of liberation. And we realize how fortunate and also how enslaved we are—whether by habits and patterns, relationships that no longer suit us, or memories of the past. We feel the tension between the ritual world—how things ought to be—and our everyday world—the way things are. This both roots us and challenges us. And we yearn for our own liberation and that of others. We feel commanded to become redeemers ourselves.

Another powerful Jewish ritual is the blowing of the shofar on Rosh Hashana, the Jewish New Year. The piercing sound is a series of one hundred loud, energetic blasts of a ram's horn. Another year is about to begin; time to WAKE UP to what this last year has been and to walk with intention into the new one. Every spiritual tradition has a technology to call us to consciousness. Some people find this one anachronistic or frighteningly primal. I encourage them to hear it as a cosmic wake-up call or a spiritual alarm clock. If the only alarm we hear is the one that gets us up in time for work every day, then how awake are we really?

Yom Kippur, which comes ten days later, is a day of introspection, a time when we are meant to reflect on how we have missed the mark over the last year, where we could have done better or heard the commandments more deeply. We're meant to take our personal inventory. There's nothing logical, didactic, or intellectualized about this process. The rituals on this holiday have a cumulative, nonverbal power, one that penetrates and unnerves. It's the holiday when Jews pour into synagogues across the world. They want a taste of this power, and to enter deeper into their psyches and encounter a different part of themselves.

Many people who observe Yom Kippur don't realize that it's a practice in which we enact our death. For twenty-five hours we fast from both food and drink; refrain from sexual relations; don't wash or shower; wear nonleather shoes (leather symbolizes life); sit in silence for long periods; and recite liturgy that remembers loved ones who've died and sacrifices people have made. We contemplate, "What would I think about on the last day of my life, or even in the last minutes?" As the day unfolds and our defenses come down, we may think about the time we've wasted, who we love and cherish most and wish we'd spent more time with or cared for a little better. Toward the end of the service, the shofar is sounded again; just one long blast. Dependent only on the breath (and it takes a lot of it!) of the blower, it's almost as if that air were entering into our bodies, bringing us back to life, to a more integrated self.

These two holidays together are called, appropriately, the Days of Awe. We enter the new year with a new perspective. And it hasn't been easy. The sages knew how hard it is to take such a serious look at ourselves. It's painful to reflect on that which we think we can't change; we ache to leave it all behind and just move on; to rush into the new year with our hopes and our dreams. No wonder the American New Year's ritual involves getting drunk, singing a song about forgetting, and making resolutions about the future.

Every year as I stand before a congregation sitting patiently waiting to hear that dramatic blast, I ask them to remember something that happened last January, last February, last March, one thing they can re-call. It's amazing how many people can't do it. And it's amazing how many tear-filled eyes I see in the pews. The sages had an intuition that all this remembering, all this awareness of how easy it is to forget and deny, as painful as it can be, really works; it deepens our relationship to all that is, and expands our vision of who we are. It empties us out and allows us to walk into the new year ready to act in the world with re-newed wonder and intention.

THE NECESSITY OF TRANSGRESSION

ONE EVENING AFTER I GAVE A LECTURE, A SMALL, SOFT-spoken woman in her fifties approached me and asked me to join her for a cup of coffee. I was ready to say no; it had been a long day, and I didn't know her. But there was a look in her eye that told me this was definitely not about a friendly cup of joe. As we walked across the street to a café, I could see that her body was tense; though the night was mild, she wrapped her coat around herself as if to shield herself from a strong wind. As we sat among the young, hip elite of Seattle, pierced bellies showing, techno music pulsing, she told me her middle-aged story of grief and longing.

Anna had married an older man who was now debilitated by Alzheimer's. His decline in the last two years had been severe, and he could barely speak. Often he didn't even recognize her. She and her husband were both quite conservative and shared a deep respect for Jewish learning. The rabbi with whom she'd consulted had told her that even in considering doing what she was about to tell me, she'd crossed the line.

> There are no easy answers. Every question and answer is contextual, a moment truth.

On the other hand, the friends she confided in, despite their discomfort, were encouraging and supportive. She wanted to have an affair.

Anna had met a man whom she felt she could love. He knew her situation and understood her commitment to care for her husband. She blushed as she told me how much she wanted to be held again, to feel again the pleasure and comfort of being held in someone's arms. Yet she felt she'd be betraying her husband and took the commandment "do not commit adultery" very seriously. She was deeply worried that if she had this affair, something might change in her relationship with her husband, an expression of distance in the nuance of her touch or the tone in her voice. At one point she grabbed my hand and said, "Please tell me what to do."

All spiritual leaders are faced with complex questions of morality from time to time, and it's always tough. There are no easy answers. Like all religious traditions, Judaism has many laws and guidelines; yet every question and answer is contextual, a moment truth. Even the seemingly obvious questions invite conflicting answers, and require us to reexamine what we thought were ironclad precedents. There was no way I could tell Anna what to do, pronounce a verdict on her wrenching dilemma. Instead, I said the first thing that came into my head when she'd begun talking, her coat still wrapped tightly around her. Could she recall the first value judgment in the Bible, the premise for the creation of Eve for Adam? I could see her eyes soften as she answered, "It is not good to be alone."

A fifth-century sage taught, "More meritorious is a transgression performed with good intent than a *mitzvah* fulfilled with an ulterior motive. Could it be better to do the wrong thing with good intention than the right thing with wrongful intention?" To be sure, the commandments are meant to be observed, but the sages also understood that the commandment that overrides all others is "choose life." And sometimes fulfilling that injunction means breaking rules, crossing boundaries, hearing the unconventional commanding voice. This is the voice that launches us into pathlessness, into territory where the old rules no longer chart our way. This, after all, is the reality of our lives: a process that asks us to respect conventional boundaries but also transgress those limits when we need to create new, more inclusive borders.

There's a Talmudic story in which the rabbis pray for the end of the evil inclination, or as psychologists might call it, the libido. But God warned them: Without the evil inclination the world would not exist.

The rabbis persevered and so God banished the evil inclination. As a result, no houses were built, no children were born. Without boundary-shattering libido, creativity isn't possible.

The spark of historical development is rooted in the challenge to accepted boundaries. Discontinuity is vital to the success of continuity, for it allows ideas and societies to evolve and grow. Innovation begins with transgression. When I ask Jewish audiences to name the three most important Jews of the modern period they answer: Marx, Freud, and Einstein. Each was a radical transgressor of the status quo. And so, too, are the greatest intellectual and artistic heroes from Copernicus to Spinoza, Beethoven to Darwin, van Gogh to Simone de Beauvoir, who defied the norms of their times, as did our greatest religious leaders such as Moses, Buddha, Jesus, and Muhammad. The major pivotal movements of American history such as the American Revolution, the Abolition Movement, the Civil Rights and Feminist Movements, all defied the prevalent laws and ideologies of their day. By transgressing precedent, these movements produced new, life-affirming social conditions that changed all our lives for the better.

I might never have become a rabbi had I not broken the rules of the yeshiva, the Jewish high school I attended. By today's standards my misbehavior might seem minor, but in the traditional setting in which I was educated it was serious business worthy of expulsion. The yeshiva was a world apart, far removed from popular culture, seemingly immune to the sea changes in society of the late '60s and early '70s. At fifteen, I snuck out of my dorm room to go to a Bob Dylan concert, a benefit concert for Rubin "Hurricane" Carter, whom many felt had been wrongly imprisoned. I was passionate about the cause and of course I loved Dylan with that intense teenage adoration of a favorite rock band.

I also had an inchoate sense that the concert was connected to what I was studying in yeshiva. There's a line in the Talmud that alerts us, "There are times when in order to do God's will, you will need to undermine the Torah." Rock and roll at its best is about breaking boundaries in search of a new kind of wisdom. The concert was my version of the forbidden fruit, and I knew I had to eat. I had gone to Madison Square Garden by myself, scared and apprehensive, but by the time my roommate pulled me up through the window of my dorm I felt changed, invigorated, dangerously alive. I realized I could be a seeker in more ways than one, that Judaism was not restricted to an insider, elite, tribal philosophy but could flourish in the world and be of the world. I could break boundaries and return inside richer and wiser and ready for more.

Maybe this is in part why transgression plays such a key role in the biblical texts. Transgression, after all, underlies the most dramatic story of our beginnings. The very first human act in the Book of Genesis is a trespass of staggering proportions, an outright defiance of the second of the very first commandments, "Do not eat of the tree." The breach was not, however, some impulsive decision borne of base temptation but a conscious move to expand reality, a willful decision to take a giant step into the unknown. Eve knows exactly what she's doing, and is well aware of its consequences. She has heard the warning and knows that if they eat, they will die. She spends several verses questioning, hesitating, and wondering. But when the serpent tells Eve, "your eyes will be opened and you will be like God, who knows good and bad," she sees that across the boundary is wisdom. And she decides it's worth the risk.

The biblical texts are in part a series of teachings about a lineage of transgressors. The word Hebrew—*ivri*—actually means "one who crosses over"; the name of the very first patriarch is Abraham Haivri, Abraham "the boundary crosser." And so he was—smasher of his father's idols, who leaves his home and undermines the conventions of his day. In every generation to follow, transgression ushers in the next stage of evolution. One generation after Abraham, Rebecca lies outright to her husband, Isaac, in order to gain the birthright for her favorite son, Jacob. Jacob, the boy who stole his brother's blessing and whose name means "heel," eventually becomes Israel, "he who wrestles with God." And, in turn, his sons sell their brother Joseph into slavery, yet become the tribes that will populate the Promised Land.

The Bible isn't prescribing sin but rather describing the human journey. The Bible understands that as hurtful as transgressions can be, there can be no life journey without them. Most of us lead conventional lives. We want to avoid the discomforts that arise from complications. But the full, creative life must be open to unpredictability. Jewish wisdom urges us to open our eyes to the possibility of change, even to the need to break a rule. Sometimes the only way to grow is to take a bite of the apple.

Perhaps this is why the messianic figure King David, the builder of the holy city of Jerusalem, the writer of Psalms, and for Christians the direct ancestor of Jesus, came from a long line of serious transgressors— sinners of the first order. Both sides of his family include generations of women who consciously choose life over toeing the line. After all the men of Sodom and Gomorrah have been killed, Lot's daughters fear that there will be no one left to carry on their family life. And so the daughters intoxicate and seduce their father. David's mother is a descendent of this morally complex incestuous relationship.

Transgression plays a key role in the biblical texts, which are, in part, a series of teachings about transgressors.

David's father is a descendent of Judah, the founder of the tribe we know as today's Jews. When Judah's son dies tragically, his daughter-in-law Tamar is bereft. She desperately misses her husband and has been left childless. It pains her to think that her husband's line will not continue and she will never be a mother. But far from passively accepting her fate, Tamar's response is nothing less than shocking. After months of intense mourning, she hears that her father-in-law will be coming to town. Maybe this is my chance, she thinks, my chance to provide my husband with an heir, for me to have a child to hold and love. Tamar removes her widow's garb, dresses herself to look like a harlot, and veils herself so she won't be recognized. Upon seeing her, Judah is gripped with lust and gives her his seal and his staff as collateral in order to sleep with her on the spot.

Amazingly, the place where Tamar stands to veil herself is called "opening of the eyes," intentionally echoing the story of Eve, a phrase captured in the daily morning blessing, "Praised are you who opens the eyes of the blind." The place of deception and violation is also the place of revelation. Even Judah seems to intuit this: Later, when he learns of Tamar's pregnancy, he says, "You are a more righteous person than me." The seeds of transgression can bear fruit. David the redeemer is a descendent of this morally complex relationship as well.

But perhaps it is in the biblical account of Aaron that we see most dramatically how an act of blatant irreverence can create an even more authentic reverence. Aaron, Moses's older brother, has been appointed the High Priest of the Israelites, their spiritual leader, chief guard of the sacred laws. And yet he becomes an idolater, the architect of the golden calf. This provocative infraction nearly leads to the destruction of the community. How can Aaron be both a scandalous rebel and an upright, holy man? How can Aaron's descendents continue through the ages to be the nation's priests?

A radical suggestion: Aaron became the High Priest precisely because he'd been a defiant idolater. He had to experience one truth before he could embrace another. The Israelites could follow him because, like them, he allowed his yearning to lead him astray. Much like the former addict who becomes the most effective drug counselor, another kind of priest, Aaron, too, had been there, hit bottom, and climbed back up to new heights.

An astonishing story recounts a parent's frustration with a child's failure to transgress. I heard this Hasidic tale from Rabbi Rami Shapiro about Reb Shneur Zalman of Liadi, the mystic thinker who lived in the late 1700s and owned a majestic library of precious texts. There is a mystical belief that certain wisdom books have unique powers. One such remarkable book in his library featured a label "Do not open or risk losing the world to come." One horrible day a massive fire destroyed the library, and Reb Shneur Zalman turned to his son and asked, "Did you ever look in the book, the one with the warning on it?" The son, surprised and expecting to please his father during this difficult time, said,

"No, Father, I never opened it. I promise you." His father looked saddened and asked, "Are you sure you never read any of it? Can you recall even a single teaching that might now restore my spirit?" Much to the son's dismay, his father bowed his head and wept: "You weren't willing to sacrifice the world to come for wisdom?"

Unlike Reb Shneur Zalman, most of us respond to a child's infraction—be it drawing on the walls or taking drugs—by devising the harshest punishment we think appropriate. At our best, we might just lose it and scream our heads off. But at that moment, we squander a precious opportunity to draw our children closer and teach them something crucial about themselves and life. And we also shortchange our own learning and development, as well as our intimacy. What if, before we judged or punished, we asked ourselves and our child: What is the yearning behind the transgression? How can we help to address it? What might we all learn from their lapses?

The rush to externalize judgments is a clue that we haven't truly recognized our own yearnings. How instructive it is, for example, that nearly every one of the politicians who aggressively condemned President Clinton for his behavior in the Oval Office also had committed adultery while in office. How much more rewarding it would have been for our society if, instead, we looked at Clinton's offenses as an opportunity to dive into our own dualities and transgressive desires. Isn't this what Jesus asked of us when he stood in the public square about to witness the murder of a prostitute and declared, "Who will cast the first stone?" Before punishing others for their yearnings and indiscretions we ought to unearth our own.

> Only when we bring our yearnings and desires to consciousness, can we address them before acting on them.

On a national news show, I was asked to comment on a bizarre and disturbing trend occurring just two years after 9/11. New York City firemen were leaving their wives to marry the widows of their comrades. When I first saw the *New York Post* headline, I reacted with not only discomfort but also condemnation. How dare these supposedly noble men create more pain in a sick attempt to address another's?

But just before going on the air, I remembered another aspect of that article. The firemen it quoted referred to their comrades as brothers. And I found myself talking about the ancient practice of Levirate marriage which sanctions, even requires that a man marry his brother's widow. I'd always thought of this commandment as a practical solution appropriate for its polygamist times, a rule that protected the widow and insured the continuation of the family line. But could this ancient imperative be speaking to us now as well? I reflected on how I would feel if one of my own brothers died: How I would want to protect his wife, comfort her, take her in.

I might even begin to feel sexual stirrings borne out of a new kind of intimacy and her need to be loved and held. By acknowledging this possibility I then understood the yearnings of these firemen for their "brothers'" spouses, the desire of these trained rescuers to reach out to the wives of their colleagues who, unlike themselves, had not survived the horrid tragedy of that morning. This seeming archaic commandment, in fact, addressed a deep and positive human yearning.

If we were able to recognize this longing, would society and the firemen have been able to handle this situation differently? What if we had gone to church or synagogue and heard of this ancient law? What if the firemen's longing to protect their "brothers'" spouses had been acknowledged, affirmed, and discussed? What would we have all learned?

I have been accused of rationalizing transgression, and there is always that danger. However, there is no way to avoid rationalization whether we follow the rules or break them. When we simply observe the law, the rationalization has generally been done for us by parents, teachers, leaders—our culture. The boundary has been given and we unquestioningly accept it. When we choose to transgress, hopefully with awe and trembling, we do the rationalizing ourselves and so it is inevitably more apparent.

Only when we bring our yearnings and desires to consciousness, can we address them before acting on them. No wonder, then, that our religious or legal traditions anticipate transgression and build in guidelines designed to minimize harm. The biblical text makes it clear that humans were meant to be vegetarian, in accordance with the wish to protect and cherish all living beings. But the text also recognized the human desire for meat and the inevitability of transgression. And so rules develop that accept these desires but also minimize the pain and suffering of animals. These are the practices called *Kashrut*, or Kosher laws.

Jewish wisdom says "yes" to the impulse but builds in footholds along the slippery slope of transgression. The lesson here is fundamental: It is, in fact, possible to balance our boundary crossing with thoughtfulness and care. Of course, there's no way to predict the outcome of our actions. This is why we can't expect simple answers to such edgy societal issues as stem-cell research, abortion, genetic testing, and cloning. We are justified in worrying about what may follow these advances, even if the benefits are enormous. But we also need to worry about a society that refuses to take any risks whatsoever.

There is no way to predict the outcome of our actions. Life is rarely neat and predictable despite our best efforts.

Instead of allowing our fear and anxieties to legislate against scientific innovation we can see that—like our eating from the Tree of Knowledge—it is part of our natural human curiosity and, therefore, inevitable. Instead of allowing our fear and anxiety about the new to legislate against any controversial practice, we can welcome the exploration, while also preparing ourselves for its risks. Why not put in place the safeguards that might prevent the very results we fear? That way we can embrace the noble need to push, and even transcend, our boundaries, and keep ourselves from spinning out of control. Of course, even when our intentions are good and we do our best to build in safeguards or guidelines, sometimes we cause harm. This is the risk of being fully human.

As I sat in that Seattle café I wondered for a moment if it was Anna's lot in life to be unloved and lonely. After all, the law is the law, and adultery can't just be sanctioned for convenience or just to make someone feel better. But then I came to a deeper teaching, that the very purpose of the marital boundary is to preserve love, to ensure that neither mate be left alone. It could be that Anna would in some way be observing the spirit of the commandment by consciously breaking it. Most of the time, it is far better to obey the rules of a society. There is a reason they have endured: They work. Until they don't.

As we continued our conversation, I suggested Anna explore ways that she might connect with her prospective lover while protecting her husband and preserving the commitment she'd made to him. She said she could create strict limits around the time she spent with her lover, keeping their encounters to twice a week and making sure to be home well before her husband awoke in the morning. She would be open with his sister, her fellow caregiver, so that Anna didn't feel she was sneaking around. She'd give herself a time limit of three months, during which she would check in with her sister-in-law regularly to gain another perspective on her behavior; someone who could tell Anna whether she noticed any change in her behavior or attitude toward her husband.

There was a risk here. This choice might be a mistake and might cause hurt and disappointment, but there was no way of knowing, of revealing a new truth about her life, unless she tried. Life is rarely neat and predictable despite our best efforts. Others might have advised differently, but everyone could appreciate the consciousness and mindfulness behind her efforts; the footholds she attempted to create along the slippery slope. In some ways Anna had created more boundaries, more rules than existed before she considered having the affair.

We are all familiar with a more common story: an unhappy spouse who has an affair, followed by a bitter, wrenching divorce. We rush to judgment, angry at the violation, upset with the way the children were unprepared, irate with the unnecessarily vicious divorce proceedings. But this is rarely the full story. Sometimes a new passion unlocks a creative stream that a marriage had dammed. Sometimes, unfortunately, it takes all this pain to reach a new level of self-understanding.

When my brother underwent just this sort of transgression—an affair that ended in divorce and temporary estrangement from one of his children—I too had the usual response of indignation. Why couldn't he have initiated marriage counseling; why didn't he start divorce proceedings in a deliberate, conscious way, or prepare his children as best he could? It was messy, really messy. And the cost was great for him, his wife, and especially for his children, to whom he'd been a wonderful and dedicated father. His wife made it difficult for him to see them for quite some time. He paid a price. Yet for the first time I can remember, he talked about how loved he felt, how something had been awakened in him that seemed to have been asleep for an awfully long time.

Sometimes acting out is the only way one's eyes can be opened. Although his relationship didn't end up lasting, my brother's musical career took off in a way it probably couldn't have in the marriage, and he seemed to have a zest and an openness I'd never seen in him before. He also seemed to have reached a new level of self-understanding. Eventually, he was able to connect with his children again. There was a lot of hurt there, and years later the healing is still underway.

I didn't approve of what my brother had done; I wished so much that he had found another way. And his actions gave rise to a lot of uncomfortable feelings about times in my own marriage, times I've felt tempted. He'd done the unthinkable and suddenly the unthinkable became real and possible for everyone around him. How dare he! At the same time, I so much wanted him to be happy. And then one night on the phone a few years after the divorce, he recounted the many nights he'd cried, agonizing over the terrible hurt he'd caused. He was afraid that he'd never be able to put his life back together and, most importantly, that he'd never again be the kind of father he'd been before.

But he also went on to describe a recent night he'd spent with his younger son, how they'd talked for hours, how honest and loving they'd been with each other. He said, "Irwin, I wish I'd done it differently, but it was the best thing that ever happened to me." His transgression, disturbing and hurtful as it was, dimmed with the knowledge of the growth that had come with it. I felt so much tenderness for him in that moment. I was overwhelmed by an older-brother impulse to protect him from all future hurt. He'd had so much already.

Just before Adam and Eve are banished from the Garden of Eden, God clothes them with "garments made of skins" even though they'd already made coverings for themselves. Before they are sent out into the wide world with all its harshness and uncertainty, God acts out of love, despite understandable disappointment and anger with their transgression.

There's new life after Eden.

YEARNING FOR
LOVE

COVENANT

IT ALL BEGINS WITH THE YEARNING FOR LOVE. THE observation "It is not good to be alone" is the first intuition about human beings in the Bible, in the story of Adam and Eve. In this simple statement, we're taught that love is the fundamental human longing. And this is just the beginning: the entire Torah is a commentary on loving. If it were a Buddhist torah, it might have been a *midrash* on how to transcend suffering; a Hindu torah would have reflected on the awakening of awareness; a scientific *midrash* would have insights about randomness—all incredibly expansive and profound teachings. Yet all these traditions would agree that love eases suffering, awakens us to another dimension, and makes meaning out of randomness. As the prophet Isaiah observes, "Love swallows up death."

The first teaching about yearning in the Bible is told from the point of view of the God character. It's the Creator that makes this first value judgment. And the reader can't help but wonder: How does God know it is not good to be alone? Wow—God must know what it feels like to be lonely! Maybe God created human beings out of a deep need to love and be loved. The biblical author takes us into the realm of poetry, of myth, of imagination, telling a story that invites us to wonder if maybe we are here on this planet for those very same reasons.

The love story between God and humankind is like every romantic epic. It begins in paradise. Before creating Adam, which in Hebrew means "human," God made a wonderful home for this first person to dwell in; a garden of delights. Everything is perfect. And yet life must grow and evolve. Just as plants need soil to thrive, a human being needs relationship. The next loving act is to create a companion for this very first person. The paradox is that by creating Eve for Adam, God assures God's own loneliness. After the birth of Eve, the text tells us that henceforth every human being will leave the mother and father to cling to a lover. Isn't what's true for God true for all of us? Even when we love so deeply and fully, we are also still alone. We give up so much of ourselves, and we are always yearning.

The biblical poet gives us such a beautiful scene. Adam goes to sleep and awakens having been divided into male and female. It's love at first sight, and Adam sings a love song: "This one at last is the bone of my bones and the flesh of my flesh." Like Adam, don't we all long to become one with someone else, for a kind of unity, a person who will complete us? Don't we yearn for unconditional love, a love that will last forever? And don't we all enter into relationships with the expectation that love will feel good, that it will bring happiness and fulfillment, that we will no longer be alone? The poet recognized these profound yearnings, but also understood that such a love wasn't possible, nor was it even desirable if the world were to continue to develop and expand.

Maybe this is why the poet chose such an interesting, rather unromantic phrase to describe Eve: "a fitting helper." The word for "fitting" in Hebrew—ezer—is itself a paradox: it means "different and equal," "facing and separate," "in devoted opposition." Eve will not only be one with her lover, she will also challenge him, as will he her. They will help each other to become more fully human.

Eden is really a story about intimacy. It requires that we hold in our consciousness two intuitions that seem contradictory: Our lover is both "flesh of my flesh" and "a fitting helper." The experience of each seems so different. When I am in "bone of my bone" mode, it all seems so "Edenic." When I'm feeling the pull of my fitting helper it can be uncomfortable, even painful. Intimacy is a dance of sameness and difference, a dynamic container for our growth and expansion.

Whenever I counsel a young couple as they prepare for their wedding, I tell them that far from "settling down," now it's really going to be unsettling. Even for those who've been living together for a while, I feel compelled to remind them that a committed relationship is going to feel bad almost as much as it feels good. Their fights will be as crucial as their lovemaking. What they disagree on will be as important as what they agree on. Intimacy is a place of multiple truths, differing points of view, and misunderstandings, as well as romance and oneness. Intimacy is a never-ending dance between loneliness and connection; expectation and disappointment; hot sex and boring sex. There's the greatest risk of loss and the greatest hope for gain.

It's amazing how many couples come to me on the brink of divorce having never understood or accepted the wondrous, excruciating dialectic that is intimacy. It's not just that "marriage is a lot of work," as I hear so many people say. It's that marriage, or any close relationship, is a place where you learn about your self—your shadows and your light. It's a place of commandment and transgression.

> Intimacy is a place of multiple truths, differing points of view, and misunderstandings, as well as romance and oneness.

It's a place where we are meant to wrestle with ourselves, as well as our loved one, in order to give birth to a new world.

We've all experienced that moment when we emerge from, or sometimes are thrust out of, paradise, that first blissful phase of romantic love. The first fight, the first time she doesn't laugh at your joke, the first shattering of the thin glass that is romance. The wine glass that is stomped on at every Jewish wedding is meant to symbolize the wish that the couple will remain whole despite inevitable conflict. The hope is that each shattering will lead to an opportunity for growth and renewal. This ritual comes at the very end of the marriage ceremony after which everyone yells, "Mazel Tov!" Congratulations on finding a place that can withstand your brokenness.

Here's a recent example from my own life. Twenty years into my marriage, after what I thought was a lively and delightful dinner party, my wife, Dana, confronted me. "Why do you always have to be the center of attention, always talking, always performing?" I was shocked. I had always been the talker, she the listener, the observer. After most parties we went to, she would recount all the innuendos and gossip I had missed as I worked the party. We were a perfect match that way. And it had always felt right. Now I felt defensive and oddly frightened by her comment.

I experienced it as a shattering of our finely balanced relationship, a kind of ending. But we sat with it, not for days but for many weeks. And there was a strain between us that whole time, frequent bickering, criticism, an all-around unpleasantness, especially at the next few parties. Almost two months after the fight, we went to a dinner gathering. I went determined to keep my mouth shut the entire evening, mostly out of resentment. Let her carry the conversation for a change. I thought she'd look at me longingly before we finished the appetizer. But she didn't. She came alive that night, talking and laughing and reaching out to people she would have previously quietly observed. My anger turned to wonder. As I watched her I could feel love well up inside me. I felt I was discovering a whole new part of my wife after two decades of thinking I knew everything. I also had a revelation about myself. I realized that I could enjoy being quiet, that I was just as much a participant when I was observing and listening as when I was talking. When we arrived home, we made love like new lovers.

On a grander scale, the same thing happens to Adam and Eve. They're cast out of Eden, having hid from God, Adam blaming Eve for everything. Yet the first thing they do after leaving is to make love. The word for lovemaking in Hebrew is the same as the word for wisdom. They now "knew" each other deeply. They've made mistakes together, disappointed each other, failed each other, and walked out of the garden with each other. After they left paradise, that first blush of love, their journey of intimacy truly begins.

So often, like Adam, we choose a lover in order to fill something inside us, to find the flesh of our flesh, and we project onto that person our greatest hopes. This is also true with our children and our friendships, but with romantic love, the bubble is that much bigger and likely to pop. We may choose someone who we think is like us, who affirms our values, our hopes, our dreams. Someone who, literally, turns us on, at least to those parts of ourselves we want to see. Or, like me, we may pick someone who is our opposite, who will complete us, who will be our other side. Love is indeed blind. We don't see our lovers' flaws, nor do they see ours.

This is the narcissistic stage of love ("bone of *my* bone," as Adam says). We put our best sides forward in the effort to win the person we so desire; we idealize them as well as ourselves. We feel we'd do anything for our loved one. This is a crucial phase in any romantic relationship. It is the love that is automatically given to us by nature. It's what opens up our shell and softens us so that the yearning comes through and a deeper love becomes possible.

Soon after we met, I traveled all the way to Israel to see Dana—who was spending a year abroad—for just four days. But it was less about her than me. I wanted to win her, make her mine, somehow guarantee that she would love me. I wanted her to think I'd give her anything. I didn't show her the withholding part; that would come years later. And thank God, because both of us yearned for something more. Just as powerful as that first bloom of romance was a longing for roots, to go deeper into the soil, to the depths of my being and hers as well. Each of us wanted a fitting helper.

Of course, one cannot exist without the other. Unless we continue to experience our lover as "flesh of my flesh" we won't be an effective or authentic helper. And unless we genuinely help each other by challenging and being challenged, we cannot continue to feel that oneness. Neither God nor Adam understood this at the outset. Not surprisingly, God erred on the side of seeing relationship as opposition, creating a fitting helper. This is a foreshadowing of God's disappointment with Adam and Eve after they eat from the tree. God feels contradicted and opposed, the same way we all feel when those we love don't listen to us, do what we ask, or take our advice. The God character's expectations are always out of this world: In theological language, they are infinite while we are finite. On the other hand, Adam favors "flesh of my flesh" because he is young and new to love. He's intoxicated with the fantasy of being one with another. In the end, he, too, discovers the dance of intimacy. He eats the fruit at Eve's urging; only then can he begin to "know" her and himself more deeply.

The real work of intimacy comes when automatic love ends and intentional love begins; when we leave the garden. Continuing and maintaining that newness and passion (without changing lovers, which is one way to keep things fresh!) we must reveal more and more of ourselves and unveil more and more of the other person. Monogamy is not some pious rule that we need to follow. It's a depth practice—a way to understand self and other. This can be risky, which is why some people make the unconscious decision to let the passion die out. We must feel vulnerable and exposed in order to keep love alive. We must say whatever needs to be said, and do whatever it takes to keep a relationship growing.

Monogamy is a depth practice—a way to understand self and other.

At some point in any romantic relationship there is a crossroads. "Should I stay or should I go?" as the Clash so astutely sang. This is the moment when we decide if all the disappointment and vulnerability and risks are worth it. When my sixteen-year-old told me about her first breakup, describing how the relationship had become boring, I found myself trying to explain. "At some point in your life, you'll decide it's not just about pleasure and passion; 'not being boring' is no longer the point. Give yourself a while, sweetheart," I said glibly, trying to convince myself I wasn't repeating my parents' annoying and patronizing refrain: "You're just not ready yet." She surprised me by asking, "Are you and mommy bored? Do you think about leaving each other?" Now I'd done it! She was already upset, and I wanted so much to reassure her. But knowing her, she'd see right through it. I said, "Yes, sometimes. But I'm pretty sure we're 'lifers.'" I looked forward to the day that Gabriella would experience the dance that is intimacy, when she'd be able to cele-brate the dynamic range that is love: fragility and solidity; boredom and spontaneity; selfishness and empathy; acceptance and rejection.

When we can withstand those edgy times, bridge those great di-vides, even the most excruciating times of insecurity and vulnerability can themselves become incredible turn-ons. I like to imagine Adam and Eve in bed one night well after they left the garden. For whatever reason—maybe they've had a fight, maybe it's the anniversary of their banishment—Eve turns to Adam and asks, "Adam, I've always won-dered, why did you blame me? So I gave you the fruit. You're a big boy. You could have said no." Adam, of course, immediately feels attacked and exposed. He wants to lash out. "You did it! You listened to the ser-pent, not me." And then, "For God's sake, aren't you over it by now?" Blame is a big part of every relationship; it's a primal protective device, a shield against vulnerability. But imagine what the postfight lovemak-ing would be like if Adam said, "I could have said no. I wanted to make you happy. It's amazing how weak I can be and how powerful you can be. And then I was afraid. I couldn't face what I'd done. I'm sorry."

When we hide parts of who we are from our lover, we just ensure that it is not the full me that is being loved. And so love ends up feeding our doubt about the relationship. Sometimes Dana and I do a "fitting helper" practice. It's a way to get our disappointments and frustrations out in the open where we can look at them and hopefully work them through. We ask each other whether there's anything we might have felt too uncomfortable, embarrassing, obnoxious, or scary to share about the other over the last weeks or months. Of course, the first thing to come to mind is the one thing we'd rather keep hidden. But more often than not, after much discussion and sometimes tension, we're on solid ground again, the relationship more rich and nurturing than it had been before. Intimacy means acknowledging to each other, "Okay, I'm greedy, horny, arrogant, lazy, flirtatious, jealous, angry, nerdy, insecure." And then feeling loved. Of course, it's helpful to try to keep a balance. Dana and I also reverse the game. We practice sharing what is good and beautiful and pleasant about each other, and sometimes this is just as challenging; it can feel corny and vulnerable, and we may have a sinking feeling that words just don't suffice.

All of us yearn for a person with whom we can be vulnerable, and yet be embraced. We all long for a place that can tolerate the inevitable turbulence, disruption, anxiety, and anguish. And we want to feel cherished and celebrated as well. Jewish wisdom calls this kind of relationship a covenant. A covenantal relationship is an ever-deepening love born of the grit and insecurity of everyday life. Covenant acknowledges the paradox that the more deeply we love, the more expectations we have and the harder we fall; the more intimate we are the more likely we are to get hurt. These paradoxes can be really scary. We realize that our lover will help us grow, but as we grow we risk growing apart from the very person who helped us get here. The more secure we want to feel the more vulnerable we have to make ourselves. Our lover loves us, both as we are and as we can be—we're always being pushed. Covenantal love creates both incredible safety and radical insecurity.

Covenant is really a fancy word for agreement, but what an agreement it is! It's a container for loving in all its variations. It holds the promise that the highs and lows, the brokenness and healing will all be on the inside of the relationship and that there'll be enough pleasure and celebration to hold it all together. A covenant is like the thick cloth that contains the glass stomped on by the groom.

The word covenant is first used in the story of Noah and the ark, the most frightening and destructive story in the Biblical texts. It's only the third story in Genesis: It didn't take long for God to feel betrayed and lose patience! We learn early on that God's love could be a rage-full love, as it can be for all of us. In Hebrew the word "Noah" means "comfort." Noah is God's great hope: "Noah found favor with the Lord." But humankind as a whole has proven to be a great disappointment. People have lashed out at each other with murderous violence. God in turn lashes out at them, creating a flood that obliterates all living things—with the exception of Noah, his family, and two of every kind of animal

(a way for God to hedge bets). One could certainly say this manifestation of love is nothing less than abusive; I wouldn't wish it on anyone.
And yet out of this supreme act of violence emerges a covenant, a promise to never again destroy humankind. "Never again will I doom the
earth because of humankind . . . nor will I ever again destroy every living being, as I have done." This is when God creates the famous rainbow
as a symbol of the promise, and a new kind of love is born. The disappointments continue, and God comes pretty close to once again obliter-
ating humankind. But every transgression and conflict can now be seen
in the context of this tremendous promise.

Yet even then covenant is not a guarantee. Paradoxically, covenant is
a commitment that acknowledges impermanence—which is exactly
what makes the commitment real. There's a great scene in the comedy
series *Curb Your Enthusiasm* which captures this perfectly. Larry David,
the show's star, is standing at the altar with his wife of ten years, renewing his vows when the rabbi says ". . . forever, and forever for all eternity
'til death do us part." He looks puzzled and then anxious. He hems and
haws. His wife asks him what's wrong, and he says, "Well, uh, all eternity? I don't know about eternity." It's no accident that this vow isn't
part of the traditional Jewish wedding ceremony.

Knowing that a relationship can end makes it even more precious
and intensifies the yearning to make it last. Maybe that's why Judaism
not only has a sacred practice of marriage; it has a sacred practice of divorce. There's a Talmudic story about one of the most celebrated rabbis,
Rabbi Akiva, who at the age of forty had discovered the love of his life.
His passionate love affair with Rachel is utterly transforming. He was
able to see the spiritual depth of the Song of Songs, an erotic love story;
and he argued that it should be included in the biblical canon. If it
wasn't for him, this incredible text might have been lost. One day the
sages were arguing about what could be justification for divorce. Everyone agreed that adultery was the thing that would surely drive couples
apart. Rabbi Akiva laughed. "Don't be silly. It could be over the burning
of dinner." How odd that a happily married man would say such a

thing. He knew that the more deeply you love, the more you know how truly delicate it is. He understood that there's no such thing as a great love, only great loving, a never-ending process of learning about oneself and each other. He also knew that any marriage has a better shot at lasting if we sweat the small stuff, if we keep our eyes and heart open, especially when pettiness threatens to pull us apart.

Yet in our most important relationships the stakes are so high that we convince ourselves otherwise. Jewish wisdom acknowledges that even the greatest loves may not last forever. We are always on the razor's edge. We really never can know if we love someone or they love us 100 percent. We can never be sure that the brokenness won't drive us apart. Maybe that's why we need to say "I love you" so often, and why we need to hear it. We need to remind ourselves of the longing for an enduring love even while acknowledging that it's not really possible to fulfill. The yearning itself can keep the relationship strong.

I met Dana when we were teenagers, and we've been married for twenty-four years. I'm often asked what our secret is. Of course, there is none. Dana's patience and calm enable her to tolerate an awful lot. We laugh a lot. And we're honest with each other, sometimes to a fault. If there's one aspect of my personality that might help us along the rocky road of marriage, it's that I tend to respond to many of our tense moments with a question I internalized from years of immersion in Jewish wisdom: "Where are you?"

"Where are you?" is the question the God character asked Adam in the garden after Eve and he ate the fruit. We may hear the question as a judgment and so we hide as the first couple did, pulling away in our fear of being discovered and rejected. The Hasidic Rebbe Shlomo Carlbach taught that Adam and Eve were thrown out of the garden because they thought they had to be perfect in their relationship. But this is not what paradise is all about. In paradise one day we are good; one day we are bad. One day we get things right; one day we make mistakes. We can't stay in paradise if we're afraid to mess up. So the original "sin" isn't sexual. It's not disobedience. Rather the sin is letting insecurity and distrustfulness take over. Reb Shlomo said that had Adam not blamed Eve, had he owned up to his mistake rather than exposing her, they would still be in Eden. If we trust, take those risks, expose our flaws, we, too, can stay there. Covenantal love is sharing the struggle to know: eating from the tree together, and together discovering wisdom.

When "the food is burned," when the small stuff over which most couples fight threatens to blow up, my response on a good day is to enter into a silence in which I hear some variation of that same question. "Where are we coming from? Where is she now? Where am I?" It doesn't always work, and I lose it sometimes, believe me. But when it does, it's amazing what happens.

One Sunday afternoon Dana wanted to see a movie at a time that interfered with a football game I had planned to watch—a classic husband-wife scenario. I was willing to go to the movie before or after the game, but the times didn't work. When I suggested going to a different film, the fight began. Dana stormed out of the apartment and then called me from downstairs on her cell phone. She was crying and yelling: I always chose the movies we saw; she always went along with it; why did I always have to be in the driver's seat? My first response was "always?" Come on! I almost said it, which would have sent us on another round of yelling. But luckily I heard the silence and then the question, "Where is she?" And where she was, my gut told me, was with her father. He'd been diagnosed with a tumor in his pancreas the week before. Depending on what the tests told us, it could be very serious. She had no power to change anything. Suddenly, the movie took on great importance. Our conversation ended in tears, but of a very different sort. Dana went to the movie of her choice on her own. When she came home she said the film was great. So was the game.

Covenantal love means learning to support our lovers, whether silently or in words or actions, to help them discover themselves in the emotional storm. The most committed relationship is called *kiddushin* from the word "holy." To be holy is to be intensely alive; it also means to be set apart, special. So the secret to a committed relationship is covenant; a context or container in which to do our most risky loving. It's a place for our moment truths to wrestle with each other in a perpetual dance of discovery. And, more than that, it represents our deepest hope that it will all hang together in the end, that the loving will continue, expand, and nurture us for the rest of our lives.

GIVING AND RECEIVING

IT'S AMAZING HOW WE TEACH OUR CHILDREN WHAT WE ourselves need to learn. We yearn for them to understand what we never did; to be the perfect, balanced people we always wanted to be. Yet our feelings are often contradictory. We want them to have it all, but not be greedy. We want them to be giving, but not give it all away. We want them to have everything they want but to always share. I remember the incredible tension I used to feel when I took my daughters to the sandbox in Central Park; not among the kids but among the parents. The sandbox is a kind of testing ground for our feelings about giving and taking, offering and receiving.

Parents would be sitting around the edges, presiding over sand throwing, shovel snatchings, dump truck nappings, deciding whose hole was whose, who knocked over whose sand castle. Most of the parents spoke softly, coaxingly, patiently to their kids, urging them toward the right thing to do, as the parents saw it; looking apologetically at the parent of the wronged child or beseechingly at the parent who did nothing to control theirs. I myself remember seesawing between not wanting Gabriella to take someone else's stuff and hoping Talia wouldn't too easily cede territory. I'd feel flashes of anger at the child who would take too much, and embarrassment for the ones who let the others walk all over them. I also occasionally would be really touched by the child who would give a toy away without asking for one back or the other child

> The "give and take" that we all accept as an integral part of life and love is actually pretty complicated.

who would graciously accept it. I surprised myself with the intensity of my feelings. The "give and take" that we all accept as an integral part of life and love is actually pretty complicated.

I'll never forget the afternoon in the neighborhood bookstore when Gabriella brought over a copy of Shel Silverstein's classic children's book *The Giving Tree* for me to read. I'd heard of the book but had never seen it before. As I thumbed through the pages, I began to get that same feeling I had at the sandbox, and it only got worse the more I read. Fortunately, Gabriella turned to another book, because I really didn't want to read it to her. I was horrified. How could this be such a beloved classic? How could anyone read this to their kids?

The story is deceptively simple: A little boy plays on a tree eating its apples, swinging on its branches, and the tree is happy. When the boy gets older he wants toys instead, so the tree tells him to cut his branches to make them, and the tree is once again happy. Later the boy wants a house so he can marry and settle down; the tree tells him to cut more and the tree is happy. When the boy wants a boat to take him away, the tree gives him the remainder of his trunk and—you guessed it—is happy. At the end of the story, the boy stays away for a long time; when he finally returns, the tree, now a stump, tells him that he has nothing left to give. The boy, a bent old man at this point, says he doesn't want anything, he only needs a stump to sit on. And the tree is happy.

I've spent a career teaching people to dive into the stories and texts that provoke the strongest reactions. Where there's discomfort or judgment, a kind of unease or chafing, as a psychologist friend of mine calls it, that's where learning can and needs to happen. It's time to turn it over. *The Giving Tree* really disturbed me—clearly I needed to go there. So I bought the book and looked at it over a period of days. I learned that I'm far from the first person to have a strong response; there are hundreds of pages of commentary on this children's tale: feminist perspectives, religious interpretations, philosophical deconstructions. And young or old, virtually everyone I talked to about the book had an opinion, almost always a strong one. Though a children's book, *The Giving*

Tree has informed my understanding of the most important dynamic in any relationship, especially our most intimate and loving ones: the dance of giving and receiving.

There are so many strong responses to this tale, and each has a moment truth, a powerful teaching about how we see ourselves in a relationship. Shel Silverstein has given us a wonderful tool for uncovering what we most yearn for and also what we're most afraid to face. It may seem obvious—every relationship has give and take, as the expression goes. But nothing is more stressful and unnerving than seeing our most raw and honest responses to this dance. All we need do is pause and explore, and the feelings and anxieties about how we give and receive tend to come pouring out. I've found that this process can be both healing and inspiring. I've also found that there are four most common interpretations of *The Giving Tree*, each of which has much to offer.

The first is what might be called the conventional read. It is a message many of us want to teach our children, perhaps especially because we never quite learned it ourselves. It is the Christian understanding of love. It is also a transpersonal psychological read—one that takes us beyond the ego-self. Here the tree is a selfless, unconditional giver, whole-hearted, joyful, and pure of motive. Giving doesn't diminish the tree but makes it happy. It has no expectations of getting anything back, and it's not trying to prove anything. It simply loves; and love means giving all. In wisdom language, it is abiding love; in religious language, sacrificial love or offering. This love, free of any conditions, allows the boy to live a full and independent life while always staying connected, which is all the tree desires.

> Unconditional love is forever on the horizon because it is infinite and we are finite.

I've found that those who resonate with this reading yearn to be able to give unconditionally to those they love. A friend of mine told me, "I made my mother read it again and again. I remember thinking, 'Wow, the tree loves the boy so much, she only wants to make him happy.' I wanted to give that way. I still do." There is a giving self in each of us that wishes we could give all, surrender in our love. This is Christ dying for us on the cross. It speaks to a non-rational (not irrational) part of who we are.

Sometimes I wake up in the middle of the night and look at Dana, and I feel so overwhelmed with love that I feel I'd do anything for her. My daughters are teenagers now, and to this day I go into their room before I go to sleep and give each sleeping child a kiss. I always stand there for what seems like a flash of eternity, feeling a rush of wanting them to know that I love them more than life itself. Not surprisingly, the words that flow out of me are, "God, I love you so much." This is a love that echoes the divine.

We've all had these experiences. And sometimes they are both awesome and frightening. We also feel we fall short. Unconditional love is forever on the horizon because it is infinite and we are finite. The fact that I don't always, or even usually, follow through on those night-time feelings during my daytime life bespeaks my—and all of our—limitations in giving. Some of us are afraid of being taken advantage of. We've been disappointed and hurt and abandoned in love, and we've learned to protect ourselves by giving only so much. And we fear we'll empty out, with nothing left for ourselves. It takes an incredibly rooted and secure self to love with no ulterior motives. And most of us can't be in that self for long.

We hold back, and yet we long to love this way. That's why we create stories, whether it's *The Giving Tree* (or really, *The Giving It All Tree*), *The Passion of the Christ*, *The Little Mermaid*, or other "martyr"-like tales. Or we front-page stories of self-sacrificing mothers who work five jobs, denying themselves everything to give their child what they need, or the fireman who runs into a burning building. Whether the story is about unconditional love for God or for another human being, each inspires us to give a little more of ourselves, to trust that whether reciprocated or not, no love is lost in the end. We may be scarred or even "stumped," but, like the tree, the mark of love will be inscribed onto our very being and endure forever. *The All-Giving Tree* interpretation requires us to ask ourselves: Am I honestly giving enough or am I holding back out of fear or insecurity?

Then there's the more secular, modernist response that is the flip-side; the one I resonate with the most. It's a seemingly rational interpretation. One could also say it's a first wave feminist understanding; it's no accident that the tree is female. It's also a psychological or self-help read. Here the tree is a compulsive giver, perhaps well-meaning but foolish. She has low self-esteem and has allowed herself to be exploited: giving without getting anything back. She's also being irresponsible by allowing the boy to think all his needs and wants will be answered without giving anything in return. The tree is out of touch with her own needs and desires. Tragically, she is so self-loathing that she destroys herself. Clearly the tree's happiness is delusional and the book should really be called *The Victim Tree*.

Many of us respond to this reading because we feel the pain of the tree's gradual dismemberment. We are angry about not standing up for ourselves, not asking for what we need in our relationships. And yet we also feel that if we gave enough, nurtured more, we'd gain the love we so desperately lack. We can become hijackers of the giving part of a relationship, leaving no room for the other person to be generous. This may be because of some old wound; a need to feel valuable and needed; even an unconscious desire to control others by keeping them indebted. Often we don't feel entitled to ask for what we want and need. There's also the guilt trip that society lays on mothers: if we give unconditionally we are saintly and will be adored and loved forever. If not, we're unworthy of being loved. Some women buy into this; others resent it. After all, this kind of giving can turn us into a dead stump, with nothing left to give.

All of us need to pay attention to feelings of exploitation or of having unmet needs, and we need to work to change—or even leave—any relationship that gives rise to them. Any relationship in which no one ever says, "What am I, the giving tree?!" is one that is either abusive or a dead end. Neither person will grow if giving and receiving aren't always being probed and explored. *The Victim Tree* invites us to ask: Am I giving in order to avoid grappling with my own desires? Or am I really not giving enough of myself?

The third version is *The Taking Boy*. This is a story about a boy who shamelessly exploits a weak and vulnerable and caring soul. As the six-year-old son of a friend said, "That boy is the greediest person I ever met!" In more adult language, he is pathologically selfish, incapable of gratitude, and insatiable. In short, he's spoiled rotten; expecting not only every need but every want to be completely met and fulfilled. But all this taking doesn't fill him up; it corrupts him, in the end makes him a stooped, hollow, diminished shell of a man. This interpretation holds such an important moment truth. We are all susceptible to being takers, to exploiting others. When this read speaks to us, it's likely that we're dangerously close to exploiting those around us, or at least deep down we think we are. For whatever reason we may be wounded and genuinely needier. Or it may be because our loved ones seem to have a limitless capacity to give. Whatever the reason, we become takers, and we then judge others as a way to mask our own disappointment in ourselves.

Every culture has its own particular excess and pathology. Ours is competition and getting ahead; success at all costs; the quicker the better. Baby boomers in particular, who have on the whole been given so much by our parents, tend to feel a little guilty about how much we have. When not acknowledged, these emotions easily can give rise to feelings of entitlement: not only to everything we've acquired, but to what we don't have as well. We all need to regularly ask ourselves, "Am I taking advantage?"

The interpretation that in my informal survey is the least popular is *The Receiving Boy*. Here the boy-turned-man is able to voice his vulnerability and accept the care of the tree. He is unafraid of showing his dependence. He is joyfully dependent, freely expressing his weaknesses, needs, and dreams. This in turn evokes unconditional generosity from the tree. In our society, being dependent and needy tends to make us feel diminished because we value self-sufficiency and independence so highly. We will take care of others, up to a point, but we dare not let ourselves be taken care of.

Some of us feel resentful of giving too much, when really it's that we can't, or don't, receive. If we can never really feel dependent, can never ask for help, then we shortchange ourselves and those around us. We miss a whole side of life. We may even become arrogant to mask our need to be nurtured.

This interpretation touches the part of us that longs to be cared for unconditionally; to share our neediness with our hands fully open and our hearts exposed. When we can overcome our fears, and surrender in this way, the boundaries between giving and receiving can dissolve. There is an honesty and transparency between helper and helpee. When we receive, we give. When we give, we receive.

I felt this when I hurt my back a while ago. I could barely stand up and literally couldn't put on my socks and shoes. I had never been hurt like that and always prided myself in never being sick. Even when I did get the flu I'd go to work no matter how bad I felt. My motto: I pull my weight and do not accept help. But when my back went I really needed people and there was no way around it. For the first few days, I was like my daughters when they were in their terrible twos throwing tantrums when I tried to help them with something, even if they obviously couldn't do it on their own. Needing help embarrassed me, made me feel weak and, therefore, resentful of my helpers when I should have felt grateful. And then—out of the mouths of babes—my daughters came into my room early one morning and together they said, "We want to help you get out of bed and get dressed before the school bus comes." When I resisted, they said, "We love you and you need us." I wept as they put my socks on. Being a receiving boy can be nothing short of transformative.

Different interpretations of this story—or any story—are bound to resonate with us more or less at different points in our lives. The balance of giving and receiving with my children is different at five than at fifteen and then different still when they are twenty-five. When I'm an old man the balance will shift again. For lovers, the balance also shifts dramatically—from the courting stage to the prechildren years, to the career-building years and the child-raising years, and then again when the nest is empty.

There's an insightful teaching in the Talmud: Love will always upset the balance. The energy and dynamism of love doesn't allow for anything but very temporary resting places, calms before the next storm. Just when the roles seem clear and defined—the giving and receiving going smoothly without a hitch—something will upset things and throw everything into play once again. Someone loses a job or gets sick or gets that promotion or recovers from an illness. The key is not to pretend we have roles for life, and to remember that no role captures all of who we are. When we can be fluid and accepting of the imbalances, our relationships can be more nimble and lasting.

Love will always upset the balance.

It's also important to remember that sometimes the balance is off, and that's as it should be. We've all heard others or ourselves say some variation of "Those ungrateful kids (those taking boys!). We give them everything, and they don't . . ." Fill in the blanks: clean up their rooms, do well in school, defer to us, obey the rules. Of course, our kids take too much! Yes, we want them to have a sense of responsibility and gratitude, but inequity is what parenting is about. It's what we sign on for.

Sometimes when I come home after being out of town for four or five days in a row, my kids start asking for the most insignificant things: a glass of water that they can get themselves; the phone, which is across the room; help on homework that they can do with their eyes closed. Until recently I had a refrain in my head during these times: "They take, take, take!" Or I'd act out in some resentful way. Maybe it was all those readings of *The Giving Tree*, but one day I realized that my feelings were less about them taking than about my guilt about being away; about not having given what I know they needed. The giving tree in me was sleeping, but it really wanted to give.

Yet, part of what it means to be a child is to take more than you give. Sometimes children feel a kind of burden of indebtedness and obligation that comes from so many years of taking and receiving from their parents. I know I feel this every time I hear my mother joke about how she'd go for a week at a time without as much as crossing our street when we were kids. This feeling of pressure created by our obligation can be very positive if we stand back and recalibrate, rather than feel guilty. As adults, if we can focus on all that we received as children, we may feel a deep desire to give back both to our parents and to society.

Other times children feel that their parents didn't give enough. This certainly happens, and we may feel genuinely and rightfully deprived. A lot of healing may need to happen, either with our parents or without them. This, too, can inspire us to give to others in a way we never experienced. With time we may also find that we were given to in ways we may have overlooked.

All relationships are dances of giving and receiving, taking and offering. The more intimate we are, the more dynamic the dance. And sometimes it's a real challenge to give without resentment and to receive with grace. We all yearn for a perfect balance, a love that is fluid, evenly alternating between giving and receiving. We want to think each person will get what she needs and will give only what she's comfortable giving. We believe we should be infinite givers and finite takers even when we act more like infinite takers and finite givers. Not surprisingly, we tell stories about gods who are always demanding more and more and always resentful for our ingratitude; and humans who are always taking and always feeling burdened with obligation. Jewish wisdom encourages us to reach for that place of balance while knowing that even if we get there, we won't remain there for long We all give too much or take too much, and feel resentful or greedy in our close relationships.

In the fourth-century wisdom text called *The Ethics of the Fathers*, two very different forms of love are described. The first refers to the story of Amnon and Tamar, children of King David, half-brother and half-sister. Amnon becomes lovesick over Tamar and forces himself on his beautiful sister, then turns away from her in shame. The second is the story of Jonathan, son of King Saul, and young David. The sages said, "The first depends on getting something back. And when that thing is gone, the love, too, disappears. This is the love between Amnon and Tamar. But a love that is not based on some external thing will not come to an end. This is the love between David and Jonathan." The former is conditional love (born out of lust that Amnon had for Tamar and an obvious attempt to own the other person) and the latter is unconditional. Between David and Jonathan, it would seem, there's no reciprocity expected; it's a love without expectation or self-consciousness, and at least no overt sexual expectations or desires (although this is debatable). For the sages, it's a supremely pure love.

The story goes like this: David is not yet king but a young man when he slays the mighty Philistine Goliath. As grateful as King Saul is, it becomes clear to him that David, and not his son Jonathan, will be the next king. This infuriates him, and Saul fears that David might even usurp the throne before Saul's time is up. Unlike Saul, Jonathan is not afraid. Instead Jonathan's soul becomes "bound up with the soul of David; Jonathan loves David as himself." The word love is used five times to describe the relationship between these two young men, and it's the only time in the Bible that two individual human beings make a *brit*, a sacred pact, with each other, a ritual reserved for God and man.

So clearly the sages were right: the biblical authors wanted us to pay very close attention to this particular love story. In the first scene, Jonathan, who at first reading is the obvious giver in the relationship, takes off his cloak, tunic, sword, bow, and belt and gives them to David. Then things get really interesting: King Saul orders Jonathan to kill David, and instead Jonathan warns David and protects him in several elaborate plots. Eventually both Saul and Jonathan are killed in battle, and David's eulogy—a precursor to his incredible poetry in the Psalms—is elegiac. In one verse, he finally declares his love for Jonathan, as Jonathan has done throughout the story for David. "I grieve for you, my brother Jonathan. You were most dear to me. Your love was wonderful to me. More than the love of women."

It's hard to argue with the fact that theirs was a pretty amazing love.

Yet the biblical authors set up the story in such a way that the reader might well question the motives of both men. The first time Jonathan declares his love and makes the pact with David it's just after David slays Golaith, showing his incredible prowess and worthiness to be king. Could it be that Jonathan, like Saul, was afraid that David might do him harm in order to become king himself? Might Jonathan's love have been double-edged: self-sacrifice that is also self-serving? David, too, may have had ulterior motives. It certainly was convenient to have a loyal spy in the palace, reporting Saul's every move against David. After all, without Jonathan, David might well have been killed by Saul.

David seems to be a bit like the boy in *The Giving Tree*, taking, and also receiving, but not giving anything back or showing his gratitude until after Jonathan's death. Even then, David refers to Jonathan's love for him, rather than the other way around. There's an earlier scene in which David seems to doubt Jonathan's intentions and Jonathan reassures him. Later Jonathan doubts David and is reassured. This hardly seems like undying trust.

The authors of *The Ethics of the Fathers* must have wondered about this relationship, and yet they saw this as the ultimate love story between human beings. They affirmed the supremacy of the relationship despite all the potential underlying political motives. They understood that David's and Jonathan's love was unconditional not because it was equally balanced or unsullied by self-serving motives—it was unconditional because it was transparent in its imbalance.

The rabbinic sages are teaching something quite radical. Purity of love is not about being perfectly reciprocal. It's about how honest people are to each other as to how they are giving and receiving. David, the powerful and charismatic king-to-be, could be totally vulnerable with Jonathan. He's the only person David lets his guard down with and to whom he shows his fears and doubts. Jonathan is able to give support and provide strength in a way that makes him very powerful. Their giving and receiving in its inequality creates a depth to their relationship that is unmatched in the Bible.

The message here seems to be that all loves have ulterior motives lurking somewhere, and all loves have imbalances. There are always reasons that we fall in love; it's never by accident. Even our love for our children can be conditional: As deep and enduring as it is, we expect to be loved back, and we usually expect that love to be demonstrated in particular ways. Mothering can become smothering with indebtedness, and fathering can become about expecting accomplishment, or vice versa. There really is no pure love, no pure action. As much as we give, it's impossible to know if we do so wholeheartedly; we'll never know what motivates us under the surface. Don't we tend to offer what we perceive to be ours in the first place? And don't we expect that the gift be recognized? Don't we sometimes want power over the other person? Don't we want praise?

Although the Bible has been called one of the greatest love stories ever written, the love between God and human beings is wrought with conflict over what is given and how it is received. We might expect the God character to be like the giving tree, an endless well of plenty, overflowing with and bestowing gifts. But the God character's gifts are always double-edged, abundant yet full of tests, conditions, and obligations.

Purity of love is not about being perfectly reciprocal. It's about how honest people are to each other as to how they are giving and receiving.

The very first gift of life—what gift could top that?—isn't a very gracious story on either side. Like a good parent, God provides everything the first couple could possibly need or desire, and yet it isn't enough. They take more than they've been given: The one forbidden fruit just can't be resisted. At first reading, the story seems to be a parable about our greed and insatiability. But then one has to wonder why God didn't offer them that fruit; why did God hold back? It seems the giving tree had its limits; God's giving came with expectations articulated and unarticulated. Although the post-Eden God does continue to give, now human beings are going to have to share the burden, providing for themselves and caring for each other. And the dynamic quality of giving and receiving will enliven their and our ongoing story. God will never be sure about us and we will never be sure about God, ourselves, or each other. That is the exquisite insecurity of love.

The very first time the word love is used in the Bible is in the story of the Binding of Isaac, called the Akedah. This is among the most disturbing stories in the entire text. Abraham is commanded to bring his beloved son Isaac to the top of Mt. Moriah and offer him up as a sacrifice, which Abraham does. Isaac is bound to the altar, a knife at his throat, when at the last minute Abraham replaces him with a ram, and Isaac's life is spared. What kind of God would make such a demand? And what kind of father would actually be willing to give such an offering? Centuries of interpretations try to make sense of this story, from Kierkegaard declaring Abraham a Knight of Faith to Woody Allen, who declares Abraham mad.

What if the Akedah is a meditation on giving and receiving? "God put Abraham to the test." But what is the test really about? Here are some of the questions it raises. What does Abraham need to do to prove his love? Is he willing to give it all? What does it take for any of us to trust the selflessness of our love? What do we have to give to know that we can love unconditionally? And then on the other side, how much does God need in order to trust Abraham's love? How much proof do we need to feel we are loved? How much do we need to be given to by those who love us in order to feel secure? There's madness in imagining what we would be willing to give in order to finally and unambiguously prove our love. And there is madness in imagining what we would need in order to clearly and unequivocally know that we are loved. We can be driven crazy by the self-doubt and insecurity of love. All this madness is present in any passionate relationship.

In the end, Abraham and God come to their senses, saving Isaac. Maybe they've learned what they need to know about love and mystery, giving and taking. More than a thousand years later, just a short walk from Mt. Moriah, where this binding takes place, another son will be bound—and this time it will be love to the end. The power of

Christianity is this demonstration of giving all for love. It creates the ultimate indebtedness, one which can never be paid off and leaves us all
yearning for grace.

In our contemporary, largely secular times, sacrifice is a bad word.
It's frequently associated with the violent, seemingly senseless taking of
a life; an anachronistic religious brutality from another era long behind
us—or perhaps only a part of "unevolved" cultures where religious
fanaticism reigns. Sacrifice in a nonreligious context is usually used to
indicate a quality of selflessness: giving up something precious for the
benefit of someone or something else, often a belief or an ideal. The
self-sacrificing mother; the soldier killed in battle; the giving tree. But
there is no word for sacrifice in the Hebrew Bible. The word used is *korban*, which means "to come closer," "to bring near"—an intimacy
maker.

Korban is an act of love as well as the product of a deep longing to
feel embraced, if only briefly. In the ancient days of the Temple in
Jerusalem, the practice of *korban* took the form of animal offerings: sin
offerings, gratitude offerings, life-cycle offerings. Whether in times of
vulnerability, security, joy, sadness, or loss, these expressions of awe involved giving up what is most precious; what in agricultural times sustained life itself. After the destruction of the Temple by the Romans in
70 C.E., this form of *korban* came to an end and was replaced with acts
of loving kindness. In other words, sacrificing time and money, giving
from the heart to another human being became a way to create intimacy, or what I call cosmic closeness.

I'll never forget the first time I donated more than my usual $50 or
so to a cause I believed in. At the time, I was earning a very modest
salary. I had attended a meeting at the State Department about the possible rescue and airlift of thousands of suffering, oppressed Ethiopians.
Money needed to be raised immediately to bribe public officials and
pay for the flights. It cost a thousand dollars to rescue one person: This
was a real stretch for me. I remember calling Dana to ask how she felt
about it, half hoping she'd object, telling me I had gotten caught up in

the moment. She didn't, and as I wrote the check my hand trembled and I literally felt expansiveness in my chest—my heart was opening. I understood *korban* just then better than I had in all my years of studying.

The most powerful form of *korban* in contemporary times—the only thing we can give and know we can't get back—is time. This is why volunteering and activism are such profound offerings. There have been studies that show the enormous psychological and even physical benefits of *korban*: When we give to others we feel closer to them, but also to some deeper place within ourselves. Giving is actually sustaining. This is especially true in our intimate relationships. From the small things in life like getting up night after night to tend to a crying child to caring for a sick parent who can no longer care for himself, we all make offerings in the course of our lives. They are no less powerful, maybe more so, than the *korban* at the Temple altar.

A friend of mine described how making her husband's lunch every day made her feel as close to him as lovemaking; quite a surprising statement. She told me how she'd been a feminist from a very early age. This stance was born from decades of watching her mother serve her father to the point where he seemed to do nothing for himself, not even make his own breakfast or dress himself in the morning. His clothes were laid out; and her mom would be pouring the milk in his cereal as he sat down to eat it.

My friend's marriage had always been one of "equals," tasks divided down the line so that one person wouldn't feel more burdened than the other, but mostly to protect herself from feeling the resentment she'd had as a child. Yet during a challenging financial time, she decided to make not just her own, but her husband's lunch every morning to save money. When things improved financially she found herself continuing the chore, even on the most rushed, pressured mornings when she had a deadline or an early meeting. She felt that lunch was even more important than it had been before. Now it seemed that in making that sandwich she was actually giving of herself. I'm guessing that her husband felt that same closeness.

Jewish wisdom has an ethics of giving. Even someone impover-ished and hungry should be able to experience the intimacy and joy of giving. There's a homeless man named Robert who usually hangs around my building, and to me he embodies this law. He's a poet, and he won't accept money unless he can recite a poem in return. One morning when Talia was about six I stopped to speak with Robert and to give him a few dollars for coffee and a bagel. Before I could walk away, he pulled a dirty teddy bear out of his bag and said to Talia in his raspy voice, "This is for you, dear." Clearly Robert understood the necessity of giving and the nobility it can bestow. Just as a poor person needs to give, no matter how little, the rich are encouraged to give, but only so much. A wealthy person is to give no more than 20 percent of what he or she possesses. Giving can be so intoxicating, such a high that it can do more harm than good: The giver can become depleted, and then what would there be left to give?

> Our yearning to give generously and receive gracefully is at the heart of our quest for intimacy.

In the Temple days there were three kinds of offerings; three ways of becoming closer to God, to expanding one's consciousness of reality and self. The first is called *olah*, which means "going up." Here the entire animal was burned at the altar. The second is called *minha*, which means "gift," and it entailed the same ritual at the altar, except part of the offering was given to the High Priests of the Temple. What's inter-esting is that this offering was considered no less important than an *olah*. The third kind, *shelamim*, means "wholeness" and is even more amazing: The animal was killed yet the entire thing was eaten by family and friends. Our ability to receive, to take in sustenance fully and joy-fully, is actually a way to express gratitude for the gift of life, which ex-plains why the meal is such a central part of every Jewish celebration. In religious language, if we don't partake of the meal, if we can't take it in, we've disappointed God.

Our yearning to give generously and receive gracefully is at the heart of our quest for intimacy. Intimacy in turn demands that we hold the tension of opposites: the yearning to love unconditionally and the craving to be loved for just being; the lust for control and the desire for surrender; the dread of entrapment and the longing for engulfment; the vitality of creative partnership and the deadness of status quo routine. George Orwell wrote, "The essence of being human is that we are in the end prepared to be broken up by life—which is the inevitable process of fastening our love upon other human beings." The yearning to love asks us to live with the fear that we may burn up in our giving and receiving—but it's worth it.

We are all needy. We all want to give. If we're lucky, we will work at it for a lifetime, taking and receiving from those around us and giving and offering to just as many. We'll be forever learning that in giving, we receive and in receiving, we give. May we all be able to recite wholeheartedly the 2500-year-old mantra: "Blessed is the giver and blessed is the taker. May he be blessed."

FORGIVENESS

"LOVE MEANS NEVER HAVING TO SAY YOU'RE SORRY" ARE the words spoken by Ali MacGraw in that classic '70s movie, *Love Story*. This line captures a yearning so many of us have, even if we don't want to admit it. We long for someone who understands us and accepts us so fully—despite all our faults and mistakes—that apologizing seems beside the point. The ultimate relationship, we can't help but think, is one in which forgiveness is easy, free-flowing, and immediate; where it requires little or no effort from either party, even when the hurt may be deep.

Of course, it's just the opposite. Our most loving relationships are those in which we say "sorry" continuously. Forgiveness is central to the workings of love. If we're not seeking and receiving, being asked for and granting forgiveness on a regular basis, it's most likely that our relationship is not as intimate, dynamic, or alive as we think it is. And it's likely that we're holding in plenty of bitterness, resentment, guilt, and shame. Quite simply, things aren't messy enough. One could say that forgiveness is the glue of loving relationships, holding them all together and constantly renewing and repairing them. But there is no such thing as "an act" of forgiveness. Forgiveness is a process, a way of being in the world.

Forgiveness is a process, a way of being in the world.

I hear so often about the hurts that won't go away: the person who holds a grudge, who nurtures a resentment; or the one who never admitted his wrong, who simply can't humble himself to ask for forgiveness, although it's clear he's burdened by the not asking. The yearning to for-give and be forgiven is palpable. We want to make our relationships right, to make things whole again. A recent Gallup poll reported that 94 percent of Americans say forgiveness is one of the central virtues. Yet 48 percent of those same people say they've never had a forgiving expe-rience. How can this be?

Perhaps it's because the forgiveness so many of us yearn for is to-tal and complete. When people talk to me about forgiveness, they want so badly to be able to start again, to have everything be okay, to wipe the slate clean. Before they open themselves up again by either granting or seeking forgiveness, they want some guarantee that it will all work out. They imagine a single conversation that will end in tears or laughter, at the end of which both parties will be able to go on as if nothing had ever happened, the hurt and disappointment having been erased or healed. When this doesn't happen, one person may become defensive, giving up too soon. Some grant forgiveness too quickly, wanting to let the other person off the hook, wanting to feel better themselves, to retreat from the pain and the uncertainty. Others tell me they want to simply let it go, to forgive someone on their own without interacting with or confronting the person at all. Or they think it's possible to forgive themselves. Anything but approach or confront another person.

This is understandable: Few things make us as vulnerable as admit-ting our mistakes, especially to someone we have every reason to think will be angry at us or, even worse, unreceptive or shut down. When we ask for forgiveness, there's no place for defenses, for justifications. We have to make ourselves naked. At the same time, to forgive is an act of faith and trust. There's little reason to expect that the transgression won't happen again; once someone crosses a line, what's the guarantee they won't again? We live in a culture of avoidance; few of us have had models of forgiveness or were taught that feeling vulnerable and taking risks is a necessary part of intimacy. So, instead, we seek a kind of cheap grace.

There are no guarantees, no absolutes, no lasting sense of complete-ness. We get hurt; we're vulnerable; doors shut in our faces. And yet we are obliged to seek forgiveness anyway. Jewish wisdom has an expansive understanding of the process of forgiveness and a method born of cen-turies of practice. The sages taught that most of the time it's not possible to have our offenses wiped away, to have that feeling of starting over, of being whole again with ourselves and the other person. But there's a lot that *can* happen. We can realign our relationships, initiate some healing, and reconnect, sometimes more deeply than we ever have before.

The twelfth-century philosopher Maimonides offered a practice of forgiveness that I call the "four Rs" of forgiveness: Recognition; Regret; Resolution; Reconciliation. The premise of this pro-

To forgive is an act of faith and trust.

cess is that forgiveness is not some pious command-ment that compels obedience. It's something to be striven for, and it must be practiced in the context of a relationship. It is as much external as internal. We must dive into the muck together.

Love Story really had it wrong: Not only is it ridiculous to believe that love is never having to say we're sorry, many times it's not even enough to say we're sorry—not even close. We must recognize what we did, how we hurt the other person; we must genuinely regret our ac-tions, and resolve not to repeat them. Sometimes we need to do more than just talk, actually demonstrating that we'll behave differently when we're in the same situation again. And if we've been hurt or di-minished by another person, we should communicate our needs, en-couraging the other person, as a friend of mine says, "to walk the walk and then come back and talk." Only then is real reconciliation possible. Jewish wisdom assumes people can change, that we want to grow and deepen our relationships, that breaches in intimacy are always oppor-tunities.

I had the opportunity to practice the four Rs recently in the midst of an ongoing struggle with my daughter Talia. She'd always been a night owl, just like me. These late hours with everyone else asleep could have been a time of closeness—daughter and father talking into the night, or at least keeping each other company as we did our own thing. But I'd always resented her presence. At a certain point, during an especially stressful time at work, my frustration got the best of me, and I began to lash out at her, berating her for spending so much time watching TV and playing on the computer. "Go to sleep, already!" "Can't you read a book in bed?" "You won't be able to focus in school!" But, like me, she couldn't just go to bed, and one night I really lost it and she crumbled in tears. I apologized profusely. How could I make my little girl cry like that? What was my problem? As she said, she was a straight A student and never missed the bus in the mornings. I felt terrible.

Much as I hate to admit it, a few nights later I lost it again. Once again I apologized. And Talia nailed me. "Don't say you're sorry. Just don't yell at me anymore!" Clearly, sorry wasn't good enough, not when she knew nothing had really changed. This got me thinking. What was this really about? Every parent needs time to themselves, but the extent of my rage, my inability to stop myself from screaming at her, clearly was coming from someplace else.

I sat with my anger for a few days and realized that it wasn't really about Talia at all. I recognized a pattern from childhood—isn't that always the case? As the eldest of six brothers, I had never been alone. We shared a room and I spent a lot of time caring for, talking to, and studying with my siblings. It seemed every minute of the day there was someone around: You couldn't use the bathroom without someone knocking. I hated the lack of privacy. As an adult, I seemed to be bent on making up for lost time. Hadn't I earned it? Wasn't this now my house where I could finally have my own space! I finally *recognized* where my bad temper was all coming from. That was a moment of realization for me, and the first stage of forgiveness.

Blaming Talia was a defense against feeling pain. Now my *regret* took on another dimension: I was burdening my child with baggage from my own childhood. I was taking fifteen years of childhood frustration out on her. I explained this to her one night after yet another outburst, and she listened with genuine interest to stories from my youth. I could see she understood. Now it was time for *resolution*: I had to show her I could act differently, that the recognition and regret actually meant something.

There's a big difference between regret and guilt, and yet the two are often confused. Guilt more often than not keeps us from action. It is often paralyzing and self-destructive. "I feel guilty" can become an indictment. We beat ourselves up, but rarely do we do something about it. On the other hand, regret generates action; we are compelled to make things better. "I regret what I did" inspires us to do it differently next time. When we regret, it becomes possible to genuinely resolve not to do the same thing again when confronted with a similar situation. Only then is reconciliation possible.

As I write this, it's been weeks since that last fight. Talia's still at the computer, in front of the TV, or reading by my side on the couch late into the night. I still long for time alone, but the edge is gone. The other night she looked up at me, and said with that ironic smile of hers, "Now isn't that better, Dad?" We both laughed; *reconciliation* at last. Although Talia probably knows I might lose it again some day, the struggle was resolved for now, and it even seemed to have strengthened our relationship. There was a new understanding between us, a kind of expanded consciousness and renewed bond. As the Hasidic Rabbi Levi Yitzchak of Berditchev said, "When one repents out of love the previous evil acts are considered changed into good deeds."

Guilt keeps us from action, but regret inspires us to be different next time.

Here's a far more powerful example of the four Rs—one of the most moving stories of brothers in the biblical texts. Once again sibling rivalry is at the center of a family conflict. This is the story of Joseph, the eleventh of Jacob's twelve sons, his first child by Rachel, his favored wife. When Rachel died, Jacob understandably turned his affections toward the eldest of Rachel's two sons. Also understandably, the hurt among Jacob's other sons was nothing short of excruciating.

Hence the Broadway musical of *Joseph and the Amazing Technicolor*

Dream Coat. It wasn't enough that Joseph was more loved; Jacob had to go and give Joseph a fancy coat on top of everything. And, of course, Jacob gave his other sons nothing. To make matters worse, Joseph was a special child who had prophetic dreams, and he told his brothers about these dreams which foretold the power he someday would have. When Joseph shared the images of his brothers' bowing down to him, their resentment and envy grew into hate.

One day while out in the fields, his brothers plotted to kill Joseph. They stripped him of his beloved coat and threw him in a pit. They surely would have murdered him had the eldest, Judah, not convinced his brothers to sell, rather than kill, Joseph. A caravan of Ishmaelites came by and the brothers sold Joseph, who was taken to Egypt. Remarkably, once again Joseph was favored, this time by his owner, and he quickly rose to a position of power in the household, a status that again gave rise to envy among the others in the house and, this time, to a false accusation. He was accused of trying to seduce his master's wife and was sent off to prison.

While there, Joseph's skill in interpreting dreams came to the attention of the Pharaoh, who invited Joseph into his court as an adviser. Yet again Joseph rose to great heights, becoming second to the Pharaoh himself. His dreams came true. Years later Joseph had the opportunity to exercise his power. At the time, he was in charge of administering food to all of Egypt. A seven-year famine struck the entire region including Canaan, where Joseph's family lived. When word got out that food could be bought in Egypt, Jacob sent his sons there. All except Benjamin—Joseph's younger brother and Rachel's other son—who Jacob favored as he had Joseph.

Imagine Joseph's surprise when his brothers showed up. Joseph had changed so much in dress, speech, and demeanor that, combined with his elevated role, his brothers didn't recognize him. But Joseph knew them, and he must have been overwhelmed with emotion as they bowed down to him. In a flash he may have remembered the years of slavery and imprisonment; that agonizing time in the pit as he waited to be murdered; his dreams; his father; his younger brother; his dead mother. All that loss and pain must have felt like a kind of eruption. In response, he decided to take revenge, calmly and methodically. He accused the brothers of being spies and threw them into prison for three days. After interrogating them and learning about Jacob and Benjamin back home, Joseph insisted that they prove their honesty in a kind of test. One of the brothers was to remain there as a hostage while the others returned home to bring Benjamin to Egypt.

Perhaps underneath his rage and bitterness, Joseph had some longing for reconciliation. He could have killed his brothers or kept them in jail. Instead he decided to create a theater of revenge to see how his brothers would respond. The brothers agreed to Joseph's demand. But before they left his court, Joseph heard his brothers whispering among themselves about the crime they had committed against Joseph years earlier. They wondered if this cruelty on the part of a stranger was some kind of payback for their betrayal. Joseph turned away from them and wept. His plot had set into motion two unexpected reactions: His brothers began to recognize and regret the terrible thing they'd done, and Joseph began to feel a longing to connect with his brothers. The theater of revenge now became a dance of both vengeance and atonement.

The brothers minus one returned home with food and told their father everything that had happened. After the food was finished, Jacob, threatened with starvation once again, with great reluctance and fear, agreed to let the brothers take Benjamin to Egypt to procure more food and redeem their older brother. As soon as Joseph saw Benjamin, he was overcome with feelings and rushed out of the room to weep again. Later, he threw a feast and sat his brothers in order from youngest to eldest. Understandably, the brothers feared he was playing with them. But that was the least of it—Joseph was far from done.

As they prepared to leave again for Canaan, Joseph had a royal silver goblet placed in Benjamin's bag. Then Joseph called his brothers before him and accused them of stealing his cup, threatening to kill the person responsible. Joseph had set a cruel trap in which they would have to decide the fate of another brother. And Judah rose to the occasion. When the cup was found in Benjamin's bag, the same brother who years earlier had argued to sell Joseph into slavery stepped forward and, in an eloquent plea, expressed his love for Benjamin and his empathy for his father, who would be broken by this loss of the second favored son. Judah offered himself in Benjamin's place. Jacob's favoritism, this time for Benjamin, was no longer a source of murderous bitterness; Judah's love for his father and brother trumped his jealousy. Put in the same situation again, he proved he was capable of acting differently. Judah would be his brother's keeper.

Upon hearing Judah's words Joseph couldn't control himself and sobbed openly. This time he cried out, "I am Joseph!" Suddenly Joseph was able to see the betrayal of him in the largest possible context, telling his brothers, "Do not be distressed or reproach yourselves because you sold me here; it was to save life that God sent me ahead of you!" If Joseph hadn't wound up in Egypt he would not have been able to save his family from starvation. There was a purpose to all that conflict and suffering.

And yet life can never be made perfect, and relationships sometimes don't completely heal. When Jacob died, the brothers feared Joseph would now take his revenge. Understandably they wanted their relationship with Joseph to be repaired, to have the whole thing behind them. So they lied to him. They told him their father's dying wish was that Joseph forgive them. The very first time the word "forgive" is used in the Bible, it is as part of a deception. Sometimes our

> **Anger is not always the enemy of forgiveness. What we do out of hurt and rage can actually sometimes lead to reconciliation.**

yearning to be forgiven is so great that we may go to great lengths to attain it. We want to do it perfectly or with pure intention. But there is always something self-serving about asking for forgiveness.

Unaware of the lie, Joseph responded by comforting them and

speaking kindly to them; by helping and sustaining them. But he never used the word "forgive." We can only assume it wasn't granted. Reconciliation doesn't wash away all the hurt, eliminate all the fears, nor diminish all the doubts. And isn't this the way things usually are? Forgiveness is one of the most complex processes in any intimate relationship. Maybe saints and enlightened beings forgive neatly and fully, but for the rest of us, when we are seriously hurt and betrayed by jealous siblings, abusive parents, or unfaithful spouses, forgiveness is rarely achievable in some fairy tale way.

Like Joseph's story, our forgiveness stories have many faces and rhythms, different outcomes and conclusions. Each time we open to another person, no matter how small or incomplete the opening, we become more intimate with them and with ourselves. When we are asked to forgive, sparing the other's life as Joseph did—literally or figuratively—may in fact be a remarkable first step. Rage, the desire to lash out, plotting revenge, testing—all may be subtle movements on the forgiveness continuum. Our desire to hurt back is actually an expression of our love, a kind of distorted yearning to stay connected.

Contrary to some "religious" views, anger is not the enemy of forgiveness, and what we do out of hurt and rage can sometimes actually lead to reconciliation, as it did for the brothers. Joseph saw the humanity and vulnerability of the very people who had hurt him only after expressing his anger, however dramatic and painful. I have seen so many instances of people who felt wronged opening their hearts to forgive when they saw their abuser suffering emotionally or ill or on a deathbed. It may take many years to reconnect, to allow someone to apologize, to gain confidence in them again, but if we don't eventually unblock the dams, forgiveness will remain an unconscious yearning. It's always there whether we acknowledge it or not. And even if we do, sadness and hurt, resentment and regret—although lessened—may still be part of the relationship. Amazingly, that pain can coexist with healing and forgiveness, becoming softer and less central over time.

Often we ourselves emerge stronger, clearer, and wiser when we wrestle with forgiveness, no matter what the outcome. Joseph's two sons gave rise to two of the twelve tribes of Israel from whom the Jewish people emerged. And Judah became the leading tribe from whom King David descended.

The sages taught that there are three kinds of forgiveness. One of them is called *selicha*, and it is the kind Joseph granted. It's a forgiveness born of a heartfelt empathy for the transgressor, and an ability to see the widest possible context, even the positive outcome of the conflict. As Joseph said, if his brothers hadn't betrayed him, he wouldn't have been able to help his family survive a bitter famine. More often than not, *selicha* doesn't happen right away just as it did not for Joseph and Judah. It takes time, especially when the hurt is great. And it's not something we can ever expect or ask for. Quite often, unforeseen circumstances are the impetus for it. There are so many stories of family members who've been alienated for years forgiving each other and reconnecting after the death of a parent. As painful as it is, a death creates an interruption of old patterns, an opening and a perspective in the midst of the grief.

Selicha also can unfold in the course of living and growing together. Typically, it's a process rather than a moment in time. This was the case for Freddie, whose mother had been an alcoholic all through Freddie's childhood and teenage years. I was surprised when she told me the story. She and her mother seemed very close. She said her mother had been neglectful and hurtful during those drunken years, leaving Freddie to serve as a buffer between her parents as they fought and struggled in a bad marriage fueled by addiction. As a young adult, she'd gone through periods where she didn't speak to her mother, and felt enraged even years after her mother joined Alcoholics Anonymous and began the recovery process. Didn't her mother recognize what she'd done? Why hadn't she approached Freddie and her sister to ask forgiveness and begin the healing process?

But her mother never did. As the years went by, she just "showed up," as Freddie put it: During Freddie's breakups with men, her mom was on the other end of the phone. Job disappointment: Mom was there. When Freddie had children of her own, her mother proved to be an exceptional grandma, down on the floor playing through long afternoons despite a bum knee. One day Freddie was listening to a talk of mine about forgiveness, and she had the thought, "Wow, I guess I've forgiven my mom." Freddie knew that those feelings of resentment and hurt hadn't disappeared. The way she described it, every time her mother disappointed her, and each time her mother showed up, Freddie forgave at deeper and deeper levels. What mattered most was that her mom was doing her best to make up for lost time. There was no moment of tears and reconciliation between them as there was in the Joseph story. There was simply living day in and day out with the hurt and the resolve to make it right.

Forgiveness so often comes into play in bold relief when it comes to our mothers and fathers. Everyone has to come to terms with negative or conflicted feelings about their parents, no matter how loving the relationship. What makes it so difficult is that we have three sets of parents: the ones who raised us and with whom we actively struggled; those who live in our memory today; and our living parents (assuming they are still alive). The parents in our memory have larger-than-life dimensions. They are the ones who adored us and ignored us, whom we idealized and demonized. Our parents today are people like us, with fears and flaws, trials and conflicts. And they likely will never live up to our childhood expectations and hopes, which are often still with us in adulthood, whether we're aware of them or not. Our job is to separate these three manifestations and work as best we can toward reconciliation, trying not to carry too much of the baggage of the past into the present, while always engaging with it. Our first great shock is when we realize that our parents are not God, and our next shock is when we realize that God is not our parent. This realization is the beginning of forgiveness for our parents and for God.

Even when reconciliation occurs, it doesn't mean the relationship continues where it left off. Another story of brothers illustrates this in a

scene full of pathos and suspense: the reunion of the previous generation of warring siblings, Jacob and Esau. Many decades after Jacob, the
younger twin, stole his brother's birthright in a plot devised by their
mother, Rebecca, Jacob and Esau come face to face with each other in
the desert.

Both men are now well established with large camps rich with animals, servants, and children. Jacob is journeying back to Canaan, his
home, when he's told Esau is approaching. Jacob is terrified, and his
guilt is palpable. After he sends ahead gifts and promises of more to
Esau, he spends the entire night before their meeting in a torturous
wrestling match with an angel (who in his dream may have been Esau
or himself). The fight leaves him wounded and limping in the morning. What happens next is remarkable: When they finally encounter
each other, Esau weeps and then hugs and kisses his brother.

The scribes found this level of forgiveness so hard to believe that
they actually played with the Hebrew word for "kiss," hinting to the
reader that the word might also be "bite." Then Esau refuses Jacob's
gifts, saying that he has enough. He invites Jacob to travel and settle
with him in town just ahead. Jacob agrees, but he never joins Esau. His
camp moves right on past that town, and the brothers see each other
again only at the death of their father, where the Bible simply says,
"Isaac was buried by his sons." We're never told and can only imagine
how their lives might have been changed by this startling reunion in the
desert. What's clear is that both of them go on to create great nations.

The second kind of forgiveness is the only kind we can ask for and
ever expect to receive. It's called *mechila*. Although we may not recognize it as forgiveness, most of us grant and receive it regularly. *Mechila*
is a kind of pardon. In legal language *mechila* is a relinquishing of a
claim or debt: You don't owe me anything for the wrong you have done.
And, contrary to the common understanding of forgiveness, it's not
necessarily a profound or heartfelt experience for either person. Certainly it's far from having the slate wiped clean. It's not the forgiveness
most of us yearn for, but the sages taught that it was enough. Let's say a

coworker cuts you off in a meeting, or dismisses something you said. She comes into your office later to apologize, and you tell her not to worry about it. There's no need for tears, although you may have been very upset with her. You don't want to know what was going on in her head or her heart. You don't need to go there. You let her off the hook. She owned up to her mistake and that's enough. *Mechila* also happens countless times with those close to us—a spouse doesn't pay attention to us as we tell him the details of our day and when we call him on it, a simple "Sorry, honey" does the trick. A child writes on the wall and, when confronted, seems to understand what she's done. Forgiveness granted.

Not every apology need be full-hearted and transforming. Apologies can be partial and still be real. There is something to be said for an apology that is done honestly just because that's what we should do and not as some great admission of guilt and shame. I have found that the key to this kind of apology is to not make any excuses. There should be no explanations of extenuating circumstances and no "I'm sorry but . . . ," which actually undermines the apology. We all do things that are thoughtless, inconsiderate, selfish, and mean, and thus we have a debt to the other person that we need to own up to as much for ourselves as for her. Sometimes an apology comes first and our feelings follow, but much of the time, we aren't even aware of our offenses. The truth is, rarely a week or even a day goes by when we don't annoy, disappoint, or hurt someone. Jewish wisdom has a system for addressing even these relatively minor or unconscious hurts, and it's one that can inform our everyday interactions. Every year before Yom Kippur, the Day of Atonement—of forgiveness—there is a centuries-old forgiveness practice. We are to speak to those close to us and say, "If there's anything over the last year that I've done to hurt or offend you, I'm sorry." These days it's often done over the phone (I'm not sure about e-mail). And it's literally a mantra, which like any mantra can seem rote. But when we make a few of these calls it's amazing the impact it can have. Most of the time, the person grants *mechila* and asks for it in return.

When they don't, that's when things get really interesting. When we're lucky, that's when the process of *selicha* can begin.

Sometimes we hurt people more than we imagine: A joke at the expense of a coworker at a meeting, a slight of a family member at the dinner table, teasing a spouse at a party. These things may barely register on our guilt meter, but it cuts to their heart. These hurts often take more than one apology to mend. The *mechila* practice is to ask for forgiveness three times. As random as that number may seem, practices can be like that. The onus is always on the person seeking forgiveness to keep trying. And if in the end forgiveness is not granted, you can feel you've truly given it your best shot. There is no knowing what eventual effect our asking will have.

One day not long before the High Holidays, I got one of those calls. It was from the former vice principal of my old high school, who I hadn't even thought about in decades. Obviously, I remembered how much he had upset me, though, because I didn't return his call; not until my assistant, uncomfortable with his frequent calls over the course of a week, asked me why I wasn't calling this guy back. Her question embarrassed me. It wasn't like me to not return a call. I couldn't imagine what he wanted, but I reluctantly picked up the phone. As I did, I could feel old feelings of resentment and anger coming back from more than thirty years ago.

I had been fourteen at the time. It was my first year away from home at a very traditional and rigorous parochial high school. Like most of my classmates in that first year, I longed for the weekends when I went home to my family. Every Saturday I went to synagogue with my father, who was a cantor there; this weekly ritual was particularly comforting and grounding at that vulnerable time. Then, one day, the vice principal called me into his office. He was young for his position and had a friendly demeanor, but behind it he was very rigid, strict, and judgmental. He told me I should no longer pray in my father's synagogue. He insisted that it wasn't traditional enough and, therefore, I wasn't fulfilling the obligation to pray. I completely lost it. "Are you fucking crazy?"

I yelled. Cursing at the vice principal was already unthinkable, but then I pushed him, and we ended up wrestling on the floor. His secretary had to separate us. I have no idea why I wasn't expelled, or how I got the nerve to write him an angry letter after this episode. I remember making a vigorous argument challenging him ethically on the grounds that the commandment to honor one's parents trumped the obligation to pray in a traditional fashion. He dropped it, but from time to time he'd needle me about not fully observing the Sabbath.

As an adult I understood that his demand was nothing personal against me or my father. All ideologies demand that we break or weaken our blood relations, that we be willing to reexamine our loyalties and make sacrifices in order to realize new truths. But even with this adult understanding I couldn't help but hold the principal's extremism against him; he'd used his power and authority in an insensitive and uncompromising way.

Thirty-one years later, there was his voice on the other end of the phone. He explained that he'd been sorting through his belongings, preparing for a move, and had come across my letter. He told me that it was a "beautiful" letter, and that he wanted me to know who he was now, how he'd changed. He told me about his years directing a different school, about the ways he'd "loosened up" and opened the curriculum to new approaches and ideas. He apologized for how he'd treated me: He'd been immature and just plain wrong. His last words to me were, "You'd be proud of me now." I was really touched, and I told him so. Without effort or hesitation, I granted *mechila*. When I hung up the phone I felt some small part of me was healed, and I really hope he felt forgiven, that maybe he experienced *selicha*.

Sometimes, we need to be rebuked in order to understand that we need to ask for forgiveness. Without the letter in hand, it's doubtful that the vice principal would have made the call. But all those years later, he was able to hear my reproval differently. We all know the famous verse from the Book of Leviticus that says, "Love your neighbor as yourself" but few of us remember that this intuition begins with the following words: "Rebuke, rebuke! Criticize your neighbor, but do not hold a grudge in your heart." Confrontation is a practice. An essential part of loving is critiquing. This is especially important to remember when we feel we're nurturing an injury, when our resentment is keeping us from living fully, or when it's stunting the growth of a relationship. It's incumbent upon us to criticize when we feel the person could benefit from our doing so.

I had a major wake-up call born of rebuke when I was a young rabbi in St. Louis. I was especially ambitious at that time, in a promising position at a synagogue of one thousand families. I was high on my new role; it was all so intense and alive. And I had a balance problem. There was always one more thing to do before I left the office, one more call, one more letter to write, one more sentence to add to that sermon. Even when the wonder of it all wore off, I was chronically late. It was a habit, and I really didn't think much about it; I was always gracious and apologetic when I finally arrived. People knew I didn't mean anything by it—at least I thought so.

It took my leaving the synagogue for me to realize that this was anything but the case. My realization came just in time for me to begin a new chapter in my life, but it was incredibly painful, however deserved. I had arrived at my good-bye dinner close to an hour and a half late. All my friends were in the middle of eating their entrees as was my wife, sitting there next to my empty chair. I did my usual round of apologies, assuming it was no big deal: Everyone knew I had this lateness thing, and this time I really needed to get everything done before we moved; I was being a responsible rabbi. As I went up to everyone, talking them up as is my usual way, I began to realize that no one was paying any attention to me, literally. They continued their conversation, eating and drinking as if I wasn't there.

Could this really be happening? I kept trying to engage people, then finally gave up, sat down, turned to Dana, and asked her what was up. Then the fun really began. She told me how hurt she was by my continual lateness, and one by one my closest friends laid into me about how insulting it had been to them all these years; how egotistical and self-important it was for me to assume all should be forgiven no matter how late I was, no matter how important the event or meeting. Weren't my wife, my friends, more important than the speech, the filing, or whatever it was that kept me from being where I'd promised to be? They were palpably angry.

I broke down in tears. I turned to Dana and apologized through my sobs. She nodded and kissed me, but her eyes were still full of hurt. I felt incredibly humbled. Of course, they were right. My lateness was a retreat from intimacy and an arrogant control move. I had a lot of repair work to do. Not even a heartfelt apology would make it any better. I had to change. I had to be on time. And I'm happy to say that, for the most part, I am a pretty prompt person these days. Years later, whenever I'm late I see Dana's eyes and hear my friends' angry voices. Theirs was an incredibly effective rebuke; a true intervention, a sacred practice.

There is an ethics of rebuke that my wife and friends intuitively understood. It is also an art. Of course, things had gone so far on my end that it was clear more harm was being done to my loved ones and me than any rebuke could cause. But they also knew that I could handle the intensity of their criticism. In the second century, Rabbi Tarfon exclaimed, "No one knows how to give rebuke, and no one knows how to hear it!" Too often we are accusing and humiliating when we confront someone, so angry the person can't hear us, can't take it in. There's another verse in Leviticus that says, "Reprove your brother but incur no guilt because of him." We should rebuke only if we're pretty sure we won't make the situation worse, or do more harm than good.

As a student of mine noted, the phrase in Leviticus uses the word "rebuke" twice. As in our dreams, repetition is always significant in sacred texts; it indicates that there's more than one meaning to a word or more than one person or consciousness it's addressing. Perhaps we're meant to rebuke the other person only after we've rebuked ourselves. If we're thoughtful, if we take confrontation seriously, before we pick up the phone and tell someone they wronged us, we generally need to take a good look in the mirror. What we find is that often our anger has masked our complicity in the hurt. Our inner drama has colored our perceptions.

This insight helped me understand why I'd never confronted the person who damaged me professionally more than anyone I know. For typical corporate political reasons, and perhaps leftover childhood jealousies and insecurities, he had rather viciously and adeptly undermined me with a few of my institution's financial support-ers. For more than two years I harbored such re-sentment against him that I rarely allowed myself to be in the same room with him. When I did have to greet him it was with a barely professional cool-ness. And then I decided I would confront him. Before calling him I re-viewed exactly how I was going to rebuke or criticize him, but as I thought about him in the context of the meditation from Leviticus, I re-alized how instrumental I'd been in our struggle.

> Perhaps we're meant to rebuke another only after we've rebuked ourselves.

Unbeknownst to him, I had actually strongly recommended him for the major position he now had, the one from which he'd been so de-structive. I asked myself why I had recommended him, and it came to me. I thought his toughness, even his meanness, would be an asset to a man I saw as kind and generous but not strong enough to make a dif-ference in the world, a difference I thought he genuinely wanted to make. And I knew that if I recommended this candidate he might even be loyal and give me better access.

I never called. I saw that I had much more to gain by rebuking my-self for being complicit in the very events that had hurt me. If anything, I, too, had amends to make; not to him, but to my old patron. I'd rec-ommended this person against my "better" judgment because, ironi-cally, I felt there was something in it for me.

The third mode of forgiveness is called *kappara*, and it's the one we all yearn for. In religious language, this kind of forgiveness can only be granted by God. In Christian language, this is grace. It can't be earned or asked for—it comes after all the asking and all the work. It can't be predicted or expected; rather, it seems to be granted from the depths or on high. When we say "To err is human, to forgive is divine," this is the kind of forgiveness we mean.

Kappara is the kind of forgiveness that wipes the slate clean. It cancels out the offense. In psychological language it's an inner experience of return, of feeling whole again. We are able to integrate our transgression into a more expanded self. And we literally have a sense of expansion, of tremendous relief and elevation. *Kappara* is a transpersonal experience in which we simultaneously understand our finitude and our infinitude. It's a vision of our widest range of selves at that point in time.

The word *kappara* comes from the same root as the word *kippur*. Hence the sacred day of Yom Kippur, the Day of Atonement. On this holiday, which comes one week after the celebration of the Jewish New Year, we're meant to reach deep down into our selves and consciously yearn for *kappara*. It's a twenty-five-hour forgiveness retreat. Only on Yom Kippur is the goal *kappara*.

It's no wonder that more people come to temple on Yom Kippur than on any other day. Millions of otherwise secular Jews who never go to the synagogue pour through its doors in order to make themselves naked, to look into their own Book of Life, as the liturgy calls it, and see themselves more clearly. I'm often asked about the symbolism of the day: why do we meditate so many times in the service on the phrase "inscribe us in the Book of Life?" I tell people to imagine their entire year on film; pretend they can look in a Godlike way, frame by frame, at themselves, their interactions with people, their mistakes, their lovemaking, their fights, their triumphs. This is their Book of Life, their record of what they did and didn't do. To be inscribed is to take note, to become conscious of ourselves, the authors.

The central metaphor of the day is a court being convened. This image may seem cold or intimidating. But don't we all have a deep desire to be judged, to be held accountable? Don't we want our actions to matter? Since we were children in school waiting for that report card, we've wanted to know where we stand. The problem is that we confuse judged and judgmental. We imagine all judgment is through harsh and severe lenses. But where did that come from? Perhaps it's a projection of how we tend to see ourselves and others. There is a paradoxical power in this metaphor of standing in court when no external authority is on the bench. The things we feel most guilty about are not the illegalities but the stuff we try at our inner court that no one knows about. And the most severe judge, whether consciously or not, is the only judge that ultimately counts, the Self, Reality, God—whatever you choose to call this higher or deeper consciousness.

The major practice on Yom Kippur is to fast for that twenty-five hours as a way to loosen our ego boundaries and make us more receptive; to open up to new truths. I have often thought that we are also reenacting our death. This is an especially important place from which to ask for forgiveness. So often we stand on ceremony with loved ones and friends waiting for them to apologize first; to humble themselves so that we can feel bigger. And then the resentments only congeal, and weeks, months, years go by without speaking—even after the cause of the fight may be forgotten and irrelevant. Every so often, it is a good exercise to ask oneself: If one of us died before we made up, would I really want to hold that grudge, not having spoken, have it all end without an attempt at reconciliation?

In my experience as a rabbi, there is nothing sadder than officiating at a funeral at which a child is burying a parent she hasn't spoken to in years. Or a brother burying his brother who he hasn't had contact with in decades. It happens all the time. Sometimes we need to apologize even if we feel we are wronged. We can be the one who has the larger context, the furthest vision, and with that the responsibility to start the process.

By the end of Yom Kippur, after fasting, meditating, chanting, studying sacred texts, and reviewing their lives over the last year, most people's boundaries are pretty thin. They are weak and tired, not quite their ordinary selves. During the last part of the service, I invite everyone, whether alone or with their families or friends, to stand before the open ark where the Torah scrolls reside; in other words, to stand before his or her open heart. In the service, I ask hundreds of people, unafraid to inhabit themselves, unafraid of what they might find inside their Holy of Holies (at least for a minute or two), to come up to make a personal prayer. Often, as someone comes forward, there is a split second in which my eye catches his or hers. I can see that for many of them it is an intensely powerful time in which all the shared memories or the past year's hard truths become palpable—whether it's the job that was lost, the parent with Alzheimer's, the marriage that ended, or the child who is ill. It's amazing and awe-fully humbling to see and hear so many people praying, or simply talking softly to each other, some of them visibly crying. One year I overheard a mother wishing healing on an addicted daughter; a husband and wife whom I knew to be on the brink of divorce holding each other, whispering. I also saw a teenager normally sullen and distant become wide-eyed and teary, holding his father's hand. Whether one has fully engaged with the practices and rituals leading up to that point of the day or not, one's perception shifts. Somehow one can enter the year with resentments diminished, bitterness eased, and a sense of possibility.

One would think that by evening, after the long blast of the shofar which marks the end of the day, we'd just be able to go home and eat. But a few minutes after that final blast, when technically the day is over, we once again pray for *selicha*. It isn't possible that we've misstepped yet; that there's anything to be forgiven. Yet the sages had an insight: We're going to walk out of that synagogue and err again. So just in case we think we're free and clear, here's a reminder that Yom Kippur is not a preventative ritual. There is no ultimate moment of forgiveness. We're always making mistakes and correcting, offending and asking for forgiveness. We're never permanently guilty, nor permanently clean. Welcome to your humanity. Welcome to the new year.

Yom Kippur is a process of re-covenanting, of reestablishing our connection to others and a deeper level of awareness. There's a story about the Israelites receiving the second set of the Ten Commandments on Yom Kippur. The story goes like this. After forty days atop Mt. Sinai, Moses came down with the tablets. What could be more holy? But contrary to popular belief, these are not the set the Israelites received. When Moses saw the people worshipping the golden calf (a blatant defiance of the first three commandments), he did the unthinkable. He smashed the tablets in rage. Then he returned to the mountain for another forty days, during which time he managed to convince an even more enraged God not to destroy the people. When Moses returned to the Israelites he brought new tablets that he himself had created. These were the commandments the people received, and this is the event Yom Kippur remembers.

There is no great moment of healing or repair in this story. Yes, of course the people show regret but, as in our own lives, the slate is not wiped clean. Something even more amazing happens. Moses places the old, smashed tablets into the Holy Ark along with the new, intact ones. The relationship continues; the covenant is renewed with the brokenness on the inside. There is no perfect reconciliation, no permanent forgiveness, no forgetting. But betrayal is not the last word. There is a larger context: Love and betrayal can merge into and out of one another in astonishing ways. There is always a more enveloping pattern—and forgiveness is the most enveloping of all.

The mistakes we make and the wrongs that are done to us needn't imprison us in some dark place. Rather we should always remember that wholeness and brokenness can be held together in a sacred place. The tradition teaches that in the days of the ancient Temple, the Ark resided in the innermost chamber called The Holy of Holies. This place was so powerful that only the High Priest could enter the room, and then, only on Yom Kippur. On this day we are meant to remember our brokenness; and this alone is healing. As the Hasidic Master Menachem Mendel of Kotzk taught, "Nothing is as whole as a broken heart."

YEARNING TO
CREATE

INSPIRATION
AND ILLUMINATION

"In the beginning God created heaven and earth—
the earth being unformed and void,
with darkness over the surface of the deep and a wind
from God sweeping over the water . . ."

THE POET WHO WROTE THIS BREATHTAKING NARRATIVE was someone just like us, someone who wanted to understand, to imagine the origins of life itself. And what a vision: The world began with an act of supreme creativity. Something was made out of nothing, and life began its glorious unfolding. There's such a wonderful order to it all: each day yielding a new form of life; every day seeming to reach such a satisfying conclusion; then humankind, created "in the image of the Creator."

It's no wonder so many people over so many centuries have wanted to take the opening of Genesis literally. How incredible to think the world emerged from a fourteen-billion-year "week" of awesome power and sheer inspiration. How marvelous to imagine that humankind was made in the image of an artistic genius worthy of being named the Creator, God, or "all that is." St. Thomas Aquinas called God "Artist of Artists."

The first chapter of Genesis is a meditation on the yearning to create; a yearning, the Biblical author intuited, that is our very birthright. It was actually a unique mythological innovation to imbue human beings with a creative spirit. In the Greek myth, Prometheus rebels against Zeus, steals fire from him, and then gives this symbol of the creative

> The world was left unfinished so that humans could have a part in Creation.

force to humans. In Genesis human beings are invited into the creative process on Day Six. After the rest of the world unfolds, human beings are created in order to tend and protect it. The world was left unfinished so that humans could have a part in Creation.

These wonderfully poetic passages invite us to imagine that we, too, can create with purpose and intention; that we, too, can craft worlds. The Creation story is so powerful in part because it awakens this yearning. It taps into a basic human desire to connect with something larger than ourselves, to feel like we contribute to the continuation and evolution of the universe.

There's a daily meditation that reminds us that Genesis happens every morning when we open our eyes to the light that marks what is always the first day. This meditation is an expression of gratitude for the continuing renewal of the act of Creation. It expresses the intuition that by simply waking up we are part of the rhythm of life. Then we really can wake up: We can consciously participate in the creative process.

The poet understood that we are all world builders. When we write a poem, give birth to a child, build a home, or help launch a company, we are acting from that same Godlike impulse. We are answering that overwhelming, wondrous yearning to be creative, to contribute something of value, to make a difference.

Whenever I teach the Creation story from this perspective, describing the wonder of the creative impulse, I get a mix of reactions. "Would it be that creativity was always that way! I'd be out of business," a therapist who counseled artists and actors for a living once said to me. Like her, I often hear people bemoan their creative output. Some people talk about those wonderful, productive times when they feel at one with their project, whether it's an art piece, a yoga class, or a strategic plan. But then they inevitably speak of the disappointment and anxiety when they don't have that experience. If creativity is our birthright, why aren't we always creative? Or, as a writer friend of mine put it, "creative on command"?

So many of us see creativity as some kind of magic spell, rare form of genius, or external energy we should be able to tap into if only we escaped the mundane demands of life, had the right space, enough money, lived in the city, the country, out of the country! Perhaps our expectations are so high in part because we live in the most creative and productive time in human history. We have become the kind of world builders the Genesis poet could never have imagined. Technological innovation, medical breakthroughs, and scientific discoveries are regular occurrences. Contemporary museums are overflowing with masterpieces. Whereas it once took hundreds of years to build a cathedral, now we plan to rebuild the World Trade Center in seven years.

It all seems so amazing, so intoxicating, so full of possibility, that we forget how complex and contradictory the process of creativity is. We want that feeling of flow, of being at one with our work, not sometimes but all the time. I noticed recently that creativity occupies its own shelf in the Personal Growth section of Barnes & Noble. We want creativity to be self-actualizing without being self-sacrificing. We want it always to feel good.

But creativity is so full of anxieties and failures, boredom and drudgery. When we resist these experiences because they are painful or frightening, we deny ourselves a rich aspect of life. We also may not realize how creative we are already—because we expect creativity to look and feel a certain way. We want creativity to only be that experience of flow, that feeling of boundarylessness and becoming one with our project. In fact, we misunderstand the experience of flow, that seamless creative moment; that feeling of mastery we so desire.

Mihaly Csikszentmihalyi, the psychologist who coined the term "flow" and researched its characteristics, showed that one of the primary impediments to this experience is our expectation that it will feel pleasant and fulfilling. Only after the fact does the champion swimmer remember those hours of laps, those times her muscles burned, and those fiercely competitive races as the best times of her life. The renowned cellist Pablo Casals spoke about his "tyrannical" twelve-hour practice sessions, his bleeding fingers. Gymnasts describe their calluses and swollen knees. Of course, there are those moments of losing oneself in the process, but most of the time the experience of flow is only in retrospect. It comes at the end of the process.

There are so many aspects of creativity and so many manifestations of the creative act, and when we really think about it creativity entails a complex array of feelings: exuberance and anxiety; fear and hope; dissonance and harmony; discomfort and determination. I've found it helpful to identify four basic stages: Inspiration, Preparation, Incubation, and Illumination. Each has its own feeling tone and none of them has a schedule: We can't control or predict how long each stage will last nor what our experience of it will be. We are always being creative—but it's not a command performance.

I've never known anyone who couldn't report at least one experience of being creatively inspired. Inspiration is commonly mistaken for being the moment of finding a solution, but actually inspiration is the moment we recognize a problem that needs solving. Inspiration is about yearning, not finding. We've all felt inspiration, that need to create order out of chaos; that experience of seeing a void and wanting to fill it. We want to find a new way that will yield different and better results. The spirit of creation arises in us: We are inspirited—inspired. Inspiration is truly a holy experience, not because it's transcendent or wonderful, but because it's an experience of the intensity of life, a reminder that there is so much more to be discovered, to be known. Suddenly we're submerged in the too-muchness of life.

Inspiration is about yearning, not finding. It is the moment we recognize a problem that needs solving, not the moment of finding a solution.

Of course we feel anxiety and fear! We've been inspired to see the problem, and that is always uncomfortable. Innovation is almost always born of a feeling that something is missing or wrong. It's the post office worker who thinks there's a better way to sort the mail. It's the writer who stays up night after night after her kids go to sleep to try to get that opening chapter right. It's the parent who sees that the old ways of disciplining his child aren't working. Or the spouse who sees the patterns in her relationship that need changing.

Creativity demands that we break from our habitual forms of thinking and acting. The conventions and rules we grew up with, the old solutions, just won't suffice. And we must divert our energy from the known to the unknown. We must turn possibility into actuality. Nothing could be more daunting; which is why there's almost always a period of resistance, of self-judgment, of fear of failure. We may just up and abandon the project at this point—often we do so without being aware of it. Maybe we're not ready. Maybe we'll come back to it. Maybe we'll move on to the next thing. Inspiration can be that scary.

But when we decide to go for it, when we step away from our pre-programmed reactions to the world, we have the opportunity to launch ourselves into a whole new landscape, a new reality, whether in our work, our relationships, or the wider world. The Hindu tradition describes this process so beautifully: When we can overcome our primal nature or libido (*rajas*) and our past conditioning and habits (*tamas*), we can be creative; we can achieve a new world (*sattawa*). Victor Havel said, "The ultimate creativity is to choose one's attitude in any set of circumstances." Creativity is not a gift or a personality bestowed upon us from on high or by our DNA; it's a conscious choice to enter the realm of the unknown. To be inspired is to enter the spirit of life in all its messiness and awesomeness.

Once we choose to follow our inspiration, to heed the call, it's time to do the work. We've opened ourselves up to the possibility of new ideas—now it's time to find them. This is the information-gathering stage, the period of preparation. We need to study the inner workings of the problem and the other solutions. We need to listen to and watch other creators who've traveled similar paths. We must research and learn. These are those hours at the library, on the internet, consulting experts, observing and absorbing.

It's also a period of practice, of skill development, a time during which we develop our craft. I remember talking to the father of a Little League champion pitcher about how she got to be so good: She'd just pitched a no-hitter, and we were all in awe. He told me she watched hours of base-ball, both live and taped games, on television and then went outside to the yard and imitated each move. She did all this for the entire off season two years in a row. It's like those thou-

> Creativity demands that we break from our habitual forms of thinking and acting. And it demands a high tolerance for failure.

sands of jump shots Michael Jordan had to take before he made the one from that impossible angle; the hours in the lab trying different combinations; the pages and pages of notes scattered around your office.

No innovative idea comes out of nowhere. There really is no such thing as a true "aha" moment, although we may experience it that way. There are always incredible amounts of preparation involved in any creative project. We may see the jump shot and hear the announcer call it magic, the most creative move ever, but we don't see the six-year-old, the twelve-year-old, the twenty-year-old standing in front of that basket day after day. As Ben Hogan, the golf champion, said, "The more I practice, the luckier I get." On a grander note, before the ancient Israelites experienced their revelation at Mt. Sinai, we're told they prepared themselves for three days. We can't encounter a new idea, have that "eureka" moment, or experience the silence that is everything until we do the work, walk the walk, step-by-step until we reach the mountainside.

Then it's time to incubate, to allow those ideas to swim in our consciousness, to rub up against each other, even bang against each other occasionally. Ideas are germinating and settling in, giving rise to new ones. We are outlining, drafting, playing, guessing, experimenting. We're uncovering contradictions, impious meanings, different combinations. We may come up against obstacles, both internally and externally: people who resist our ideas; ways we judge ourselves. We're doubting as much as we're discovering; eliminating as much as we're generating. We're struggling and wrestling with both new and old

truths. We can sometimes be difficult to be with during these periods—
the most creatively engaged people usually are.

For every breakthrough that we have, we have hundreds of periods
of drudgery and boredom. A writer once told me that when it was time
to start a new chapter after weeks of research, she'd have the overwhelming desire to take a nap. The task seemed simultaneously overwhelming and mundane; quite simply not worth it. "I'd rather be doing
anything but this," she said. And then when she did take a nap, things
incubated in ways she never expected. Thomas Edison would doze off
in a chair with his hands draped over the armrest. In each hand he held
a ball. When he drifted into a state between sleeping and waking, his
hands would relax and the balls would drop. He'd be awakened by the
noise the balls made and he'd immediately make notes on whatever
ideas had come to him. That's the meaning of "sleep on it." Our seeming
diversions are so often part of the incubation stage. We may experience
these as distinctly uncreative times. We may even judge them and ourselves, thereby disrupting or preempting the creative process itself. For
many of us, boredom equals disengagement and failure, especially in
the context of this stimulation-driven culture.

Then there are those infamous creative blocks: the periods when we
don't produce anything at all. These times of tedium, even despair, are
often precursors to some great discovery: periods of dormancy that actually give birth to extraordinary output. Boredom is really an invitation to be creative. The drone of the Xerox machine, the endlessly long
meeting, the moments staring at a blank screen—if we stay open and
receptive, these can lead us to new plateaus.

When I was working on my first public-television series, I often felt
blocked and afraid. I found taking a different walk to work made a
world of difference. It allowed me to break from routine ways of thinking and feeling—to create on the inside what was happening on the outside. The night before the first show was to be filmed, my doubts and
fears turned into overwhelming anxiety. I was to stand up in front of
the cameras and talk about ideas I'd been developing for a lifetime;

I had no idea how I was going to do it, how to be Irwin on camera. I lay in my bed sobbing; I felt so alone, so inadequate, so frightened. I was convinced I couldn't do it, and to top it off I was ashamed of such a seemingly lame response to a creative challenge. I got up and took a shower and then went for a long walk around the harbor outside my hotel.

During my walk I remembered a scene from the movie *Broadcast News*: The producer, played by actress Holly Hunter, is a great innovator in a whole new media form—live television news. But in this scene she's sitting hunched over at her desk before what was to be an incredibly intense workday, one in which failure in front of the cameras faced her at every turn. She's weeping loudly and uncontrollably. Then she simply gets up and begins her day. I wondered if she'd have been as good as she was if she hadn't lost it on a regular basis. Creativity means being on the edge. When we can acknowledge and fully experience that, we can be all the more creative. She took her vulnerability and anxiety with her into her day—and that's in part what made her so amazingly effective. Fear and uncertainty are inside the incubation process. I realized when I came back from my walk that if I could be as honest the next morning as I was just then, the show would be great. Suddenly the possibility of failure seemed dimmer and much less important.

Creativity demands that we have a high tolerance for failure. In our celebrity-oriented culture, we tend to mistake creativity for success and fame, when creativity actually very often means failure. We all know the stories. Edison tried thousands of different light bulbs before the first one worked. Einstein once said, "I have not failed. I've just found ten thousand ways that would not work." He said he loved mistakes, because it meant there was one more thing he understood.

Making mistakes is messy, unnerving, and sometimes discouraging—especially during these times of preparation and incubation. Sometimes we have to throw out those first drafts and start from the beginning. We have to clean up the messes we've left in our path in order to start with a clean slate. As a teacher of mine used to say, "Even Leonardo da Vinci destroyed some of his canvases. Even he had to clean his brushes and start over."

At one of my talks about Creation in the Genesis story, an artist asked a great question: "Where were the mounds of dried-out clay thrown in anguish into a corner?" Creation seems so quick and effortless. Maybe da Vinci had to clean up after himself, but what about God? What kind of model for creativity did that Genesis poet create after all? It all seems so glorious, so neat, so perfect, so unrealistic, especially when seen in the context of our own creative experiences. But there's a Talmudic teaching that imagines that God created ten worlds, destroying each one, then trying again, until finally having that one wonderful, productive week. And in the Book of Job, there's that very different creation story in which chaos is always at the doorstep of creation, and God is continually keeping things from falling apart. Besides, there was plenty of dried-out clay in the first Creation story—Adam was created out of dust. Earlier failures became the stuff of innovation.

This emblematic story of Creation has a powerful underlying message. Embedded in this seemingly idyllic fairy tale is a surprising teaching: Our work is never really done; no creation is ever perfect. One would think words like "excellent," "awesome," or "complete" would describe the acts of Creation. This is the very first scene in the Bible in which all that is comes to be; what could be more awesome than that! Yet the word used to describe each day's creation is simply *tov* or "good." If there were creative highs or declarations of triumph during that first week we don't hear them. On the sixth day, we read: "And God saw all that God had made and found it very good." Creation is less than perfect, but good is good enough.

We have images of the lonely artist; the isolated writer in his garret; the scientist late at night in her lab. The Creation story turns this on its head. No worthy project can be completed alone. At the end of that first week, human beings join in the effort. The Creator makes cocreators or coevolvers. The God character is no longer the only one making it happen. God's next job is another supremely creative role: nurturing and teaching other creators. Creativity and innovation are always collaborations of some kind. We are always responding to the work that has preceded us, even if we're departing from it. Most of us have colleagues or partners who either support us or contribute directly to the goal. And we're always inspiring our successors.

So many of the tensions endemic to creativity are captured in the story of the Israelites at Mt. Sinai. There are two paradigms of creativity juxtaposed in this one scene, one coming right after the other as if to invite our comparison. The first is the story of the golden calf, followed by the building of a tabernacle in the desert. That moment at the base of the mountain was wide open with possibilities for human expression and realization. Both stories have so much to teach us about our process, the dark side of creativity and the light.

As the ancient Israelites stood at the base of Mt. Sinai, they experienced the full dimensions of the creative moment. Having been freed from slavery in Egypt, they were now free to create their lives. They were given an opportunity to experience a new sense of their own capacities, which they simply couldn't have had as slaves. They'd left their old identity behind, broken from their past, and now had to construct a new future. Meanwhile, on top of Mt. Sinai, Moses received instructions for building a tabernacle, a temporary temple in the desert, a sanctuary for the divine presence. In Hebrew the word "tabernacle" also means neighborhood, a dwelling place for a people, a community.

What kind of world do you want to create?

Below, the people had an encounter with the Creator that was dramatic and fiery, as creative inspiration can so often be. Everything seemed altered. Time stood still, and everything hung in the balance. Their senses fused: We're told they saw thunder and heard lightning. They were in a different reality. Then they heard the *aleph*, the great silence, and experienced the vast openness of life. The questions they heard in all that silence were, "What now? Who will we be?" The fear of the unknown is central to creativity. Will the Israelites be able to rise to the creative challenge? To follow the inspiration? To become a people? We, too, face similar turning points. We all have our Egypts. When we're freed from the authority of our parents, the expectations of our bosses, the limitations of a dysfunctional marriage—what now? Do we really want the power to create our own lives? When it's time for us to run the company, create our own family, construct a new relationship—are we up to the challenge? Or would we rather stay in Egypt, where the landmarks are familiar, if confining?

For the Israelites, the encounter was overwhelming. They shuddered, were knocked off their feet, and fell back from the mountain. They retreated from the questions. The problem of freedom seemed too difficult to tackle. And then they tried to fill the silence with their old script; to resurrect the past. Instead of building a tabernacle, they built the golden calf. At that moment of unprecedented freedom they engaged in what was a magnificent act of creativity and construction. But it was an old image, one that was worshipped in Egypt. Just at the moment when they were invited to create something new, they preserved a deadened form of the past. They literally recast it. They affirmed what they already knew rather than stretching into the future. Inspiration aborted.

Of course they were attracted to the golden, glittering calf: The past is compelling. Their idolatry was the creation of what had been rather than what could be. They didn't yet know that creativity dissolves the system of givens that one inherits. Instead of facing their discomfort and fear, in the confusion of the inspirational moment, they regressed. After building the calf out of their own golden jewelry, they eat, drink, and dance. The biblical author chose such a telling word to describe this dance: "circle dance." They were dancing around in circles. The Israelites had chosen to go around in circles rather than reach toward the future.

Often, after we see the challenge, our first move is to retreat. Only then can we step forward. Sometimes we need to reach backward before we can reach toward something new. The key is to not mistake our first move as our last. Just because we misstep doesn't mean we preempt illumination. We can be loyal to our past and still transcend it. When Moses came down from the mountain and saw what the people had done, he was enraged. Is this what you do when you're invited to create your own lives?! Moses destroyed the calf, and then something remarkable happened. A different kind of construction began. It was the onset of illumination.

It was as if the people heard the question once again: What kind of world do you really want to create? This time they heard it as an invitation rather than a demand; an evolution rather than an abrupt break from the past. The golden calf might not have been a failure, but part of the preparation. And the language in these passages is so markedly different than in those which precede them. The construction of the calf takes only a few lines; you don't need preparation and incubation if you're simply repeating the past. The people bring Aaron their gold rings and the calf is built. But the tabernacle takes six chapters to build.

Before that there are six chapters of instructions about how to build it and what it should contain. The people are to use gold once again, but also hundreds of other materials to be combined in many new and intricate ways. This is the information-gathering stage; now they are willing to jump in and learn. This time their response to the unknown, to the call of inspiration, has been to prepare. Rather than creating a solid idol, they construct a space, a safe place for creativity to continue, for the Creator to dwell.

Craft, design, make. These words are used eighty times in these passages describing the building of the tabernacle. They're the same three words used to describe the acts of Creation in Genesis. Now it's the people who are working hard to make a world; a house worthy of containing all that is. The people are clearly in a state of flow, which Csikszentmihalyi describes as "a sense of participation in determining the content of life."

We, too, can create with purpose and intention. We, too, can craft worlds.

The poet's language so beautifully captures our creative yearnings. Everyone "whose heart so moves him" is invited to bring gifts with which to build. The Israelites contribute their gold and silver, their yarns and linens, and their oil and spices and wood as a "freewill offering" until there's more than enough. The people are called "inspired artisans, carvers, designers, weavers." They use their expertise to address their new challenge of freedom. The women spin blue, purple, and crimson yarns as the men build the grand tent in very specific dimensions, with silver sockets and bars of acacia wood and planks of gold.

One commentary describes a tapestry with a different scene on each side. When you've been inspired, prepared, and incubated, there's an element of impossibility to the next stage—illumination. We can combine fragments of our imagination in untold ways. What a glorious world! What amazing creators! Miraculously, in the middle of the desert there's a tabernacle: illumination in the midst of a barren landscape. Creation in the shadow of idolatry now becomes creation in the shadow of God.

The head architect of this monumental and complex structure is Bezalel, whose name actually means "in the shadow of God." He's "endowed with a divine spirit of skill, ability, and knowledge." In Hebrew the word for knowledge is the same word as that for lovemaking, intimacy. Bezalel combines materials both old and new to create. The sages say he pulled himself loose of all the forms of Egypt to build something new.

Moses told Bezalel to make the tabernacle according to God's instructions, but he made it according to his vision of his own time and place. The tabernacle is an improvisation. But you can only improvise after you've been inspired and gone through all the preparation and incubation. Then you can integrate and leap into the future. The commentators say that when Bezalel was praised, he said none of it had anything to do with him. As so many artists describe it, he became a channel for creativity itself.

We are all Bezalels. We are lovers and weavers; architects and poets. The playwright George Bernard Shaw once said that life is not about finding yourself but creating yourself. Like the ancient Israelites, we always have a choice: Will we build golden calves or tabernacles? Sometimes it's hard to know the difference. The good news is, we can always start again.

THE PRACTICE OF BEING

"MOMMY, WHY DO YOU GO TO WORK?" A FRIEND OF MINE told me her son asked her this question as she rushed out the door one morning. It was what she'd always dreaded he might ask, and as she described it she had a serious pang of that all-too-familiar "working mom's guilt." She dropped her bags, took off her coat, and began to explain. She told him that her job paid her money which gave them the beautiful house they live in. "But, Mommy, why do we need a beautiful house?" To each answer, he had a question: "Why do we need so much food?" "Why do I need all these toys?" Finally, the killer: "Why is work more important than me?"

She described how in a flash she'd realized his questioning had nothing to do with her going to work every day: He'd never known her to do anything else. In fact, she'd come home from work early the previous day, as she sometimes did, to spend time with him. But had she really spent time with him? As they'd sat on the floor playing with LEGOs, she remembered feeling antsy, distracted, and worried that she'd left so many e-mails unanswered, that she might not meet next week's deadline—and she found herself thinking that work was way more fun and engaging than LEGO. To top it off, her son couldn't make the pieces fit, couldn't really make anything at all. She'd not only been disinterested, but felt unable to help him in any constructive way. After a while she told him she'd be right back and went to the kitchen to get a jump on making dinner.

I remember thinking how honest she was, how self-aware. But the obvious pain it caused her made me want to ask, "Why in the world can't you cool out? Why can't you just be?" I restrained myself only because I knew she was asking herself the same questions and that the answers were anything but simple.

I hear so many people complain that they don't know how to relax; that they just can't seem to "let it all go" so that they can enjoy the rest of life. At the same time, they talk about how much they fear falling behind at work, that it's gotten so much more intense, jobs so much less secure. They really can't afford to step away, not even on weekends. They may compromise by limiting their after-hours work to "just e-mails." I know others who are quite wealthy, who really

We all yearn for a sense of completion, of accomplishment.

don't need to be working so hard, but who can't seem to bring themselves to slow down. Their identities are so wrapped up in what they do, and they fear they won't be able to maintain their "standard of living," a turn of phrase I find ironic since their standard undermines their living. And even when people do take time off, they often don't find it all that relaxing. One mom told me guiltily, "When I go to work on Monday, I feel like I'm going to a spa!"

Of course, parents seem to struggle the most. The balance issues facing working mothers and fathers today are real; society simply isn't offering the support and services families need. But there's also a kind of addiction to doing, an epidemic of busyness that seems to plague many families, often without them even realizing it. Soccer practice, play dates, errands, home improvement, working out—you name it; there's always an activity or project that needs doing, even on the days supposedly set aside for family. The kids have to do what their friends are doing; they just can't fall behind—go to museums to become cultured, or participate in after-school activities to keep stimulated. Others compensate for their lack of relaxation by buying more stuff, trying to make their homes more beautiful and comfortable, plopping down in front of the TV with an indulgent snack in hand, or going out to a bar. On Sunday nights, so many people lament, "Where did the weekend go?" None of this is news; there've been countless articles and books about simplifying our lives, the overscheduled child, and the health benefits of relaxing with friends and family. But our drive to achieve and our inability to rest seem to get the best of us nevertheless.

Even those of us who love our work, who have found creative expression in our vocations, have a hard time stopping, even if the demands of the job itself are not that great. Because of advances in technology and education levels, more and more of us see our work as an end in itself, a creative act that connects us to something larger than ourselves. We've become intoxicated with the effort and addicted to the financial rewards (which for some levels of society have become so much greater in the last fifty years). We want a sense of completion, of accomplishment, and when we don't have it, we feel unfulfilled and even more determined to get it the next time. Work can crowd out the rest of life and become a kind of idolatry. Eventually our work, too, will suffer. We're in danger of burning out. America's work ethic is out of whack and so, of course, is our ethics of leisure. We yearn for a break but we don't know how to take one.

Although modern society has greatly exacerbated the problem, burnout is hardly new. There's a scene in Exodus which captures this syndrome perfectly. Moses has succumbed to the allure and pull of his own creative efforts and responsibilities. This might seem appropriate; after all, he is the leader of the people and teaching people to live responsibly when they've been slaves their entire lives is no easy task. Leadership positions can be especially intoxicating, as there's often the desire to be a hero, to go it alone. The best of leaders tend to be simultaneously self-important and self-sacrificing; that's, in part, what makes them great.

At one point Moses's wife Zipporah and their two sons, accompanied by Moses's father-in-law Jethro, come to visit Moses at his encampment in the desert after many months of separation. Moses had left his family behind when he returned to Egypt to free his people. In the scene, Moses embraces only Jethro. This is a painful, glaring act of neglect.

Later Jethro sees Moses standing before a line of thousands of Is-raelites who are waiting to hear his wisdom about their life challenges and questions; to get his judgments; to tell them what to do. And Moses speaks to them one by one well into the night. Jethro is clearly con-cerned. He's just seen Moses ignore Jethro's daughter and grandchil-dren. He says, "You're going to wither up." He sees that Moses's flow has gotten the best of him, and he's headed toward burnout. He's not even serving the people well by making them wait. Things have gone too far.

Perhaps Jethro sees an arrogance that can't possibly serve Moses or his people in the long run. He approaches Moses and asks him what he's doing taking care of so many people on his own. Moses is mystified: These are his people; he's got to attend to them. Jethro encourages Moses, practically insists that he appoint deputies and judges—a kind of graded delegation of authority—who he can train to issue judgments in his stead. Remarkably for a workaholic, Moses immediately insti-tutes Jethro's plans. The rabbinic sages knew the price of work subsum-ing all else. They described Zipporah crying out to the wives of Moses's appointees, warning them that they'll never make love again.

Even the most meaningful work can become a form of slavery. It can trump the rest of life. We all need people like Jethro in our lives; people who understand that being is an essential aspect of our human-ness, as important as any other. But most of us don't have Jethros, and so the yearning for rest and replenishment is ignored and buried. We may feel guilty about or dismiss this need as secondary to our produc-tivity and our commitment to helping others and contributing to the world.

Rabbi Joseph B. Soloveitchik, one of the most important Jewish thinkers of the twentieth century, taught that there are two human ty-pologies portrayed in the two different Creation stories at the begin-ning of Genesis. In the first, human beings are told to master and rule the land. This represents our drive to produce and transform, design and build, improve and control, achieve and accomplish. And it's an es-sential creative mindset.

In the second story the language and mood are markedly different. The story is softer, more gentle. There is nothing to do or accomplish. The garden is already planted and flourishing, and humans are there to enjoy it. Everything is provided: The rivers overflow, the fruit is ripe and ready to eat. In other words, part of being human is pausing to marvel at and partake in all that is. We are to relate to the world in all its glory. We are to breathe deeply, rest, reflect, lounge, and love. We are to *be* in the garden. This, too, is an essential creative mindset.

The Genesis poet gave life to human beings on the last day of Creation because he saw us as being at the very cutting edge of evolution. We are after all the only creatures to reflect on our own creative impulse; the only ones conscious of our need to create. But you need to be careful when you're on the cutting edge. It's easy to experience oneself as being somehow superior to the rest of the world rather than being a part of it, and also profoundly responsible for it. Making time to experience, rather than rule, over nature is so essential. It's a reminder of the broader context of creativity. When you're on the cutting edge, you'd better stand back and gain perspective or risk destroying what you are meant to protect.

Together these two Creation stories teach that we are meant both to do and to be; and both require creativity. Creativity is more expansive than we imagined, and relaxation requires as much discipline and effort as work. Just as God doesn't ask Adam and Eve to sweat over their role in Creation or work hard to improve themselves, they're also not encouraged to just lie around, let it all go, and mellow out. When we aren't busying ourselves, many of us think a day off should be effortless, fluid, simple; that we need only give ourselves permission and we'll enter a different head space, and that peace and relaxation will come flooding in. But the first two humans were encouraged to "till and tend" the land. There's creative effort, although it's of a very different kind. They move from master to tend-er.

It's no accident that Sabbath has been recovered, reappropriated, and in some cases re-envisioned in the last few years. A number of books have been published recently about the Sabbath as an antidote to hectic, modern living—and as a stopgap to the unceasing desire to create and contribute to the world. More and more people are coming to me for advice about how to make Sabbath a part of their lives. They see it as a way to alleviate or cure their workaholism. They desperately want to learn to take a genuine break, and without exception they resonate with the four qualities of Sabbath: rest, reflection, relationship, and replenishment. We all need a breather, a time to literally experience our breathing, to take it in fully and let it out. We need an opportunity to reflect on our lives, to remember other parts of who we are, to spend time with our loved ones, and to gain perspective on the week so that we can wake up on the next workday, our "doing" energy restored.

Even the most meaningful work can trump the rest of life.

Sabbath is a time to attend to the nonwork aspects of life, but here's the other side: There's nothing more creative than rest. Being is as essential as doing. Sabbath is another way in which we can become partners in Creation. And just as there's a discipline to creative work, there's a practice of creative rest as well. In fact the same verb "make" is used to describe both the work of creating the tabernacle in the desert and the Sabbath day. As Abraham Joshua Heschel wrote, on Sabbath we are to build a sanctuary in time, a place to just be.

New skills and expertise are necessary to "make" any project. All creative acts involve entering different levels of awareness in which we can access new insights and perspectives. The art of being is no different. Yogis study for years before being able to rest still in "corpse" pose. Meditators describe the effort and skill it takes to focus on a mantra. Sabbath is a day-long "being" practice that calls on four levels of consciousness, and they, too, take time and practice to cultivate. They correspond to the four verbs used to describe the first Sabbath day in the Creation story: cease, rest, bless, and make holy.

The first level of being is to cease doing. Quite simply, we need to stop the work of the week. This can be a lot tougher than it sounds.

Sometimes I find myself sneaking in a few extra minutes at the office even when I know it's time to leave. I call it the "one more" dance: one more phone call, one more e-mail, one more paragraph, one more minute. A minute can turn into an hour before we know it. I know many people who just can't leave work behind even when they do leave—they'll pile their bags full of work to do at home; e-mail them-selves additional files; if they don't actually get to the work, they feel better knowing they can.

The Genesis poet invites us to cultivate a stopping mindset. If God can stop working at the end of that first cosmic week, surely we can. The poet tells us that on the seventh day God is "finished" when obvi-ously this isn't the case. It's the very beginning of the larger project of Creation, of humankind's unfolding. And yet the Creator was "done." Like the God character, we're encouraged to suspend disbelief; to have a fantasy of completion. Can we have that sense of being done even when we know there's always more to do, so much toil and struggle ahead of us? If we're willing to try, we enter the second level of being; we can be-gin to rest.

For many of us, making believe our work is done and stepping out of the rat race is really tough. The first thing people notice when they begin a Sabbath practice is how work and material desires crowd out other thoughts. What I say to them is, "Congratulations, you've reached the second level of Sabbath consciousness." Even when I physically stop working, worries, thoughts, and insights about my day or week keep popping into my mind, sometimes gnawing at me. As with any medita-tion practice, I try to gently observe them, to breathe through them. When work mode grips me, I start again. Eventually these thoughts soften and recede. I begin to feel clarity of mind and a fuller range of emotions. It helps when I can stop working before sunset so that twi-light becomes a transition not only between day and night, but between doing and being. Other people I know take an earlier train home once a week or they walk along a more scenic route, even if it takes longer to get home.

The more we abstain from our work week activities over the next twenty-five hours, the deeper we can sink into rest consciousness. I try to abstain from anything related to business, producing, or any economic activity through the next day. I don't shop, clean the house, or answer the phone. For those beginning to think about a Sabbath practice I ask: "What activities would you need to stop in order to have one day out of the rat race?" It could be a day that you cease the work for which you get paid. In our culture that's already a tremendous accomplishment of being. Maybe you'll put your Daytimer away; not look at your BlackBerry; set your cell phone to silent. Some people find it meaningful to cease from being a "consumer" as well; they cook meals with the food they have, or leave the dry cleaning for another day. They allow for a one-day fantasy that they have everything they need.

> There's nothing more creative than rest.

For others, even imagining "not" doing anything seems stifling and oppressive, the very opposite of creative. You know how much one more day of work might further your career goals; how much easier your week would be if you could do the laundry. If you could drive to the mall and grab a burger, wouldn't that be more relaxing than having to prepare your own food beforehand? And if you love your work because it engages your mind and heart, isn't that a more sacred way to spend the day? I encourage you to try it all—doing and not doing a number of different activities to see how your consciousness shifts or how it doesn't.

Like most disciplines, a Sabbath practice can't be designed or adopted overnight. No one has an "aha" experience every time, or even most of the time: that perfect day of rest, a profound twenty-five hours of reflection, or the feeling of being totally rejuvenated. And when one first begins a Sabbath practice it can feel uncomfortable, odd, or even unnecessary. But as Ram Dass teaches, give any practice forty days before deciding whether it's working. And if you're fortunate to have an inherited practice—whether it's a Friday, Saturday, or Sunday Sabbath, or a meditation or prayer practice, I encourage you to reexplore it before trying something new. There's incredible richness to be found in rituals that have a connection to your past and your community.

Whether you decide not to work, not to shop, whether you spend the day reading a novel, socializing with friends, or playing with your kids (really playing), the most important thing is your intention; *kavanah* in Hebrew. It's important to become conscious of your actions and the meaning behind them; to slow down enough to do so. Sabbath actually is not at all about letting go, and it's not just about stopping. It's about inviting in: It's about *doing* being.

The next level of being is blessing consciousness. We expand our sense of who we are and treasure our lives. On my day of being, the first act of blessing is when my family lights candles to usher in the Sabbath before sundown. So many wisdom traditions ritualize light, whether votive candles or candles on a Buddhist altar. Candlelight casts different shadows and gives off different light. Candlelight dinners bring couples closer. Candles create a magical, romantic, separate space that evokes and awakens feelings that stay under the surface in brighter light. The psalmist says the candle of God is like the soul of the human being. Light brings the soul out of slumber.

There's a tradition of closing one's eyes and ushering the light toward you with your hands, awakening oneself to the interior light. With our eyes closed we always can see more clearly. What do I want to see more clearly? I want to see myself in a wider context, connected to something more than just my ambitious, work self. Sometimes, when the candles are lit, I imagine that brightest of lights fourteen billion years ago: the big bang that brought us all to this moment standing together at this table.

What a blessing it is to reconnect with those we love, rekindling our most cherished relationships. Some families also reach out beyond their smallest circle to offer hospitality to acquaintances and sometimes strangers. In our home, we eat a leisurely, special Friday-night meal—perhaps from a new recipe or with some new delicacy—at a beautifully set table. When I sit down in the candlelight, a home-cooked meal before me, and look across the table at the glowing faces of family and friends, I find myself thinking how little I saw of them during the week; how fast I grabbed those meals before rushing out the door; how rarely I checked in with my kids; how little I spoke with friends; wondering if I even kissed my wife all week.

We've all experienced times with those we love when we feel so grateful to have them in our lives, aware of how lucky we are. During the week we rarely have time to stop and feel thankful for even the most pleasant and wonderful things; and gratitude is such a central quality of being. There's a Friday night meditation in which each person gives thanks for one thing that happened during the week. As you go around the table you learn so much about what happened to everyone during those days. You feel you somehow know them better—and your gratitude is deepened.

Every family has a favorite saying, some maxim, some teaching, a song or expression that captures the uniqueness of the group. Singing a favorite song, telling a familiar story, or having everyone share a thought or observation from the week can be a way to create a different environment, a specialness to the evening meal. A family I know has a member who attends Twelve-Step recovery meetings. They say the Serenity Prayer together over dinner to usher in every weekend: "Grant me the serenity to accept the things I cannot change; to change the things I can; and the wisdom to know the difference." What a wonderful way to let go of the anxiety of the week.

I bless my children with words from the most ancient recorded blessing: "May God bless you and keep you. May God's light shine upon you and be gracious to you. May God's presence be lifted upon you and give you peace." My wife thinks of something during the week that she wants to emphasize about each child's goodness, some unique quality, some story that she tells them quietly. Lovers also bless each other on Sabbath eve. I sing to Dana a traditional love song. It's important to each of us, but also to our daughters, who get to see their normally busy parents stopping to offer public affection and kind words.

Some people resist these practices: Why should there be some specific time to tell my kids or my mate that I love them? Shouldn't it be
natural and spontaneous? Yes and no. Our culture highly values spontaneity and tends to ignore ritual practice, but
most of our lifestyles don't actually allow for   **Our actions change our**
much spontaneity at all. The intuition behind   **thoughts and feelings.**
the Friday night ritual is that when we practice expressing love, it becomes more natural. When we bless or intentionally express love to our
partner or our children once a week, we are actually more apt to be
spontaneously affectionate during the other days.

Our actions change our thoughts and feelings; this is, in fact, the
purpose of ritual. There have been many times when I've fought with
my wife during the week and the tension is still there on Friday nights,
or when my kids have been driving me crazy to the point where I'd like
nothing more than to get away for the weekend. But when blessing is a
discipline, when you observe a ritual of loving, it's incredible the way
feelings of resentment and anger can be softened, even transformed by
the meal's end. We're reminded of the wider context of these relationships, of how blessed we are to have each other, how even the struggles
and conflict can add dimension to life.

Some of the things we do on Sabbath are not all that different from
what we do during the week. It's the way we do them, the shift in intention. We may go to sleep a little earlier and awaken without an alarm
clock; rather than watching the news, we read that novel that we've been
wanting to get to; we might walk more slowly or get up from the couch
less often; we talk about the joyful things of life, tell jokes, laugh at
ourselves—keeping the arguments and complaining to a minimum.
And we spend time reflecting, taking long walks, studying sacred texts,
or praying.

Here's my Sabbath in a nutshell: I eat, sing, take walks, nap, meditate, tell stories, read for enjoyment, listen, watch the sun set, and see
the stars come up. And I make love. Traditionally, sex is a key activity of
the day. We're encouraged to return to our bodies, to take full pleasure

in the sensual parts of life. Making love is slow, luscious, playful. I remember my parents' Saturday "naps"; the sound of music floating down from upstairs; how they'd emerge from their bedroom so happy and relaxed. Our Saturday night dinners were some of the best times we had as a family—the many qualities of the Sabbath had sunk in, but also the joyous, satiated mood of my parents infused the evening with a kind of softness and generosity.

Actually, napping itself is considered a sacred practice. It's a way to refresh and replenish. But it's also a means of entering a different mindspace, of integrating the different parts of ourselves. Wisdom traditions always have understood that there are multiple states of awareness. In our dreams, different selves are revealed. When I wake up from a Saturday afternoon nap, my house seems aglow. I feel simultaneously languid and refreshed; settled into myself.

And then there are those rare moments of grace; those times when I experience the fourth level of consciousness; when I feel a sense of sacred stillness and release from all worry and anxiety. I'm subsumed in love and gratitude. I feel a sense of completeness, of all-encompassing holiness and joy. I call this the "flow of being," as it can only be matched by the creative flow of work at its best. There's no way to make it happen. This level of consciousness only can be reached after experiencing the other three; after practicing being and accomplishing not-accomplishing.

When we make being a practice, whether on Friday or Sunday or Tuesday, whether for twenty-five hours, twelve hours, or two hours, we come to realize that being isn't simply an antidote to the frenzy of doing. It not only counteracts our productive obsessions but actually can mitigate the fever of the week before it descends on us. And it can become the nurturing ground for all kinds of creativity.

Before the Israelites began building the tabernacle in the desert, they were reminded of the Sabbath. This seems kind of odd: Why talk about rest before the work has even begun? You'd think the Ultimate Manager, the Creator, would try to motivate the people by telling them how amazing the work will be, how incredible the result, getting them focused on the task at hand. After all, they're being asked to give up the precious possessions they painstakingly took out of Egypt; they're being invited to undertake a Herculean effort: building a structure worthy of their God in the middle of nowhere.

But would they have had that marvelous, masterful work experience if they hadn't remembered the Sabbath? Would they have built such a breathtaking sanctuary if they hadn't first experienced the blessing of being? Don't we all want to contribute more to the world when we know we can enjoy the fruits of what we've created? Just imagine how much more glorious our world would be if we all understood that Sabbath is the reverie that precedes Creation.

THE SABBATH OF WORK

THE AVERAGE AMERICAN SPENDS 65 PERCENT OF HIS OR her adult life on the job. Work takes more time than all the other wakeful activities combined. Yet 50 percent of us claim not to be happy with our work, according to recent studies. I hear people describe their jobs as overwhelming, dead end, suffocating. Recent articles report that some of the most educated women are leaving their well-paying careers to stay home with their children in part because, as one book title summed it up, *Work Doesn't Work Anymore*. There's more turnover at most companies than there ever has been: People are being laid off or quitting to find something better. The cynicism about work has turned to bitterness for some as companies like Enron and WorldCom have taken such brutal advantage of those who work for them.

Sayings like "I survived the week" or "Thank God It's Friday" capture the widespread depression and anxiety about what much of work has become. And some of us aren't surviving the week; most heart attacks occur between 8:00–9:00 on Monday mornings. Even those of us lucky enough to be engaged in fulfilling and creative work also feel there's too much of it. In America it's par for the course to complain about the burdens of work; being busy and overwhelmed is a badge of honor. For many of us, work is a four-letter word.

Yet for the first time in history, many of us have a choice about the work we do. Most of us don't have to start at sunrise. Most of us don't have to do backbreaking labor. Most of us have enough to eat when we don't work for a day. Many of us have the opportunity to engage our minds and hearts in creative projects. Even in our disillu-sionment, few of us would deny that work is an aspect of our identity and has an impact on our sense of self-worth. In many communities the first question we ask when we meet some-one is, "What do you do for a living?" And there's no greater cause of depression in this country than being unem-ployed.

> The yearning to produce something of value, to contribute to the unfolding of the world, is apparent in the smallest child.

Burdensome as it can be, work is central to our sense of dignity. The yearning to produce something of value, to contribute to the unfolding of the world, is apparent in the smallest child, as Maria Montessori taught. There's the three-year-old who asks to set the table and then smiles with pride when she puts the spoon on the right side and the napkin just so—even before she's looked to you for approval. There's the teenager who earns his first five dollars mowing the lawn and who does it so much more carefully when he knows it's a real job. The young adult who proudly tells you she landed her first position. The lifelong employee who finally gets up the courage to start his own business. The retiree with a good pension and a strong golf swing who nevertheless chooses to spend every afternoon tutoring high school students. It's not just that work brings out our creativity. It's not just that we have to earn money to live. Work has intrinsic value. It is an integral part of the hu-man journey.

Until very recently, spiritual leaders were required to have other vo-cations. In some traditions, many still do. Work on the material plane was considered essential and it didn't matter how holy you were consid-ered to be. Monasteries and nunneries still produce wonderful wine, bread, and arts and crafts. Hillel was a porter; Rashi was a winemaker; Maimonides was a physician. There was an intuition that to make one's only work spiritual seeking was to try to live in Sabbath all the time, and this is not what the fourth commandment intended. Most of us forget that the first part of the fourth commandment says "you shall work."

The biblical author of those famous commandments chose to give work incredible primacy. The work and rest commandment comes before the ones that tell us to honor our parents, to not murder or steal. Work is directly connected to the acts of Creation; a way to expand the self and the world. The workweek is no less sacred than Sabbath. Perhaps what's missing is that we haven't yet made work a practice, a discipline, a spiritual art. We haven't yet developed a work consciousness, a way to bring more of who we are to the job. We need to imbue our work with as much intention and enchantment as the Sabbath day.

There's a meditation of gratitude for every weekday morning. The opening of this prayer is for some reason rarely translated into English and so is overlooked: "On this first day of the week of Sabbath . . ." "On this second day of the week of Sabbath . . ." This simple phrase invites us to take that profound appreciation for the world we cultivated on the Sabbath into the world of work. It urges us to create a Sabbath of work; in other words, to really *be* on the job.

In Hebrew the word for meaningful work, for work that is a service to Creation, is *avodah*, which is also used to mean prayer and Torah study. The Greek word for work comes from the same root as the word for energy and orgy. If we want our work to contribute to the vitality and unfolding of life, if we want our vocation to be a source of fulfillment and dignity, maybe even ecstasy, we need to develop a practice of work. We need a litmus test of the soul with which to question and probe our chosen work on a regular basis.

Whether we're an orderly or a surgeon, a clerk or a CEO, a teacher or a techie, we all can benefit from standing back from our work and asking some simple questions. When I consult with business owners and executives, I encourage them to do so at the same time as they're evaluating their quarterly earnings statements. I urge them to produce quarterly consciousness-raising statements as well. Here are four basic questions every worker should ask:

The first question is: Am I being fairly compensated or fairly compensating those who work for me? Profit is the oxygen of any work endeavor—we literally have to make a living. Salaries are the subject of so much anxiety but they are rarely seriously or openly discussed. When we reflect on compensation, when we research competitive salaries, and consult others in similar positions, we may begin to value our own and others' work differently. Money and work are inseparable; rather than denying it or resenting it, we can make salary discussions and budgeting a regular practice.

The next question to ask is: Am I proud of the product? Is what I'm working to create something of quality; does it have a purpose and benefit? If we're simply producing to produce, selling to sell, we have work without purpose; work that is disconnected from the work of Creation and evolution. It's in danger of becoming pure drudgery.

There's an exercise I encourage people to do that helps them meditate on the value of the product they make and the contribution they feel their job is making. It begins with the simple question: What is the purpose of your work? Usually money is the first answer. Then ask: What do you get from money that is even more valuable than money itself? I get to buy what I need. What do you get from buying what you need that's even more valuable than that? With every answer, the same question is asked. If within a few rounds the answer doesn't grow wider in context, entering into the emotional or spiritual realm—joy, fullness, freedom, pleasure—chances are your work is lacking.

The third question: Is my work contributing to my personal and spiritual evolution? Am I perfecting my talents and gifts? It's possible to be employed in work that makes a genuine contribution to the world but feel inwardly stalled or stifled. Even the most seemingly challenging or creative work can eventually deaden our imagination. Then we have a choice: We can reimagine the existing work, taking greater risks from where we are standing, or we can stand in a different place and find new work that will take us someplace new. No one can tell you which would be the right move, although they may try. But in the end we need to ask, "Am I being stretched?"

I think one of the reasons so many people are starting new businesses on their own today is because they are asking this question. They may make less money in the short run and have all the hassles and risks involved with self-employment and employing others, but they feel they can put their heart and soul into the process. They can bring more of their selves through that office door. Not only is the product more in their control, but the group dynamic and work environment is likely to be more aligned with their values.

Of course, our individual experience is shaped in large part by the group we work with and the relationships we have on the job. The fourth set of questions is about this very issue. What is the currency or energy of the group I work with? Do the values of the group reflect my own? Do these relationships allow me to be more honest—or cause me to be less honest? Is the energy between people alive and electric? Is there as much cooperation as competition? Does the competition motivate me or paralyze me?

Some of the first work advice I ever received was that I should keep my emotions out of the office. And it couldn't have been more wrong. A healthy work environment invites everyone to experience the full range of emotions. We should feel happy and sad, excited and afraid, angry and grateful, guilty and proud. When I became president of my organization, I felt I had to narrow my emotional range in order to be a leader. I tried to be moderate and consistent in my responses. What happened almost immediately was that my own enjoyment began to diminish—and I was far less engaging to others as well. If you want people to feel passionately committed to their jobs, there's going to need to be exuberance and disappointment in equal measure. A workplace can be largely orderly and efficient while also making room for the dialectic of emotions involved in any creative project.

I always worry when someone explains her actions at work with the often abused phrase, "It's just business." Whenever anyone says this, it means they are compromising their values. There is no such thing as a business value that is any different than it would be in the rest of life. Care and compassion, and honesty and responsibility all belong at work as much as they do at home.

When we can answer these four questions, we'll have a much clearer idea of the nature of our work. On balance, is it serving the world; is it serving me? There are four people who to me embody the Sabbath of work. They are masters of *avodah*, although they manifest their creativity and sense of purpose in different ways.

First, there's Daniel, the guru of taxi drivers, who I was lucky enough to study with for an unforgettable forty-five-minute ride. He was lively and cheerful, even at five o'clock in the morning on a rainy morning in humid, stifling Washington, D.C. When I got into his car, I was struck by the fancy-looking computer set up on the dashboard. I asked him what it did. He told me he kept an updated list of every regular customer: who expected him to come a few minutes early; who was always late; who typically asked him to stop at the ATM; what kind of bagel and coffee they liked, which he provided. I asked, "Why do you do all that?" "I get people from here to there," he said with a smile. "Whenever you take people from here to there, it's more than just a taxi ride." I thought to myself, "Wow, this guy sees taxi driving as a metaphor for the journey through life." The rest of the ride was a delight—he'd also made it his business to know everything there was to know about Washington, its highlights and history, which he shared with me as we drove.

When we got to the airport and he was taking my bags out of the trunk, it occurred to me that this bright, ambitious, affable man could have done anything he wanted with his life. I thought to say this to him, asking him if he considered going back to school, which he told me he'd never finished. Then it hit me that he was already doing everything anyone could aspire to. I got a chill as I realized I had just met a *baal agalah*, which means "wagon driver." In mystical literature, the person who takes people from town to town is almost always Elijah, who is the harbinger of the messiah. The mythical messiah ushers us into the next world, the next evolutionary moment. Daniel was doing more than I could have imagined. I told him the story as I handed him his tip. I expected him to be so grateful for my insight, to tear up, to understand his purpose more deeply. Instead he simply nodded appreciatively and knowingly and said under his breath, "*baal agalah.*"

So often we denigrate or glorify the work of others. When we find ourselves thinking, "He's not maximizing his potential" or "That's the ultimate work," it means we're masking our feelings about our own profession. I wasn't feeling much like Elijah when I took that trip; I was on my fourth consecutive week of lecturing, and I'd not yet realized that my sense of purpose was fading and burnout was on its way. I found myself feeling jealous of the vision Daniel had of his work and the clarity he had about its purpose. What if we all took the care he did in getting ourselves from here to there in life and helping others do the same? What if we could find such a broad context for our work and allow it to make the most of our gifts and capacities? He had given his work nothing short of cosmic significance.

Although his story may seem grander, Aaron Feurstein also saw his business in the context of Creation—as a lifeline for a community and a sacred collaboration. Mr. Feurstein is the owner of Malden Mills in Lawrence, Massachusetts, producers of polar fleece and Polartec. When the mill burned down in 1995 in a devastating fire, he could have walked away with $309 million in insurance payments. Lawrence was a depressed area, and the loss of the 2,500 jobs would have devastated the community. In an era of downsizing, Aaron Feurstein made the radical decision to up-size. All employees were paid full salaries while they set about rebuilding the plant. Outsiders contributed whatever they could to the building, as that, combined with the salaries, would cost more than the insurance payments. One year later, everything was rebuilt. Feurstein and the people of Lawrence had a modern plant that, within a few years, was doing $425 million in annual sales. And needless to say the group dynamic—the employees' sense of accomplishment and connection to each other and their work—was nothing less than inspiring. It's no stretch of the imagination to see that in the Enron and WorldCom era Aaron Feurstein was an Elijah.

Perhaps my most moving and surprising work encounter of all was with yet another rabbi of work: the young orderly who took care of my grandfather when he was dying of prostate cancer. I was feeling helpless and sad that morning when the orderly came into the room to empty my grandfather's bedpans and wash his body. I'd seen this orderly two or three other times, but I'd left when he entered, not bothering to engage with him at all. As I watched him this time, I saw that this muscle-bound man who looked barely twenty was handling my grandfather with incredible gentleness, singing quietly as he washed my grandfather's bottom and legs. At first, my grandfather grimaced with discomfort and humiliation, the embarrassment of being washed up by a stranger. But when he heard the singing, he looked up and smiled weakly.

As the orderly left, I quickly followed him out of the room and awkwardly and inelegantly thanked him for taking care so beautifully. I felt painfully aware of how little I was doing for my grandfather in the face of how much this orderly had done. I said I was sure it wasn't the easiest job in the world. He looked me straight in the eye and smiled, "Don't worry, my friend. Remember, your shit is my bread and butter." Suddenly, in the face of sadness there was sacred comedy. We both laughed. Here was a man who wasn't just making money at this job. Bread and butter, I couldn't help thinking, is the staff of life. His work was primal, corporeal, intimate: soothing and cleaning people as they entered the next stage of their lives, as they declined. His work wasn't all that different from a midwife's. My interpretation of his joke and his easy laugh was that cleaning this eighty-year-old man's excrement was also an affirmation of the sacred cycle of birth and death.

I realized as I left the hospital that part of my discomfort before I spoke to the orderly was about how disconnected I'd become from the labor, grit, and sweat of work. Work isn't only a calling. Work isn't always *avodah.* Work isn't only energy and orgy. Work is burdensome and dirty. It sometimes stinks. And the truth is that most of us don't make meaning of our own grit, even though it is as central to the fullness and dignity of work as service. Without labor there's no birth; there is no Elijah. For us "white collar" types there's a kind of lie of work—that we should have a higher purpose, a sense of energy and creativity all the time. White collar is a way of imagining that we are above, or immune from, the toil of labor, which in turn keeps us disconnected from the pulse and effort behind Creation.

Unlike the orderly, most of us don't make meaning out of the crap of our own jobs. Instead, we divide up the world into management and employees; faculty and administration; orderlies and doctors. We all have to get our hands dirty, either literally or metaphorically, in the intimacy and messiness of human relations. We need to fully face and enter into "bloody" office skirmishes; confront or actively filter the nonsense of corporate bureaucracy; spend time on those assembly lines, in those warehouses, or on those switchboards. If we don't, *avodah* becomes an empty illusion, a glorified narcissism.

When we take on the full dimensions of our work—the pain and the pleasure, the messiness and the order, the triumphs and the failures, the grit and the gold—we can transform just about any work situation into an opportunity for connection and deepening for both ourselves and the others around us. I read a story in the *New York Times* that described a high school teacher in the South Bronx, one of New York City's toughest neighborhoods. She was a new teacher at the school, and the kids were giving her a particularly difficult time and learning practically nothing as a result. Not surprisingly, the rate of teacher turnover at this school was incredibly high. But this young teacher did something amazing.

> When we take on the full dimensions of our work—the messiness and the order, the triumphs and the failures—we can transform just about any situation into an opportunity for connection and deepening, for both ourselves and the others around us.

She asked each child to write down one good thing about another child in the class, handing out names as assignments to each student so that everyone would be covered. Then she collected the cards, shuffled them, and redistributed them. Each student had someone else's interpretation of a classmate. She asked each of them to read that card. This group of kids who were always being dumped on, called failures, and coming to school with little expectation of being taught, were now hearing about their strengths and assets. The effect was nothing short of miraculous. The energy of the classroom completely shifted; there was laughter, embarrassment, and recognition as each of them read the comments. There was palpable gratitude to this teacher for creating a moment of remembering the "being" in each of them in the middle of the school week. She had brought a Sabbath consciousness to the most stressful of work situations and transformed it in the process.

Sometimes, like the teacher, we can shift our attitude and others' as well, imbuing our work with meaning. We can answer those four questions and change our perspective. Other times we can't, and we need to be honest with ourselves and switch jobs or careers. However we choose to do it, we are all obligated, as philosopher Thomas Berry says, to "connect our work to the great project," to the work of world-making. There actually is a practice designed to have just that effect. It's called *havdalah*, and it's a mirror of the Friday night ushering in of the Sabbath day. It is both the closing practice of Sabbath and the beginning practice of the workweek.

In short, *havdalah* is a TGIM (Thank-God-it's-Monday) practice. It's designed to make sure that our work makes a difference in the world; to remind us that our work can always stretch us and connect us to people more deeply—if we make it a practice. Like any ritual, it also surfaces what we don't feel we have, enabling us to see when our work isn't allowing that connection to happen so that we're more likely to make a change.

Havdalah is a ritual for entering the workweek; a celebration of creativity in the external world. We are literally being asked to join hands with the mythic Creator to begin the job of building once again; to be a partner in the evolution of the planet. *Havdalah* also acknowledges the complexity of creativity and world-building. It ennobles the dialectical relationships between Creation and destruction, doing and being, meaningful work and drudgery.

Havdalah actually means "distinction." There's a difference between rest and work, but they do so much to inform each other. When we observe some form of Sabbath, a time of self-reflection and rest, we are far less likely to create golden calves and much more likely to use our creativity to expand and deepen, rather than reduce or narrow reality. The ancient ritual of *havdalah* encourages us to integrate the being consciousness of Sabbath into the doing consciousness of the week.

The ritual is performed one hour after sunset on a Saturday evening, and it's every bit as mystical and beautiful as the Friday-night practice. There are three practices contained in the ritual. Just as we welcome in the Sabbath, we welcome the workweek with the same kind of joy—by drinking wine. Next, a container of fragrant spices is passed around and we are meant to deeply breathe in the scent. The sweet smell of the Sabbath, the spirit of being, is inhaled deep within. This is a symbolic way of bringing that consciousness we reached on the Sabbath into the workweek. It's an invitation to take a deep breath and the intentionality that comes with it into our work. It's a breathing meditation with a fragrance; a perfume for the week.

The Sabbath is opened with candles and it's closed with candles, but there are important differences. Whereas on Sabbath, two single-wicked candles are lit, on *havdalah* there is a single candle with multiple wicks wrapped together to create one; an invitation to remember that we do not enter the workweek alone, that all of our creative work is in the end collaborative. We have collaborators in the present and from the past; people we've been inspired by, whose work we are expanding upon. Because of the size of the wick, the fire is wild and big, the effect quite dramatic. It evokes the fire of creativity—a fire that can create and destroy, consume and enliven. It's the fire of illumination.

To enhance the drama, the candle is lit in a completely dark room. It awakens the hope that our labors will bring light to darkness; a poetic way to describe the yearning for meaningful work. Rather than closing our eyes as we do on Friday nights, our eyes are wide open. We are entering the external world again. We cup our hands and bring them close to the candle, creating a shadow. Then we open them; a way of saying that our hands can be vehicles of life.

> There's a difference between rest and work, but the two do so much to inform each other.

The ecstatic flame of the candle always reminds me that the dance between being and doing is the most creative act of all. *Havdalah* awakens us to the ongoing construction of ourselves and the world. Unlike other holy days which come around once a year, we need to practice Sabbath and *havdalah* every single week. We need to recalibrate and rebalance, and in the end, even the richest rest and work consciousness won't ensure that we'll get the balance right. We're learning how to *be* better doers and *do* being better.

There's a story told about Rabbi Zusya lying on his deathbed. His adoring students surrounded him, comforting him as he wept. One student asked, "Why are you crying?" He said, "I'm scared." His students said, "Why? You were like Abraham, like Moses to us!" But instead of being soothed, he wept louder. "God won't ask me why I wasn't more like Abraham or Moses. He will ask me why I wasn't more like Zusya!" The rabbi was articulating the exquisite yearning to fully manifest who we are, to reach our creative potential—and the realization that we're always going to fall short. The study of being and doing teaches us that we can celebrate our finitude as we seek the infinite. This is in fact the very essence of creativity.

YEARNING FOR
HAPPINESS

THE BLESSING
OF PLEASURE

IN AMERICA, THE YEARNING FOR HAPPINESS MAY BE THE most all-encompassing yearning of them all. Whether it's the Dalai Lama's art of happiness; cognitive scientists' promises to find the "happiness set point" in the brain; or the latest iPod advertising campaign, the messages that happiness is attainable are everywhere. Happiness is yours if you have an open heart, a set of talents or skills, the right genes, or even that latest product. We should be happy in our relationships, at work, with our bodies, and if we're not, something is seriously wrong. We'd better fix it quick—medicate it, soothe it, or drown it out with the multiplicity of delights and "cures" available in our "advanced" culture.

The intent of the founding fathers when they wrote about the right to pursue happiness has been much debated, but few would disagree that this promise is unique. No other nation in history has held out the hope of self-fulfillment and individual freedom. Most also would agree that with this freedom, many sometimes-conflicting ideas about how to find happiness have arisen: versions those erudite gentlemen could never have imagined. And they undoubtedly would **When we seek happiness for its own sake, it will most likely elude us.** have been mystified by the fact that in the wealthiest, most privileged country in the world, twenty-five million Americans report being depressed. Clinical depression is undeniably a syndrome that demands treatment, but is that really all that's going on?

If the founding fathers could spend one week in contemporary America, one wonders if they might have agreed with another distinguished gentleman, John Stuart Mill, who said the search for happiness is one of the chief sources of unhappiness. When we seek happiness for its own sake, it will most likely elude us. Perhaps unhappiness is not the problem at all, but rather our understandings of how happiness should look and feel—and our expectation that we somehow can find the golden key.

Critiques of modern materialism and its accompanying excesses are prevalent, and there are shifts in this dynamic, from the "simplify your life" movement to the widespread disillusionment with corporate greed. But on the whole it's clear that Americans want to feel good by living big at all costs: big cars, luxury goods, beautiful homes—and the accompanying credit card bills. It used to be that credit was something you earned: you were a regular customer who could be trusted to pay later. Now, credit really means debt. It's a way to satisfy desires at all cost. What Freud called the pleasure principle has become a central code. Material and sensual pleasure has become a prescription for all that ails us. Our other needs—our spiritual longings, our relational needs, our yearning to serve or contribute—have been trumped by our desire to experience immediate happiness.

I was a witness to the birth of this very syndrome at, of all places, a five-year-old boy's birthday party. His extended family had gathered to celebrate, bearing an astounding number of gifts. His face was full of light and joy as he opened the first one; an action figure he'd been wanting forever (as he put it). He carried it around for every guest to see and then began to play with it. After a couple of minutes, a relative handed him her gift, which, much to everyone's surprise, he put aside. With some urging, he opened it, and then the next and the next and the next, ripping open the paper, putting each present down, sometimes throwing it and reaching for another. At the end of what was nothing short of a gift orgy, he cried for more and then completely melted down and was given a time out. I heard one guest remark to another about how spoiled and ungrateful he was. What had really happened, of course, was that this joyful child wasn't allowed to savor his beloved toy, to enjoy it fully and express his gratitude. He was learning to be a good little consumer, to always want more.

The intensity of popular culture's celebration of happiness through consumption is matched by another cultural perspective, one that goes back centuries. This is the religious perspective, and America is among the most religiously focused countries in the world. Religions tend to be suspicious of personal happiness and judging of excess. Fulfillment and sensual pleasures will keep us from pursuing grander and more transcendent goals—and finding the ultimate happiness. Satisfying the needs and desires of the body, acting on our impulses, and following our id will subsume our yearnings to connect to something larger; we will cease to long for God. Christianity, Buddhism, and Hinduism all urge us to get in touch with our "noble" and "higher" yearnings. And with rare exception they universally diminish carnal or "lower" desires. There's an idealization of asceticism and self-denial.

The ancient Greek and Roman philosophers were in part responsible for this understanding of the potential dangers of all things sensual. They taught that the transient nature of pleasure makes it inferior to what is lasting, unchanging, or transcendent. Spirit is separate from body; mind can control desire. Christians picked up on this and took it a few steps further, pitting morality against the body. Rather than God being a metaphor for everything, God became elevated, outside this world, not to be experienced by most mortals. This God judges and condemns the sensual; what feels good is, by definition, not good. The most puritanical strain of Christianity took hold early in America's history; perhaps in part because the country's first immigrant inhabitants were struggling in a new land without material comforts.

The lust for the spiritual can be as intoxicating and consuming as the lust for the material.

Of course there's truth to the claim that the yearning for pleasure can crowd out other experiences of life: There's an intoxicating effect of plenty. It creates a fleeting happiness that can lead to the desire for more and more. And it can be a distraction from mindful and spiritual pursuits, as we constantly seek new and ever more exhilarating and satiating experiences to get those endorphins going. We need to shop, eat, or drink too much in order to have the same experience a toddler gets from looking at a leaf.

But the lust for the spiritual can be as intoxicating and consuming as the lust for the material. The enemy of happiness is the tendency to be consumed or devoured by any one impulse. When materialists neglect the spiritual, they become narcissistic pleasure seekers and eventually create a wasteland. When the religious neglect the sensual, they can create body hunger and abusive religious leaders who take their material desires underground.

Of course, we all have both spiritual and sensual longings. Happiness is about having the full range of yearnings in dialogue. It may seem like a funny example, but there isn't a currency in the world that doesn't represent these two sides: One side of a coin or bill has a secular or national symbol, a wordly reference, and the other side has a spiritual invitation, whether it's the pyramid or "In God We Trust." There's an understanding that this world is the place where we can struggle with these two yearnings. Happiness is the ongoing process of wrestling with and integrating these sensibilities—our spiritual strivings and sensual needs. We need to embody spirituality and spiritually enliven the corporeal. Happiness is the product of the conversation among our many desires, needs, and wants; becoming more fully aware of them. As Plato said, "There is no happiness that's not somehow rooted in the task of systematic self-examination."

Critics of our over-the-top, oversexed, buy-your-happiness era actually miss the point. The American problem is that we misunderstand and diminish sensual and carnal pleasure, whether we reject it or indulge in it. We don't take the sensual and material seriously enough. The polarities created by this society's Puritan roots, combined with its modern consumer-driven economy, create a dangerous deflection from what pleasure is really about. We tend to float between indulgence and guilt, consumerism and self-restraint, bingeing and fasting, desire and shame, overdoing it on both ends of the spectrum—devouring or denying rather than savoring, and often not really feeling very good at all. Materialism is not a sin but an error of perception. Pleasure is deeper, more expansive than we imagine—and it can create genuine and profound joy.

I often surprise audiences by saying that Judaism is first and foremost a system of enjoyment. Most spiritual traditions in some way engage the senses to communicate the spiritual, whether with beautiful churches, incense, music, gardens, tea ceremonies, or art. Jewish wisdom actually embraces and celebrates the carnal for its own sake. It urges us to delight in sensual pleasure and pursue it in all its possible incarnations. The very first commandment to the first humans is, "From every tree of the garden you must eat." The Talmud, the classical Jewish text, tells us that if we don't enjoy life's pleasures, we will be disappointing God. In other words, we'll diminish reality itself.

When I ask the average audience what comes to mind when they think of the Garden of Eden story, almost everyone says it is Adam and Eve, their heads hanging low, clothed in fig leaves, being cast out of paradise. Once in a while someone will mention Eve being created out of Adam's side. But few have remarked at the gloriousness and lusciousness of Eden, at "every tree that was pleasing to the sight and good for food," at the gold and the four flowing rivers or Adam's love song to Eve just after she is created. The word "Eden" means "delight" in Hebrew. It is a world of sensuality and abundance. In this country, we are so focused on original sin that we've forgotten original pleasure and the endless opportunities for personal fulfillment it has to offer.

Most don't know that the fruit from the tree of good and evil is called "good for eating and a delight to the eyes." Rather than being referred to as a forbidden fruit, it is "desirable as a source of wisdom." Eve eats it because she wants "her eyes to be open"; she wants to "be like divine beings who know good from bad." Hers is not so much an act of defiance as much as an act born of an overpowering yearning to experience a wider reality. When you delight in the fruit, you may discover more of who you are.

Why was the fruit so desirable; why was the tree placed in the center of the garden anyway? Perhaps the biblical author decided that God wanted humans to leave paradise to learn to create pleasure on their own terms. The contemporary Christian philosopher Mathew Fox calls the Creation story a tale of "original blessing." When Adam and Eve leave Eden, the first thing they do is make love and have a child. Perhaps toiling on the soil—as Adam must now do—or perhaps pain during childbirth for Eve actually will create more pleasure in the end. It will be pleasure earned "by the sweat of their brow."

The garden metaphor entered my life in bold relief when my family moved to St. Louis and had a backyard for the first time. A city boy through and through, I was determined to grow our own tomatoes. And my first time out with the hoe, I got the worst case of poison ivy you can imagine, from head to toe. I kept at it after the cortisone did its job, and that first tomato of the season tasted just so divine. In reality, it was probably not all that different from the tomatoes in the grocery store, but it tasted different to me. On a grander scale, when Eve held the first baby for the first time, the pain was undoubtedly more than worth it, and the joy was all the greater. Rather than dwelling in Eden, Adam and Eve and their descendents would now always be "Eden-ing."

The biblical author clearly knew and appreciated the importance of the material. All the blessings God gave to the patriarchs and the covenant itself are essentially "stuff" blessings. Abraham is promised a great nation if he leaves to go to "a land I will show you." The blessing that Jacob and Esau fought over so bitterly is nothing if not sensual. It opens with the lines: "May God give you of the dew of heaven and the fat of the earth. Abundance of new grain and wine." The dream Jacob had later in the desert is not about ascending or transcending, leaving what is earthly behind: It's about going up and down the ladder, bringing earth to heaven and heaven to earth.

All the patriarchs are quite wealthy and acquisitive. It's only the descendent of the wealthy and powerful King David—Jesus—who is born into a poor family. Christianity has such important teachings about relinquishing the material to discover other aspects of our being, to find different forms of abundance and love. But there are equally important teachings about enhancing and expanding pleasure.

Material goods have an inherent goodness. We're not meant to feel guilty for having enough, or even more than enough, money, a beautiful home, great sex, lovely clothes, and delicious food. There isn't a single holiday that doesn't have a meal attached to it, not even the Day of Atonement, after which the feast is as much of a *mitzvah* as the fast of the previous hours. In Hebrew the word for such a celebration is *oneg*, which literally means "pleasure" or "enjoyment." Jewish wisdom teaches that we need a lot of sensual pleasures. When we really enjoy them, we will ongoingly feel we have enough. The hunger, the need for more, will be less. And when we feel full, we have more to give. We'll be that much more creative, joyful, gracious, and alive.

There's a practice of putting something sweet—candy or honey—on the first page of the very first Bible a child receives. You'd think the honey would be on the last page, or midway, to reward the child for hard work, but the hope is that the entire ride will be a pleasure-filled experience, that the taste at the beginning will motivate the child to read on.

Imagine if schools put something delicious on the first page of every math book. How would it change the experience of that first-grader who is nervous about the first day of school? What would the message of that candy be? So much pleasure awaits you. There's no difference between the delight of a new idea and the burst of sensation that a lollipop provides. What this is teaching us is that the intellectual and the spiritual, the religious and the physical, are integrated. They feed and support each other. This is the very meaning of holistic.

The body is, quite literally, our temple, as the Bible tells us. There is no distinction between body **We're so focused on original sin that we've forgotten original pleasure.** and spirit. There is only holy embodiedness. In fact, there is no word for spirit or soul in biblical Hebrew. There is *nefesh*, which translates as "breathing body spirit." The medieval philosopher Maimonides warned against negating the body, and he instructed us to take care of it before attending to any other needs. There's a concept called "service through the material"; we are serving God, expanding reality, connecting to a deeper self when we experience the sensual. The more intense the pleasure, the closer we are to God. As the poet W.H. Auden wrote, "It's the pleasure haters who become unjust." By denying our bodies, our "God-given" gift, we will deny others as well.

It seems that in America, we're cut off from this wisdom about our innate sensuality, particularly when it comes to sex. We either demonize sex through religion or express our carnal desires without restraint, whether in our own lives or vicariously through the entertainment industry. The paradox is that so many of us don't enjoy sex, and so we look for more and more titillation or we hold back, dulling our senses and protecting ourselves from the stimulation all around us. There's a proliferation of taboos and an accompanying yearning to break them. The result is that we have become a voyeuristic culture with a high divorce rate.

Marriage and committed romantic relationships have suffered from what's been a domestication of sex in recent years. Sex has been watered down, tamed, dulled. All relationships struggle with the tensions created by two often conflicting needs. One is the need for steadiness, trust, reliability, security, stability, and predictability—all of which are necessary for commitment to be real. The other is the riskiness, seduction, friskiness, unpredictability, mystery, unruliness, and instability necessary to maintain desire. For so many of us, sex becomes less exciting, the range of intensity so much lower than when we were single. We all know that committed relationships can get boring, and we know that sex can get routine and that erotic pleasure can be diminished with time. In a committed relationship we're always available to each other, so why bother to seduce?

When we think we don't need to seduce our lover, we'll end up seeking seduction outside the relationship. When we don't have erotic adventure within our relationships, we'll seek it elsewhere. When our illicit fantasies are banished from our own bedroom, when we play it safe at home, we'll look for danger somewhere else. And so sex with someone new and forbidden becomes so appealing. Or if we don't dare do that, there's always the titillation of *Desperate Housewives*, or pornography.

What if we could stop dualizing and separating our need for commitment and our need for lust? What if what we really yearn for are lusty commitments and commitments to lust? In order for monogamy to work, monogamy has to be "dirty." If the forbidden is what's exciting, we have to work hard to bring the taboo into our most intimate relationships. If transgression is so titillating, we have to learn to transgress where we're most safe.

Our committed relationships can be nothing less than pleasure chambers. But we need to create situations and take risks that are out of the ordinary and push the envelope. Dana and I once took a trip to Northern California to celebrate our seventeenth wedding anniversary. We took a beautiful hike in Big Sur, climbing a winding path to the top of a cliff. It was foggy and yet still sunny, as it can be in that part of the country. There was a bench at a scenic overlook. It couldn't have been more romantic. As we sat there, I knew what I was thinking, but I didn't say anything. Instead I leaned over and took a risk. I started kissing her. And then . . . It turned out we were both thinking the same thing. The illicit, transgressive lovemaking in that public space was far more erotic and pleasurable that any first-time sex could ever be.

Of the hundreds of times happiness, *simcha*, is used in Jewish wisdom texts, the majority are in regard to committed lovers. It's really pretty simple: If we don't have great sex, we can't have a great spiritual life. Jewish wisdom has a kind of Torah of seduction; a *mitzvah* of foreplay. There's a funny story from the Talmud about a teacher, Rav, and his devoted student, Rav Kahana. One night Rav is making love to his wife, and he hears something under his bed. When he calls out, Rav Kahana answers that it is he, and he is here to learn at the feet of his master:

"This is a matter of Torah, and I must study." Rav and his wife must have had a lot to teach about sex for Rav Kahana to want to hide under the bed. Rav Kahana knew that if you want to understand the Torah of life, you have to study the Torah of sex.

There's also a text written by the famous thirteenth-century philosopher Nachmonides called the Holy Letter, which is an actual Torah of sex. Nachmonides recommends that we talk about our fantasies in order to increase our desire. Lovers are encouraged to invite new positions. Foreplay isn't fore-play; it's the play. Nachmonides suggests foods and menus to stimulate desire. Holding back one's orgasm to deepen pleasure is a sacred practice.

Committed relationships are where we are literally obligated to be vulnerable and make mistakes, to experience sexual pleasure and even pain as long as both partners are in agreement. Sex is a dance between the masculine and feminine, a way to join both dimensions, so nothing should be held back. We must be exposed and open, be willing to improvise. Nothing is off limits.

The Talmud says that when committed lovers cleave to each other, the *Shekinah*, or divine presence, is a third partner. It is a kind of cosmic *ménage à trois*. The first blessing said at every wedding, which I think of as the sex blessing, is: "Be grateful for the consciousness to make love to those with whom we are meant to make love." The last blessing of the ceremony describes the multiple forms of joy that emerge from committed lovemaking: the happiness that washes over you and circles back, a kind of luxuriating sensuality; the more subtle joy that hums through your body; the dance of exultation that makes you buoyant and energetic; and the happiness that takes over, subsuming everything.

When we see our bodies as a blessing, our sensual desires as sacred, there's no end to the pleasure that awaits us. The challenge is to raise our consciousness to the delights everywhere around us; to anticipate and celebrate every momentary pleasure with intention. One of the cornerstones of the Jewish tradition is a two-thousand-year-old method for raising our awareness, and thereby increasing our pleasure: the practice of blessing.

It's nothing short of a pleasure practice. We are to say a hundred blessings a day, which is a metaphor for as many times as possible and symbolic of each of the hundred sockets that held together the ancient tabernacle, a microcosm of the world. In other words, our experience of pleasure is integral to the ongoing creation of all-that-is. It may seem like an awful lot of work, but there's such a power to all this blessing. Quite simply, it brings the sensual world to life in all its splendor—from the marriage of two people in love to a new pair of shoes; from a delicious meal to a new home. Blessing is a gratitude practice—when we pause to recognize the gifts we've been given, it's amazing how much happier we are.

The origin of the Hebrew word for blessing says so much. If you change one vowel of the Hebrew word *bracha* you have the word for "pool of water." *Bracha* also comes from the same root as the word for "bent knee." The word "blessing" was first used by a desert people. Imagine the experience of coming across a reservoir of water in the middle of a barren wilderness and then kneeling before that pool to drink fully. The ancient Israelites saw water as a blessing, and blessing as a spring of happiness. So the word for blessing was born of a sensual yearning, out of thirst and the wonder that comes from quenching it. In other words, the pool is a symbol of life itself, and blessing connects us to the energy current that sustains us.

In Hebrew, the blessings are called "blessings of enjoyment." Pleasure is God manifested, or, as Buddhists believe, form is formlessness made material. Blessings are a way of contextualizing pleasure, a reminder of the source of everything. Abraham Joshua Heschel wrote beautifully about this: "When we drink a glass of water, we remind ourselves of the eternal mystery of creation, 'Blessed are You . . . by whose word all things came into being,' whether a trivial act or a supreme miracle. When we wish to eat bread or fruit, to enjoy a pleasant fragrance or a cup of wine . . . on noticing trees when they blossom; on meeting a sage in Torah or in secular learning, we are taught to evoke His great name and our awareness of Him. . . . This is one of the goals of the Jewish way of living; to feel the hidden love and wisdom in all things."

I feel so fortunate to have grown up in a tradition that continually raised my pleasure consciousness. The first time I remember being aware of what a gift I'd been given was as a teenager when I put on a new pair of jeans. I remember relishing the stiffness and snugness, anticipating all the mornings I would put them on, how each time they'd be a little more faded, fit a little bit better. That morning, my mother had taken my brothers and me for our semiannual shopping spree. These expeditions always took place around the seasonal festivals of

Pleasure is God manifested.

Passover in the spring and Succot in the fall. They were literally a ritual. Of course, there was the practical aspect: We needed clothes for the winter and then the summer months. But no less important was the fact that we were anticipating these two important holidays by celebrating the sensual: ushering in the spiritually new with sensual delight and pleasure. That spring afternoon before I put those jeans on I said a simple blessing, which is made with any new experience. After I put them on I remember feeling a rush of contentment as I glanced in the mirror at my jeans and did a little dance.

Blessings are said before; not after. The blessing gives us a hit of gratitude even before we indulge. We feel thankful not only after having the great experience, but as a way to enhance that experience as we're having it. We surface our desire so that we feel it fully and therefore bring intention to the act of satisfying it. The blessing I said over those jeans was, "Praised are you who clothes the naked." When we really can experience the yearning to be clothed; when we can appreciate the feeling of being protected from the elements, or covered by a soft or silky fabric; we are so much more satiated than we would be after a frenetic day shopping at the mall. Clothing ourselves can then be a metaphor for clothing the world. One practice I learned growing up is to give away one piece of clothing whenever we buy a new one. When we feel blessed, we are more likely to become a blessing to the world.

There was another time several years later that really stuck with me. I was at summer camp before the campers arrived, setting things up with the other counselors. Every week, we left the grounds to go to town to buy bread for Friday-night dinner. We'd wait outside the bakery to get the first morning's batch fresh out of the oven. When it was ready and purchased, before heading back we'd sit on the curb in front of the bakery and eat some of the steaming, fluffy, crispy bread saturated with melting butter. But before I did, I said a blessing that I'd said hundreds of times before. That morning maybe the bread was especially wonderful, or maybe I was just in a great mood or happy to be in the company of my friends. But I remember thinking, wow, the blessing over bread is so perfect, so right. Just then it named exactly what I was feeling in that moment: It allowed me to really notice my own pleasure; to have it fully sink in. The taste of the bread was prolonged somehow and my tongue seemed to tingle during the whole trip back to the grounds. I don't always have such a delightful experience when I eat bread, but I've never said that blessing the same way since.

Once again the depth of my experience was enhanced by the actual words of the blessing, which are "Praised are you who feeds the whole world." Mine was a bittersweet, complex enjoyment, because, of course, everybody isn't able to eat bread, to enjoy abundance. But rather than guilt, the blessing evokes a profound appreciation for the gift and awakens an even more powerful yearning that goes beyond the sensual self. The blessing adds texture and authenticity to the pleasure. It reminds us that whatever delight is before us, it is enough. When we bless the bread, we are invited to think about how we got the money to buy it, about the people who put it on the shelves at the grocer, the farmer who picked the wheat, the baker that baked it, the rain and the sun that enabled it to grow—all of that for me? The experience of that handful of bread is so conscious and full-filling that we're less likely to want another piece.

Jewish wisdom teaches that it's a serious mistake to refuse to taste a new kind of food. There's a law that you are not allowed to eat standing up, as you can't fully enjoy your food if you are not sitting. Our mothers' "sit down when you eat" or "take a plate" or "do not drink out of the bottle" are actually spiritual insights. It's so important to energize the eating experience with intention or *kavanah*. We are all meant to be gourmets; not gourmands. When we exclaim over the chocolate, "Oh, it's divine!" it really is. But if we immediately take another piece, the pleasure will decrease. A gourmet is enthusiastic—which means infused with God's spirit. A gourmand can never get enough. When we don't savor, we want more.

A doctor friend of mine refers to the practice of blessing as a satiation diet. He calls the epidemic of obesity in this country "malnutrition of happiness." Maybe this is why there are so many bestselling diet books and only the rare cookbook that rises to the top of the bestseller lists. Perhaps if we cooked for each other more often, we'd eat less. I find it hopeful that the latest research is showing that nutrition is not about low fat or high protein. It's about feeling full. In other words, it's about feeling blessed.

People are always surprised when I tell them that there's also a blessing for when the food comes out the other end. This, too, is a form of pleasure, something to feel thankful for. And the rabbis had no qualms about acknowledging the base corporeal sensation of going to the bathroom. We've all had that experience of holding it in; for whatever reason waiting until we can barely stand it and then having that feeling of "Oh, thank God" as we finally let it go. If we tune in, we may feel a sense of gratitude that it all works. The blessing reads: "Blessed are You, who fashions the human body with wisdom and created in him orifices . . . and completely knows that if one of these holes or orifices should open all the way or close all the way we would not be able to live or stand before You who heals all bodies in wondrous ways." As my grandmother used to say, "Eat, sleep, and eliminate." Remember that it's all blessed.

There are so many blessings for the things we normally take for granted, so that they, too, become a source of joy. There are blessings for waking up in the morning, standing up straight, and for walking. There's one for seeing a crowd of people—"Oh, my God, look how many stories there are!" Awe, wonder, and surprise are all deeply pleasurable.

Among Jews, the most commonly known blessing is called the *Shecheyanu*—"who has kept us alive." It's the blessing said over any new experience: tasting a fruit for the first time in the season, the return of an annual holiday or festival, a new purchase, opening a gift. "Blessed are You, who has kept us alive and has sustained us and has enabled us to arrive at this moment." It is literally a method for keeping things fresh; of recognizing that if we really think about it everything is always new. It's also an acknowledgment that life is a series of moments, of moment pleasures, moment happinesses, and that the most significant blessing of all is that we are here to enjoy them.

THE ETHICS OF JOY

IT WAS AN UNUSUALLY COLD FEBRUARY DAY FOR ISRAEL.
I was visiting a temporary village that housed and helped Ethiopian
immigrants adjust to their new land. They'd just arrived after a long
journey and decades of struggle to leave their country where, for generations, they'd been an oppressed minority. They stood around make-
shift caravans of prefabricated housing, shivering in the new experience
of winter chill after a life near the equator.

As I walked around not quite knowing what to do to help, I spotted
two boys, about ten years old. They were standing off to the side of the
camp rubbing their hands together, their eyes wide as they took in the
landscape and all the new faces. I walked over and offered them my
gloves. They hesitated at first, glancing from one to the other until one
of them took the gloves and put them on. He immediately started
laughing: He'd never worn gloves before. It was a laugh of sheer delight
at these second hands over his, warm and scratchy. He motioned to me
to give his friend gloves, too. When it was apparent from my body language that I didn't have another pair, he took off one glove and gave it
to his friend, who also started laughing in that same wonderful way,
both their faces beaming with joy.

I, too, felt a rush of happiness, of warmth, even though my hands
were now pretty cold. When I got back to Jerusalem I bought myself a
new pair of gloves. This was back in 1984. I still wear those gloves every
winter. Although they're pretty worn-out by now I continue to welcome

the extra warmth that comes along with that memory of the gleeful laugh of those young boys each with a single gloved hand.

There was such a rich intersection of happiness for all three of us in that short encounter. The unexpected sensual pleasure of the gloves and the emotional joy of sharing the gloves with each other created an explosion of happiness for those boys. For me there was the joy of offering something of myself, a happiness born of giving pleasure and creating an opportunity for others to do the same.

Most of us have experienced feelings of pleasure and happiness that rise within when we care for others. For example, we all can feel the difference between cooking a tasty meal just for ourselves, cooking a meal for ourselves and a loved one, and cooking that same meal with enough to share with a friend or neighbor who is ill. The same food tastes so much better, our pleasure intensified. So too, giving charity is a joy, perhaps even more so when our donation exceeds our own expectation. The pleasure of getting a holiday bonus is often less pleasurable than giving it away to someone who desperately needs it. Or compare the enjoyment of sitting down and reading a good book with the deeper enjoyment of then passing the book on to someone else when we're done, or reading that very same book to an elderly person.

Mahatma Gandhi once observed, "Consciously or unconsciously, every one of us does render some service or other. If we cultivate the habit of doing this service deliberately, our desire for service will steadily grow stronger, and it will make not only for our own happiness, but that of the world at large." Whether through random acts of kindness, planned gifts, routine caretaking, or generous lovemaking, acting from concern for others makes us happier human beings; our lives more satisfying and meaningful. It might sound like a platitude, but it is true nonetheless: Being happy isn't only about feeling good, but also about doing good.

Being happy isn't only about feeling good; it's about doing good.

Nevertheless, despite our own experiences, so many still insist on posing morality in opposition to happiness. Pleasure is usually associated with one's own sensual and physical pleasure—whether gastronomic, aesthetic, or sexual—not with activities directed to the welfare of others. Too often, we assume that any self-serving motivation, such as our own personal happiness, automatically undermines the morality of what we do. So we tend to be reluctant to admit and even to feel embarrassed by the joy that comes from acting decently, doing the right thing, and helping others. Maybe this accounts for why so many parents, when asked what they want for their children, initially respond that they want their children to be happy and then may say they want their children to be kind or good—as if happiness and goodness were disconnected. But can our children genuinely feel happy about themselves without developing character and being ethical?

We have gotten ourselves into a strange bind. When we indulge in sensual pleasure, we often feel guilty. And when we do a good deed, we tend to ignore the accompanying sense of well-being. But ignoring the joy of being ethical can lead to a sense of self-righteousness or entitlement. Self-righteous, because if we do not genuinely feel personal joy we will wind up feeling we've acted from some purely selfless state. Entitled, because if we feel we're acting from some purely selfless state, we are superior. We may give of ourselves because we want to be profusely praised by our friends; or in wealthier circles, want our name on a building or to be honored at a gala. Or we wind up creating models of generosity that are completely selfless, as if we aren't really giving unless we are sacrificing and suffering. Think of Mother Teresa. In so many ways, she is our culture's exemplar of pure generosity. When she's our example, we can become so discouraged about ever living up to her or someone like her, that we may do nothing. And so either way, when we're really honest with ourselves we aren't as good as we would like to be. As Gandhi said, if we all brought happiness born of goodness to consciousness, our lives—and the world—might be transformed.

What accounts for this pervasive disconnection between happiness and goodness? The answer traces, I believe, to three deeply imbedded ethical presumptions in our culture and, as a consequence, in our individual unconsciousnesses as well. The first is a religious inheritance which distrusts carnal pleasure and teaches that what feels good can't be good. This reflects the old body-spirit divide bequeathed to us by the Greeks and traditional Christianity. This separation between physical pleasure and spiritual happiness often leads to our being painfully torn between wild indulgence and rigid denial of our physical and sensual desires. But is this truncated notion of happiness and morality really true to our experience?

The second is the philosophical legacy of Immanuel Kant's duty-based ethical theory. Kant wrote, "It is one thing to make a man happy, it is quite another to make him good." He drove a wedge between happiness and goodness and, in the process, made the search for happiness empty and denied the ethical life its real pleasures. In fact, he argued that if we perform a moral action because we are emotionally moved to do so, that act has no moral worth. For example, Kant thought that although love between parents and children is natural, it has no moral weight because morality has to involve a struggle against the self. (It should be of no surprise that Kant had no children.) When duty calls we must be prepared to yield our personal interest and fulfill our obligation. Doing the right thing then becomes associated with the inflexible demands of duty unspoiled by thoughts of happiness. This idea that happiness and morality are in conflict sometimes leads to an almost pathological conclusion that if something makes us happy, then that is evidence it is morally suspect.

The third legacy is the psychological theory of Sigmund Freud. A pioneer of explicating sensual urges, he also argued that acting morally requires sacrificing a degree of happiness. For Freud the only meaningful notion of happiness is the satisfaction of our instinctual desires. Because we need to live in society, we must repress our desires and can never be genuinely happy. As Freud put it, "Civilized man has exchanged a portion of his happiness for a portion of security." Discontent is the price we pay for civilization, thus his book, *Civilization and*

Its Discontents. We have a choice: We can have a good life that rules out happiness or a happy life that makes being good problematic. (It should not surprise us that throughout his life Freud suffered from bouts of depression and near the end of his life asked, "What good to us is a long life if it is difficult and barren of joys . . . ?")

These three legacies teach that if we hope to attain true, wholesome happiness we have to rise above our born inclinations. I suspect this idea is mostly a handy excuse for those who would rather critique others for their selfish behavior than face the shame of their own self-centeredness. It's also a useful tool to manipulate others into donating to a cause, be it political or religious. But are these divides true to our experience?

The truth is, I don't spend much time calibrating how much pleasure I receive from doing good deeds, and I doubt you do either. My decisions tend to be taken up with choosing between such things as getting TiVo and buying great tickets to the Rolling Stones, or spending my limited funds on a dining room table or a vacation. But I do know that when I visit a friend in the hospital rather than spend hours in front of the television watching my favorite shows, my contentment is richer and more abiding. I can say with certainty that the joy that comes with spending a Sunday morning raising money by participating in the AIDS Walk is truly more sustaining than the pleasures of sitting with a perfect cup of coffee reading the paper. We all seek this enriching, self-affirming joy that comes with caring for others. We long for the kind of happiness that will keep us warm during colder seasons, like those worn gloves.

Acting from a place of generosity and compassion creates sustaining happiness.

To be sure, the intensity and flash of happiness that flows from a sensual experience is more brilliant and enlivening than the experience of doing for others. The intensity of finer pleasures, says Freud, is mild compared with that from the satisfying of crude, primary, instinctual impulses. I recall the ecstasy and heightened perception I experienced from tripping on LSD years ago. It's no accident that drugs are called intoxicants and spirits. But with sensual pleasures, both the joy and the insights quickly evaporate. In contrast, the higher state of awareness and understanding attained through an ethical practice is always more sustaining and embracing. Such practices can give rise to perceptions that last a lifetime. Doing "good" demands intention and the delay of gratification; yet the ensuing pleasure is so much greater and so much deeper.

All spiritual traditions teach that acting from a place of generosity and compassion creates sustaining happiness; whether it's the Eightfold Path for ending suffering in Buddhism, the practice of good works in the Christian tradition, or the ethical commandments of Judaism. Abraham Joshua Heschel wrote, "The experience of bliss in doing good is the greatest moment that mortals know." Doing good is a practice and it takes discipline, but the discipline is an ingredient in the joy. When we hold together the truths of sense and heart, we realize that we need not minimize our material delights to attain the greater joy of giving. One informs the other. If we don't have pleasure in our lives, the world seems barren. If we aren't sources of happiness, our pleasure is fleeting.

There are spiritual practices designed to heighten our awareness of abiding happiness. The Jewish tradition, for example, urges us to begin our day with a contemplative practice, what Hindus call *jnana* yoga (inquiry and discrimination). We are asked to study the very first paragraph in the Talmud: "These are the deeds that yield immediate fruit and continue to yield fruit in time to come; honoring parents; deeds of kindness; providing hospitality; visiting the sick; helping the needy bride (which in ancient times meant providing dowries); making peace between people; taking care of the dead; study; and spiritual introspection." The Talmudic sage understood that lasting happiness can only come from deeper self-awareness and commitment that extends beyond one's self.

Paradoxically, when we do good deeds, when we act ethically, we tend to enjoy our material pleasures even more. When we don't, we may feel guilty or even ashamed, as if we haven't earned or merited such abundance. We feel a gnawing emptiness that precludes the happiness we seek and causes us to yearn for more and more. Then there's that unconscious feeling of indebtedness that crops up in all of us from time to time, a kind of existential angst: After all, what did we do to earn the greatest gift of all—our very lives? It is almost as if there's a switch inside that flips when we get something for nothing, which then keeps us from enjoying the world in all of its sensual beauty. These feelings can be mitigated by the simple act of giving: by offering our service, kindness, and love and transforming ourselves from receivers to givers.

There's a teaching called *simcha shel mitzvah*, which means "the joy of doing good deeds" or "the pleasure in acting as we know we should." Underlying this concept is the recognition that happiness does not depend on feeling good all the time, but on the ability to reflect on what is worthwhile in one's life. Happiness is, therefore, not just a feeling or emotion but a profound connection to the world. The wise of every generation understood this, as did Aristotle when he concluded, "A happy life is a virtuous life." The new science of happiness is now making the same discovery: Doing acts of kindness creates more happiness than just about anything else.

The Hebrew word *mitzvah* is often translated as obligation. Most of us feel constrained or burdened when we hear this word, as though freedom is now constrained and happiness compromised. But, in fact, when we heed our obligations, take responsibility for our decisions, place our duties for others before our immediate satisfactions, we actually are happier as a result.

Happiness is not just a mood or an emotion, but a profound connection to the world. It doesn't depend on feeling good all the time, but on the ability to reflect on what is worthwhile in life.

We're faced with ethical choices every day. Do I tell my husband the truth or lie to avoid conflict? Do I take the credit for what someone else did or point to whom it's due? Do I give money to the beggar or assume he's a drug addict who doesn't deserve it? Do I help my child with his homework or take a much-needed break? Do I take office supplies home from my workplace for personal use or buy my own? Do I put the unwanted product back on the right shelf, or leave it by the register and let the underpaid clerk do it for me? Whenever we face these kinds of choices—from the grand to the trivial—we hear so many voices: those of our parents, traditions, peers, wounded selves, tired selves, selfish selves, angry selves, guilty selves, generous selves, and kind selves. Our happiness depends on which voice we choose to follow.

This is why practice is so important. The sages imagined that by doing *mitzvot* regularly, eventually all acts of loving kindness and obligation would eventually become *simcha shel mitzvot*. In other words, our "shoulds" and our "wants" would become one and the same. We will want to do what we know we should. Our personal pleasure and our service to others will be aligned. On the other hand, when we know what we should do but we don't do it, we are following a recipe for unhappiness. While right and wrong may not be as absolute as fundamentalists preach, neither is right and wrong hopelessly relative either. Right and wrong may be dependent on context, contingent and open to constant change, but the distinction does exist. And although we may do a good job at denying it in the moment of decision, the ethical choice is always alive within us.

Sometimes we excuse unethical behavior because we determine no harm will come from what we do. We can think of a million good reasons—usually self-serving ones—to justify our decisions. When we hear that dialogue going on inside our head, it's time to have a different conversation, and if we're honest most of the time it's pretty hard to fool ourselves. Of course, we can choose not to have that conversation; instead, to rationalize and justify, but in the end the God inside is immeasurably more investigative, has much clearer standards, and is far more punitive than the god in the sky.

I wish I'd had that internal conversation several years ago when I took a monetary gift from someone I taught. Instead, my dialogue went like this: "I've worked hard for this man, far beyond the call of duty or the needs of my organization. He's so wealthy; the money is nothing to him. He's offering a gift of thanks; I should be gracious and receive it." And then the bottom line: "This would be one year's private school tuition for my daughter; a 20 percent increase in my salary." I was breaking no laws or overt rules. But even as I accepted the money I felt it wasn't right.

Not surprisingly, it changed the nature of my relationship with this man, who I cared about very much. Was I now his friend or his employee? Did I have to accept his invitations or requests because he was paying me? Did he see me the same way as he did before? Every quarter, I was supposed to send out a bill as a formality. Each time I filled out his bill, I had a gnawing feeling of discomfort. Once again, I'd run through my justifications, and soon found myself with a new worry: Will I still get my money next quarter? During that period I wasn't racked with guilt—obviously not, because I never did give the money back. But a chronic unhappiness hovered in the background, a bitter flavor that tainted my successes during that period. For someone else, taking the money could have been comfortable and right, but it wasn't for me. What I did was not who I wanted to be.

There will always be arguments—internal and external—about what makes for an ethical life and what generates happiness. Our unprecedented personal freedom exacerbates this confusion. For the most part, traditional, external forms of authority—parental, religious, social, and cultural—have weakened, leaving us as our own authorities to choose how we want to live. Rather than being a series of tightly knit communities with shared values—as we've been for most of human history—we've become a pluralist, fragmented, postmodern culture.

There is no agreed-upon moral position across every context and every situation. There is no moral code, no algorithm for ethics, no easily accessible precedents. As a result, the determination of what it means to lead a good life is now more complicated than ever before. But the fact that there aren't such clear answers makes it even more vital that the debate continues, and that it continues with even greater openness and honesty.

Wrestling with these central questions about the good life turns out to be the central ingredient for a flourishing, happy life. Israel means "God wrestler." Jacob is named Israel after wrestling with an angel during that agonizing night in which he grapples with having stolen his brother's blessing. There were more obviously worthy candidates to be the founder of Israel—more upstanding, more humble, more powerful—but that honor was bestowed on Jacob because he was willing to wrestle his way through his own doubts and conflicts. From the encounter, Jacob emerged limping, but also a more compassionate, always-evolving son, father, and leader.

Plato taught that happiness is rooted in an examined life and the Psalmist wrote, "Know Before Whom You Stand." In other words, happiness comes from learning to appreciate living in the gap between what we desire and what we have, who we are and who we want to be, how we act and how we ought to act. In the end, maybe a happy life is one in which we regularly reflect on what makes for a happy life.

FULL OF ENOUGH

IT WAS FOUR WEEKS BEFORE MY NIECE MELISSA'S wedding. Dana's sister, the mother of the bride, had been orchestrating a grand affair. Everyone had been buzzing about the details of the occasion for months—who would sit where, what the bridal party should wear—the usual wedding mania. Three generations of our scattered family would come together for a weekend of joyous celebration of the marriage of two beautiful people and the miracle of all being together. It made it even more special to me that my father and I would lead the ceremony. *Simcha*, the Hebrew word for "joy," also means "a happy occasion." Weddings are considered one of the greatest *simchas* of all.

Three weeks before the ceremony my father-in-law, Jules, was diagnosed with cancer of the pancreas, with a very serious prognosis. We were devastated. He is our precious Grandpa. Dana, the kids, and I are incredibly close to him. The blow hit us all very hard. Dana accompanied her parents to every appointment. In the evenings, we would lie in bed, talk, and cry. My kids couldn't concentrate on their work or sleep: This was the grandfather who ran after them when they were young; taught them to harvest the many vegetables from his garden; and coached them as they rode their boogie boards in the Atlantic. My mother-in-law, Janice, worked around the clock caring for her husband of more than fifty years. We were all racked with anxiety as he underwent a dangerous surgery, which we weren't sure he'd survive. Even if he did, the outcome was far from clear.

Dana and I found ourselves praying that somehow at least he'd make it to the wedding of his precious granddaughter. Over the course of our relationship, whenever I pictured Jules in my mind I saw him, with his full head of jet-black hair well into his eighth decade, on the dance floor—he and Janice were beautiful ballroom dancers. As I waited for the six-hour surgery to be over, I visualized him dancing at the wedding, his face radiant with health as he beamed with pride and delight.

Jules came through the surgery, although there were complications and not all the cancer could be removed. Until two days before the wedding, we weren't sure if he'd be strong enough to attend. But he did come. As we drove from New York City to Baltimore for the weekend of celebration that would culminate in a Sunday-evening wedding, the car was pulsating with life. What happened over that weekend forever changed my understanding of *simcha*. The wedding was nothing short of breathtaking. The night sparkled with candles and crystal; the wedding canopy was covered in sprays of beautiful flowers; the guests looked fabulous in their fancy attire; the bride and groom were exuberant and gracious. Every moment, every detail, was enriched by Jules's presence. I could barely keep my eyes off him as he joked with my father. After twenty-five years of being family, they were like brothers. I watched him stroke his granddaughters' hair and compliment them on how mature and beautiful they looked. Pale and visibly thin under his tux, he beamed nevertheless.

When I looked over and saw him dancing with Dana, tears streamed down my face. When they circled closer I could see Dana also had tears in her eyes and both of their faces were lit up with the biggest smiles I'd ever seen. I had watched them dance together many times but this time there was a shimmering light around them. It was a different kind of dancing than the one that I'd imagined while waiting for the surgery to be over—sadness and happiness were intertwined in every step, and no one wanted the music to stop.

The Hassidic mystic Rabbi Nachman struggled with depression his entire life. In one of his parables he describes a person watching a traditional dance at a village wedding, with people joyfully circling the bride and groom. Too sad to join in, he stands outside the circle of the dancers until someone takes hold of his hand and pulls him into the dance, despite his protestations. He finds himself dancing hesitantly at first and then joyfully; then turning to watch his sad self looking on with disappointment.

> There is no happiness without sadness; no pleasure without pain; no fullness without loss. They are inseparable.

The task, says Rabbi Nachman, is to bring that sadness itself into the circle; to see that it, too, is transformed into joy. The truth of Nachman's teaching could not be any more real than it was at Melissa's wedding. We had taken sadness by the hand and somehow transformed it into joy.

There was nothing any of us wouldn't have done to take back the last month, to have Jules's health fully restored, and yet the joy we felt during those two days was so life-affirming and richly layered. There was a depth of gratitude, an appreciation for every detail, and a feeling of preciousness. The sorrow that had overwhelmed and consumed us in the previous days—and likely would again—somehow generated a more profound happiness, a feeling of being in the pulse and intensity of life. There is no happiness without sadness; no pleasure without pain; no fullness without loss. They go together; they are inseparable. Naturally, we always want to get rid of the sadness rather than see how it works together with joy. We forget that the point is not to cultivate one thing as opposed to the other, but to see clearly where we are.

I realized that weekend that joy is deepened by sadness, and that very joy can carry you through that very sadness. This is precisely the power of the final practice at every Jewish wedding: A glass is stomped on and shattered as a reminder of the destruction of the ancient temple and the fragility of everything precious. At the sound of the shattering, all those watching the ceremony applaud and yell "*Mazel tov!*" or "Good luck"; and the marriage has begun with the brokenness brought into the circle of joy.

Happiness is about embracing the cycle of life, about seeing everything in its widest possible context and experiencing it all to the fullest. The Dalai Lama captures this in his definition of happiness: "Deliberately broadening one's outlook and finding meaning in suffering; a transformation of outlook." It's not that he sees things through rose-colored glasses; it's that he views suffering and joy along the same continuum. Our hope for Jules's recovery, for many more dances with him, sat side-by-side with our awareness that this might in fact be his very last *simcha*. Somehow, for that glorious weekend, it was enough.

There's a song sung at every Passover seder, although I've often thought it should be a daily meditation. It's called "*Dayenu*," which means "it's enough for us." The song is a remarkable and deceptively simple teaching about embracing the present, while having a keen awareness of the past and a yearning for the future. It's about feeling longing and gratitude; triumph and tragedy. It's about celebrating every single step along the way and yet fiercely longing for the fulfillment of one's dream.

The song acknowledges fifteen major Biblical events, asking us to sing *dayenu* after each one. If God had brought us out of Egypt but not divided the sea for us, *dayenu*; it would have been enough for us. If God had led us to Mt. Sinai but there had been no encounter, *dayenu*; it would have been enough for us. If we had had the encounter at Sinai but had not made it through the desert, *dayenu*; it would have been enough for us.

As I watched Jules and Dana dance, I thought, *dayenu*. If they had that one dance but never another, *dayenu*. I felt so full and so grateful. Yet at the same time, I knew it wouldn't always feel like enough. I wondered if anything would. Would two more years be enough?; would ten?; would twenty? The song can be sung multiple ways: with joy and gusto—*dayenu* as a declarative, an affirmation that every moment in life is a gift, that it really is enough; or slowly and mournfully—*dayenu* as resignation that, given the cycle of life, it would have to be enough. Or as a protest—it's not enough! *Dayenu* also can be a question; would it ever be enough for us? There's an inherent tension and edginess in the song—there's both comfort and challenge.

Anyone familiar with the stories mentioned in each verse of "*Dayenu*" knows that forty-eight hours after escaping Egypt, rather than celebrating their freedom and feeling it was enough, the Israelites were complaining that they were thirsty and there was no water. After going through the sea they complained about there not being enough food. A few weeks after encountering the divine at Mt. Sinai, after having a vision of the deepest dimensions of reality, the Israelites worshipped the golden calf. Nothing seemed to be enough. Isn't this true for all of us? We have a breakthrough in our lives: finally launching that new business, falling in love with the girl we've pursued, having that healthy child after years of trying, having our sick father-in-law dance at a family celebration—and whether it's the next minute, the next day, or the next year, we want something more.

The last line of the song is, "If we were brought into the Promised Land, and the Temple was not built, it would have been enough for us, *dayenu*." The Temple is metaphor for that place where everything is as it should be—the cure is found, love wins out, life triumphs. It is pure joy and happiness; nothing short of the ultimate. Yet the song was written well over one thousand years after the destruction of the Temple. The Temple was clearly not going to be rebuilt. How can we be grateful for what we will never have? How can we sing *dayenu* while wanting so much more? How can we parse the journey into steps and be thankful for each one, even though we don't really know where we're going?

Only by becoming proficient at both gratitude and longing can our happiness become richer and more real.

We all want to rebuild our temples, to reach our Promised Land—the place in life where our dreams are fulfilled, where our father-in-law can be cured—but we need to remember that it's called the Promised Land for a reason. It is always promised, just beyond us. And so we better enjoy every dance. "*Dayenu*" urges us to go for it, to long for the ultimate and to know that regardless of what happens, every step along the way is enough. When we become proficient at gratitude and longing, when we can experience the fullness of *dayenu*—as affirmation, lament, protest, and question—our happiness will be so much richer and more real.

After all, if we're only happy when everything works out, happiness will always elude us and our experience of reality will be so much narrower. One of the many names for God is the mystical name *Shaddai*, which comes from the same root as the word *dayenu*. Why would there be a name for the infinite one that means "enough"? One master taught that after that first week of Creation, the work was far from done and never would be done, but God was able to say enough for now. In other words, one of the qualities of the divine presence is the sense of enough. Incompleteness is a quality of reality. "*Dayenu*" is not simply about being satisfied with what we have, it's about feeling the fullness of the partial. It's about experiencing the exquisiteness of two yearnings: how very much we want the Temple and how much we long to feel "enough" even if it's never built.

If we were to practice *dayenu* every morning and every night before we went to sleep, imagine how we'd reframe our goals and anxieties; how differently we'd parse our day. "If I walk into my kids' room just before they awaken and see them stir, and nothing else happens today, *dayenu*. If I have breakfast with them, but I fail to close the deal this afternoon, *dayenu*. If I close the deal but miss a date with an old friend, *dayenu*." *Dayenu* is like a marinade for our consciousness. The more time we dwell there, the richer and more delicious life becomes.

The Talmud teaches that if one eats as little as an olive-size amount of food, one should feel gratitude. To be honest, I do not think I have ever eaten only an olive-size amount of anything, and can barely imagine what it is to feel grateful for just a morsel of food. It may well be easier to feel the fullness in the partial when we actually have less to begin with, just as one can feel deeper joy when the backdrop is sadness. I remember once, when I was about ten, eating dinner with my grandfather, who visited every week. He was literally gnawing and sucking on a steak bone and enjoying it immensely. When I asked him why he didn't take another slice of steak, he told me about how he came from Russia to this country alone at sixteen. There were plenty of days in the first couple of years when he was hungry, and sucking on bones would make him full. And so even now he enjoyed the bone as much as the steak. If feeling full and grateful when one has very little was the challenge for my grandfather, the challenge for me and many of us today is how to feel full and grateful in the midst of abundance.

By dozens of measures, life has gotten better for most Americans since the 1950s. We have achieved what our grandparents or great-grandparents could barely dream of, and yet polling data shows that we are no happier than we were back then; 60 percent of Americans feel less well-off than their parents. We have greater prosperity and yet the number of people who consider themselves depressed has dramatically increased—some social scientists say by as much as twenty-fold. We suffer what some have called "abundance denial."

Abundance poses very different psychospiritual questions than scarcity. The question of scarcity is, how do I get what I need to feel happy and secure? The question of abundance is, how do I really know what I need? How do I distinguish between my real needs and my desires? What does enough, or *dayenu*, mean when I have an overwhelming number of choices and manufactured desires for things I didn't even know I wanted, let alone needed? In our culture, wants get converted so quickly into needs that feeling satisfied becomes incredibly elusive. In other words, the question is not, how can I feel grateful for an olive-size amount of food, but how can I feel satisfied when I can have as many olives as I want? That's the *dayenu* challenge for most of us.

There's a daring Hasidic teaching that says Esau was the happiest, most satisfied character in the Bible. Esau, the same guy whose blessing, whose sacred inheritance was stolen by his younger brother? Esau, whose mother betrayed him and whose father didn't stop it from happening? Esau, the hunter who sold his birthright blessing for a pot of lentils? The sages taught that despite it all, Esau still felt blessed. He was happy with his lot and appreciated his own uniqueness. The pot of lentils was enough: When you feel blessed your blessing can't be sold or stolen. When he meets Jacob decades later, Esau greets his brother warmly, saying he has plenty in response to his brother's offers of gifts. For Jacob, not even the blessing had been enough: He wanted the more beautiful sister as his wife, a larger share of the herd from his father-in-law. Jacob could never have appreciated the simple pleasure of a pot of lentils; he could only see it as a vehicle to something else—to being more and more blessed. Yet at that chance meeting in the desert, both brothers in fact seem happy and blessed. Together, the twins seem to embody *dayenu*—wanting it all and finding enough.

Friends have sometimes described me as one of the happiest people they've ever met. "Lucky in life" is a phrase I've heard a lot. "Lucky" is the secular word for "blessed." I guess I've been a little like Esau. For most of my life I've barely ever planned anything, and I had very few dreams or visions for the future. I've missed planes because I got into engaging conversations with people I'd just met in the airport. I worked hard and trusted that I'd be rewarded with success without worrying too much about it. Happiness was to be found in the moment and things would always work out.

Then one day I was unexpectedly named president of the organization I still run today. And so I ran the Center for Learning and Leadership the same way I lived my life—by the seat of my pants. I coasted from one great adventure to another. I dealt with issues as they came up and tried to be kind and encouraging to the people who worked for me.

Then, one evening, a major donor asked me with a slight edge in his voice, "So what do you want to do with your life? What's your vision for the organization?" He was a millionaire many times over and had become very accomplished at a young age. I felt defensive, to say the least. Crazy as it might seem, it was the first time I'd ever been asked those questions, and it was the first time I can remember not having an answer. I was really uncomfortable. And then I got annoyed. How could he put me on the spot that way? Besides, the organization was growing, financially secure, and programmatically interesting. I offered some deflective answer, but over the next few weeks his question haunted me.

"What was my dream? What was I really up to?" Suddenly, enough wasn't enough.

Within a few weeks, and after much thinking—and some of the most interesting conversations with friends and colleagues I had ever had—I came back to my supporter with an answer. I had a really big dream and it felt great. I decided that the mission of the organization would be to take Jewish wisdom public, to offer a philosophical, spiritual, and psychological life-approach that could benefit everyone, whether they were Jewish or not. My job was no longer just a gig, but a tremendous opportunity. I saw my Promised Land and I was hell-bent on getting there. Family and colleagues barely recognized me as I worked late into the night, pushing them and myself to come up with a strategic plan for a center that would nourish wisdom and imagination. We accomplished so much over those many months. It was such an amazing time. Until it wasn't.

I found myself running from meeting to meeting, traveling constantly, accomplishing one goal and quickly moving on to the next. Instead of talking to people for sheer pleasure and engagement, I began to think about what I needed from them, or in what possible way they could help me and my organization accomplish our goals. In other words, people in my life became means to manifest my dream—a little like Jacob. One day, a very close friend asked me, with genuine love and hurt in his voice, why I rarely returned his calls, and when I did, it was often days later. I was always apologetic, but I wasn't really there. There was a time when I could sit with a stranger for three hours and now I was barely in touch with someone I cared about so much. I remember feeling so sad after that call. I had gone from a person happy in the present to one who lived obsessed in the anticipation of the future I was working to create.

I have come to realize that when I feel this kind of sadness about being neither here nor there, it means that I have either invested too much in transitory moments or put too much stock in the future. Most of us have a predisposition one way or the other. We're either planners or moment-to-moment people. Now I'd gone full-steam both ways. Neither had worked, and it hurt.

In the end I walked away with a renewed understanding of life; sadness often enlightens. I saw that I could strive for my goals—yearn for the Promised Land—and still savor every step of the way. I could be fiercely in the present and be fiercely building for the future. If I did, I'd have a better chance of both being happy and reaching my goals. Yet I'd never get the balance just right. There'd be many more agonizing times of disappointment and always a lot more work to do. But there also could be a kind of sweet agony. *Dayenu* is a way to discipline the dream without suppressing it. It enables us to live with great visions, and love the journey. There's no great answer but a lot of little answers. If you listen they all just might add up. And even if they don't, sing "*Dayenu.*"

Holidays, like songs and stories, are reframing practices—ways to contextualize our deep yearnings in the memory of a historical or mythical event, which in turn gives meaning and depth to our lives. The festival of Succot, which falls in the autumn, is also called the "The Holiday of Rejoicing." Originally a celebration of the harvest, it is an eight-day thanksgiving. It's a celebration of abundance, plentitude, and fullness. And yet it also recalls those difficult forty years the Israelites spent wandering in the desert; all the longing and the yearning; all the waiting to get in to the Promised Land. Unlike the American version of Thanksgiving, Succot celebrates the pilgrimage rather than the arrival. It's a weeklong party designed to expand our experience of happiness.

Succot is a journey practice—a retreat in the wilderness, both figuratively and literally. A structure called a Succah is built, in which family and guests eat their meals: It's a reproduction of the temporary shelters built by the Israelites in the desert. The Succah is made of canvas or thin wooden boards, strong enough to survive the basic elements but not able to withstand winds of unusual force. The roof of wooden slats is not nailed down and is open enough to allow the rain to fall in and to see the stars in the sky. There's a playfulness in building a temporary structure in the backyard that, for a week, we move into—or at least eat our meals in. It's like when you were a kid sleeping in a tent or tree house in your own yard, and you see the lights of your home, your bedroom window above, and you feel the excitement of being both safe and exposed.

The Succah teaches that we are neither as vulnerable as we fear nor as invulnerable as we fantasize. It's a way to reenvision our own messy, incomplete journeys, to celebrate the daily strain of pursuing our dreams. What does it mean to celebrate the forty-year journey—a metaphor for the journey that is our lifetime? As my teacher, Rabbi Irving "Yitz" Greenberg, offers: "It is celebrating pitching tents and taking them down over the course of 14,600 days. It honors forty-three thousand meals prepared on the desert trek; the cleanups, the washing of utensils . . . the gritty days of marching." If we can celebrate all of that we will be happy. The question is, can we enjoy the long strange trip? to quote the Grateful Dead. Like *dayenu*, Succot is about the joy of appreciating every step of the journey, even relishing those uncertain times before our feet hit the ground. It's a celebration of how we lose and find our way over and over again.

> Our journeys are messy and incomplete, but if we can still celebrate the daily strain of pursuing our dreams we can be happy.

It also teaches that we only can be as happy as we ourselves believe we can be—we can't reach a Promised Land that we're too afraid to envision. But the only Promised Land worth envisioning is the one that we can never reach. It only took the Israelites two years to get to the borders of the Promised Land, but they were too frightened to go in. "We looked like grasshoppers to ourselves, and so we must have looked to them," said the spies sent ahead to investigate the enemy inhabitants. The people saw themselves as weak and small, and so they were not able to enter for thirty-eight more years. Aren't most of us afraid to dream big? It also could be that a richer, more expansive happiness awaited the people back in the desert. If they'd entered the land they'd have lost the promise. There was so much more to be discovered in the wilderness, in the *midbar*. They knew that wandering is the source of wonder. In yearning there is so much fullness.

The first words God says to Abraham, the first biblical wanderer, are "go to yourself." Abraham lived an edgy, painful life: years of childlessness; then the loss of one son and almost the second; constant doubt in his God, and conflict with his wife; and a nagging feeling of always wanting more, of never having enough. Yet as he breathed his last breaths, we are told that he was "old, good, full, and contented." Similarly, the great philosopher Ludwig Wittgenstein is often described as being sad and isolated a good part of the time. He struggled with new interpretations and visions that changed the way we understand reality, yet he seemed never to be happy with himself. On a typical day of teaching, he could be heard mumbling to himself, "Wittgenstein, what a terrible teacher you are." Yet his last reported words as he lay dying were, "Tell them it's been wonderful!"

That kind of fullness and satisfaction, of knowing you led a good life, can only come after having lived a lifetime of questioning and yearning—after many dances of happiness and sadness; many moments of *dayenu*. Maybe that's why the Jewish tradition celebrates the anniversary of someone's death, but not their birth. The only character in the Bible to celebrate a birthday is the Pharaoh, who would never know what it means to feel full and good.

I've always marveled at how we Americans go to such great pains to fill our children's arms with presents and their stomachs with delights one day a year. Perhaps we do so because attaining that sense of authentic contentment is simply not possible, and yet we yearn for it. What if birthdays instead became practices to help us appreciate the steps along the way? What if they were days of storytelling and mythmaking; of introspection and (more than one) song? What if we sang *dayenu* about the last year and the next one? What if what we meant by wishing *happy* birthday is that all that *happens* will be cause for a deeper joy; that the person will live intensely and tap into the energy current of life; that she take chances and not be afraid to yearn? What if we made a practice of reframing and reinterpreting our own lives every year; celebrating our own personal harvest day? Then, just maybe, we'd feel contented at the end of it all. And that would be enough. *Dayenu*.

YEARNING FOR
TRANSCENDENCE

DYING FOR LIFE

ONCE, WHEN I WAS TRAVELING, I WENT INTO ONE OF those gadget stores in the airport. They had something they called a "personal life clock," and I was intrigued. I entered my age, my gender, and a few other facts, and it made some kind of statistical computation that told me how many hours, minutes, and seconds I had left to live. As the clock went to work computing the data, it made an unnerving *tick-tock*. I literally could hear my life ticking away. At some point I had to turn away, and when I came back to the clock ten minutes later, I remember there were about 300,000 hours left in my life, which seemed not only incomprehensible but really disturbing. It took me a few days to recover, and it still makes me anxious whenever I think of it.

I didn't feel so different than Rav Nachman, who the Talmud tells us showed himself to his friend Rava in a dream after Rav Nachman died. Rava asked him, "Was death painful?" Rav Nachman replied, "It was as painless as lifting a hair from a cup of milk. But were the Holy One to say to me, 'You may return to that world where you were before,' I would not wish to do it. The fear of death is too great." Or, as Woody Allen said, "I don't mind dying. I just don't want to be there when it happens."

> Dying, and being with those who are dying, is the ultimate challenge and the greatest spiritual opportunity.

The mystery of death is always there in the background, an ever-present anxiety that most of the time we effectively deny or push aside in order to live our daily lives. And then inevitably we're forced to confront the reality of our own or a loved one's death. Or perhaps we aren't even given the time to say good-bye to someone we care about. Either way, our fear and panic, along with our grief, surface in Technicolor.

Every wisdom system until the modern period has taught that dying and being with those who are dying is the ultimate challenge and the greatest spiritual opportunity. As Rabbi Jack Reimer says, "No one can claim to be wise about life whose wisdom does not include a relationship to death." Whether we are facing our own death or confronting the death of a loved one, there are a host of tensions that revolve around this mystery, and we can gain understanding by grappling with them. When we're faced with serious or terminal illness, we have the chance to decide whether to fight fiercely for life or surrender peacefully to death. We wonder when is the right time to let go, to prepare to die, to say good-bye. If we're a loved one, we agonize over whether to work toward closure and allow things to take their course or use every medical means necessary to keep the person alive, hoping a cure is possible. To paraphrase Dylan Thomas, will we rage against the dying of the light or go gently into that good night?

We always need to ask ourselves whether living as long as possible is the right option. I have come to trust the wisdom of the dying person. I have seen people fight fiercely for life and literally come back from comas; live years beyond the terminal prognosis given to them; gain time no one could have expected, while somehow maintaining quality of life. I also have seen people who, unable to let go, died with incredible anxiousness and lack of peace. Others seem to surrender to death when those around them felt they were giving up before their time. Still others let go beautifully, taking the time that might otherwise be spent resisting death to settle their relationships, make peace with their lives, and then die with such little regret that all I can do is marvel and learn.

When to fight and when to let go; how hard to resist and how easily to surrender: There are no rules about dying. When society tries to determine a "one-size-fits-all" rule we wind up with Doctor Kevorkian on the one side and Terri Schiavo–type controversies on the other. We turn what ought to be a deeply personal and familial time into a public spectacle and an ideological battle. Death trumps all ideologies, and anyone or any system that thinks it is 100 percent right has allowed their fear to reach a dangerous extreme and is therefore disrespectful to the sanctity of life and the intimacy of death.

In my own life there have been few moments more frightening, more life-affirming, and more enlightening than holding the hands of people who are about to find out what happens next. Sam Goldenhersch was my first rebbe of death. I was a new rabbi, and he was one of the first people with whom I went through the process of dying. Sam was a gruff, hard-nosed building contractor in his sixties. He had a strong personality, a loud booming voice, and he was no lover of rabbis, rebuking anything that smacked of the spiritual. But he was a friend whose challenging, confrontational personality kept me on my toes.

It was so painful to watch his diabetes slowly kill him, and to see how much severe pain he was in. Over a couple of years he lost one limb after another as he went in and out of the hospital for amputations. He told me there was no way he would give up; not until there was nothing left—no toes, no feet, no legs—no matter how much it hurt.

Every time I saw him, I felt more depressed and frightened. Of course, as a spiritual leader, "I knew better" than Sam: If he would just stop fighting and let go he would be so much happier. It was inevitable, and he needed to face it. But there was no taking him on: His strength and resolve were palpable, even when he was confined to his bed. I would visit on Friday afternoon before the Sabbath when I made my rounds in the hospital, usually making small talk and gauging his frame of both body and mind before I left for the weekend. I felt so helpless; I wanted to do something. Yet as things got worse, his gruffness and bitterness began to put me off. When I'd ask how he was doing, he'd answer with some variation of, "How would you be if they took you apart limb-by-limb?" He didn't make visiting easy.

One day he was in a particularly prickly mood, and after my ritualistic brief visit I wished him Shabbat Shalom and got up to leave, to which he said, "Leaving so soon?" I asked him what he meant by the question. "Did you ever notice how you conveniently visit when you have to be home in time for the Sabbath?" Trying to keep it light, I joked, "Sam, you just think that because you're so tough you don't need the Sabbath." He laughed and said, "That may be, but I smell fear. I think you are more afraid of what is going on with me than I am, which means you must be pretty frightened. Why don't you sit down?"

Over the next three months, I had some of the most uncomfortable encounters of my life. Sam taught me that waves of sadness, pity, aversion, fear, and, yes, even bitterness can be healthy parts of dying. He taught me about the subtle and not-so-subtle ways many of us distance ourselves from death in order to protect ourselves; that there is no model of a "good death" which can be imposed from the outside. Sam was honest and transparent. Every time a different part of his body would be amputated he would urge me to look at the stump; and then, in what seemed to be a strange mix of courage, disgust, pride, and resistance, he'd challenge me to physically touch the area. I didn't conquer my fears but I learned to dwell in them.

Sam never became any calmer about dying—no theology or attempts to make things better were going to work for him. He taught me that fear and fighting can be as spiritual and life-affirming as serenity and acceptance. I learned that being with the dying is not about pious answers. Sam had been a tough guy all his life, and he was going to die a tough guy. His death was as enlightening as the most peaceful, calm, and gentle deaths that I have been honored to witness.

About two weeks before Sam died, I went to visit him. When I walked into his room his wife was there. The room had that acrid smell hospitals can have when death is close; it made my stomach churn. Sam was barely conscious, and now it was painful even to look at him. A few months earlier I would have mumbled a prayer, said something appropriately comforting to his wife, and then left. Instead I stood at the bedside and looked at Sam for the longest time. I don't know what came over me but I found myself putting my hands on his face, leaning over, and planting a big kiss right on his mouth. His wife started laughing and said, "Irwin, if Sam knew you'd kissed him on the mouth he'd die!" Then we both began to cry.

There is great courage in letting go and great courage in fighting. And, of course, there are often many stages people go through during the process of dying: denial, anger, bargaining, despair, and acceptance. But they are not clean or linear. They bleed into each other and double back on each other and mask each other. Our feelings about death are moment truths; they change and evolve. Coping with death is really the ultimate humility practice, and when we can hold the various truths and experiences together, there's so much insight to be gained. There are moments of acceptance and moments of resistance; moments of fighting and moments of softening.

> **Our feelings about death are moment truths that change and evolve: moments of acceptance and moments of resistance, moments of fighting and moments of softening.**

Here's an ancient story, an example of how to hold truths together even in the midst of dying. It's the story about the death of Moses. The Bible tells us that Moses died on a mountain overlooking the Promised Land as the next generation of Israelites crossed the border. He was one hundred and twenty years old at the time, and what a life! He'd freed his people from slavery and then spent forty years in the desert as their leader. How could it be that he wouldn't even get to enter the land he spent decades yearning for! The rabbinic sages describe a scene that is far from peaceful. Moses fights death fiercely. He argues with God about the injustice of it all, writhing as he lies there, lashing out and cursing. "How can you do this to me? You've got to let me live long enough to enter the land!"

In the end Moses accepts his death and, as sages imagine, dies with a kiss from God. He faces his death as all of us must, but not before he fights like crazy. There's never a perfect time to die. There's no such thing as dying when it's your time. Moses isn't over the hill; he's on top of the mountain. He knows full well that his project isn't over, and it hurts like hell. What an amazing teaching this is. Dream big but don't complete the project. If your dream comes true you've dreamed too small. It's enough to look over a mountainside and get a glimpse of what comes next, and see how you've contributed to the unfolding of the story. What vision of afterlife can beat that?

The story of Moses's death gave me a rich context for dealing with the death of my own Moses, one of the most influential teachers I'd ever had. Rabbi Hyman was truly larger than life, with wild red hair, a piercing voice, and always a playful look in his eye. And he had such a mastery over Jewish wisdom. All of us who'd experienced his teaching loved him deeply. Midway into our second year in his Talmud class, Rabbi Hyman was diagnosed with brain cancer, and he quickly declined. One day, a group of us went to visit him in his home. The scene was so unreal. His kids were playing outside, yelling and laughing as they threw a ball around: They were so young and couldn't have known or understood how sick their father was. Their voices were so full of life.

When I first saw him, I couldn't help but gasp. His head was swollen almost beyond recognition, and he lay very still in his bed. One of us began to cry and then we all did. I can't remember who said, "You have to fight this. How can it be that you'll never teach again?" He seemed so accepting and resigned—and we couldn't help it; it made us angry. Rabbi Hyman looked up at us and that twinkle was still there. "What do you mean?" he asked. "Now I'll be able to study with God; to see it all; to finally understand all that I've ever tried to teach." I said, "That's not good enough! How can we keep going without you?" And he turned to me with a raised eyebrow and said, "Leave you? Where could I go?" As we left his room, I imagined that, like Moses, he was watching the next generation continue the journey and for him there was no greater comfort.

In the Bible the word for where you go after death is *sheol*, which comes from the same root as the word for "question." When we or a loved one is dying some of us who'd never contemplated an afterlife inevitably wonder, "Could this be all there is?" "Is there a spirit that lives on?" Even if we don't have these questions, we begin to struggle at a whole other level with our own mortality and that of others we love. We may fight against the inevitability of death or seek new ways of looking at it. Either way, death begins to inform our lives. And the yearning to understand, even transcend the finality of death, to find meaning in loss, is awakened at a whole other level. This yearning is one of the most noble, defining aspects of our humanness.

Every culture and wisdom tradition offers insights in an attempt to fill the vacuum of not-knowing. None of them resolves the mystery, but each offers moment truths that can help us through the process. In America, there's a polarity between the modern, rationalist, scientific view that death is final and this life is all there is, and every single spiritual and religious tradition that claims this life is not the end, that there is something after life.

The perception that death is final has generated a full-scale assault on illness in the last century: It's doubled life spans and dramatically lowered infant mortality. The starkness of this view has created a fierce desire to push back death. If you are a grandparent or great-grandparent who is in good health and enjoys your grandchild, you have the tremendous advances in medicine to thank. This contemporary view of the finality of death allows us to feel the preciousness of life. The scarcer something is, the more valuable it becomes—and nothing is more valuable than time.

The downside of the modern, scientific view is that it can create extreme fear—even paranoia. Death becomes the enemy and so we sanitize it, and are overly youth-conscious and preoccupied with making sure people do not take dying into their own hands. More than half our national health budget goes to the last months of life when little or nothing can be done, and that diverts resources from health care that could enhance people's lives or ease them into death. As Woody Allen said, "In America, we've decided that death is optional."

On the other side are the varieties of afterlife intuitions—immortality of the soul, the next world, resurrection, reincarnation, rebirth, heaven, hell, the bardos, Kabbalistic mansions. These mystical perceptions are based on centuries of intuitions and practices that teach that there's more than just this life, and they can mitigate our fear, providing comfort and hope. Soul, Atman, Ruach—there are so many names for the part of us that lives on or that never was born and, therefore, can never die.

There's a belief in many Eastern traditions that like the self, death is an illusion, so what is there to fear? Life isn't about beginnings and endings; it's an endless cycle of unfolding and evolution. We return to the ocean of all that is. This certainly puts things in perspective: In fourteen billion years of unfolding, my individual self is either a blip or a microcosm and it shouldn't be overdramatized. The ancient Greeks taught that there is a spirit that continues after death. Christianity was greatly influenced by this idea, and took it one step further to say that resurrection is possible and that there's a heaven, a world beyond ours where we live on in an elevated state. Islam shares this teaching, as does Judaism beginning in the third century when it was heavily influenced by Christian beliefs.

In response to the stark, modern view, more traditional views of heaven and an afterlife are returning as Christian evangelical and fundamentalist communities have grown in numbers. At the same time so-called New Age beliefs have grown in popularity. There's the relocation theory—we are just going to a better place—and the reincarnation theory—we will be coming back. Both Christianity and New Age teachings share the belief that the soul is immortal. Some believe the dead remain as spirits or souls lingering in the corners of our lives.

I've seen that those who are open to the idea of an afterlife can experience new levels of intimacy, new modes of connecting, a softening of the seemingly hard boundary between life and death. But the same afterlife intuitions that can generate hope, comfort, and meaning can lead to resignation and a dismissal of this world. And even more hurtful, many believers deal with the uncertainty inherent in any afterlife teaching by turning it into a system

The yearning for forever is an essential part of being human.

of rigid reward and punishment: who is entitled to an afterlife and who isn't.

Can we really allow ourselves to believe any of it? Voltaire said, "It would be no more surprising to be born twice than born once." After all, to even be here to ask these questions is a wild result of billions of consecutive throws of the genetic dice. What are the odds that we as unique individuals even exist? The finality of death and the afterlife are both moment truths. The challenge is to know when to embrace which and how lightly.

What guidelines can we use to determine where along the continuum we ought to be? First we need to leave ourselves open to the ever-shifting quality of the truths about what happens after we die. The tensions, mysteries, and ignorance surrounding death are actually invitations to seek unfolding levels of insight and trust our own experience. If we hold on too tightly to any one view of death, we risk losing out on the intuitions of the others. The poet Rilke wrote that we should "try to love the questions themselves . . . live everything . . . live into the answers."

After close to three decades of sitting with people who are dying, as well as their families, I have become very pragmatic. Our responses to death do not have to be intellectually sound or consistent. Rather, they need to be existentially comforting and enlightening. My criteria are simple. Does your view create less terror around death? Does your view support you as you fight for life until you're ready to let go? Does it allow you and those around you to be more honest, more hopeful, calmer, more compassionate, more loving, and even more joyful? Does it allow you to grasp the truth of the Ecclesiastes poet who wrote that there's a time for birth and a time for death; to feel the intensity and beauty of the cycle of life?

It's important to remember that all perceptions of the afterlife or no-afterlife grow out of genuine interior experiences. They can be life-changing as well as life-affirming. When you remain open, they can really take you by surprise. My dead grandfather once came back to me in a waking dream; I couldn't believe it when I heard his voice, but there it was, clear as a bell. He had always been really tough on me, pushing me to follow a conventional path to success and giving me such a hard time about my long hair. He'd often ask me, "Who do you think you are, Jesus?" Before he died I'd become an assistant rabbi at a major congregation, and I'd finally made him happy. But in my vision, or waking dream, he urged me to leave that very job to take a far more risky, unconventional one I'd been contemplating and was very conflicted about. It's not important whether or not this was a projection or really happened; the experience was real and it comforted me deeply. More than that, it released me to do something I needed and wanted to do.

Another time I attended a funeral of the mother of a student of mine. She had died suddenly of a stroke, and there was so much sorrow, so much loss and hurt in the room. As the casket was carried out of the funeral home, a flower fell loose from the spray on top; it landed at the feet of the husband, who then burst into loud sobs. At the gathering afterward, it seemed like everyone was talking about that flower. I learned that the husband had brought his wife a bouquet every Friday night for decades. For the husband, that single flower was his wife's loving good-bye; her hand reaching out from beyond.

The yearning for forever is an essential part of being human. The Adam and Eve story is, in part, a teaching about keeping the questions about death alive. There are two trees that are off limits: The tree of knowledge of good and bad is one; the tree of knowledge of life and death is the other. One of God's motivations for banishing Adam and Eve is the fear that they might now eat of the other tree and therefore be immortal. To be human is to die and to know it. If they had eaten from the Tree of Life, Adam and Eve would have lost their very humanity. Of course they had to leave that temptation behind! And yet they, like us, always will long to taste that fruit, to live forever. Perhaps this is why the first thing the couple does after leaving the garden is to make love and have a child; love can transcend death.

Jewish wisdom holds together many of the tensions surrounding death. It encourages us to fight fiercely and to let go; to face the finality

of death and then to hope the person lives on. The tradition understands that death is often tougher on those who are left to live on without a loved one than it is on the dying. It teaches that for survivors,
death causes a profound collapse of meaning that no belief system in
the world can mitigate. Whatever intuition we embrace about what
happens to our loved one next, there's no escaping the immediate devastation of death. Anything we say or do that doesn't acknowledge this
reality simply isn't true to our experience. Jewish wisdom invites us to
address the death directly, to embrace the finality of loss fully. If we can
face the stark, tragic reality of death, eventually we will heal.

In the Jewish tradition there are no sayings like "passed away" or "final resting place." We are to call death by its real name—feel the blow,
sink into the loss, let it subsume us—and we're to do so when it's most
painful and intense: in the first twenty-four hours after someone dies.
We need to deepen, rather than minimize, our sorrow and express our
anger. Only then can we hope for reconciliation and return. As psychologist Joyce Slochower wrote, "Jewish wisdom provides a structure to
address death, not to control or contain it, but to express and experience it as fully as possible."

Our first job is to attend to the dead. The body is buried in a plain
pine box within those twenty-four hours. Death makes no distinction
between rich and poor. There's no embalming, no making things beautiful or lifelike; the body is to be left in its natural state. We are meant to
see death, feel it, no pretending. "From dust to dust" is considered a sacred experience. We are to be buried so that we can return to the earth,
and we're to be dressed in a simple white cloak, with no adornments. As
Job said, "Naked did I emerge from my mother's womb. And naked
shall I return there."

There's a name for the twenty-four hours just after a death and before the burial: *aninut*, which means "between." Many people are surprised when I tell them that during this time we are not supposed to
pray. This is not the time for meaning-making, rationalizing, or making
sense of the experience. One would think the opposite; that one should

call upon a larger power as a source of comfort, a way to put death in a larger context. But when we're in the grip of such utter despair, there's no use pretending there's a larger plan, a reason, or a purpose. When your life has been completely shattered, there's no way to imagine wholeness, and trying to do so can short-circuit our grief.

Before the burial we are invited to honor the dead. During the funeral someone close to the deceased is to stand before those gathered and create a narrative of the person's life. The most common word for this is "eulogy," which is Greek for "good words" or "praise." The word in Hebrew is *hesped*, which has the same root as the word for mourning. Once again, there's no glossing over the difficult feelings associated with death. You are meant to make everyone in the room cry. And there's to be no sugar-coating; rather we're to capture the person's complexity and richness. Part of honoring someone is to acknowledge their messiness. Speak of the full range of feelings around the loss; show your rawness and vulnerability. Be honest. This allows us to preserve a relationship with the dead person in all its complexity. We are reconstructing the person so that they can live on in our hearts.

I remember a *hesped* given by a woman in her twenties about her father, who'd died in his early fifties, far too young. Her grief was palpable and she spoke of how he would never meet her future children, be at her wedding, or see her succeed and grow up. She said that at every important moment in her life from then on she would feel a cold wind blow through the hole that was once him. She spoke of his love and caring, but she also spoke of his perfectionism, how he drove his children too hard; his obsessive need for everything to be right. Like his love, this drive would always be part of her. He'd always be whispering in her ear, "You can do better."

At the gravesite there are a number of practices designed to help us integrate the finality of death and begin to find comfort from community. The Hebrew word for "funeral"—*levaya*—means "accompaniment"; people surround us as we face our loss and remember our loved one. This is the moment when we can pray or begin to try to make sense of the loss. The name for God that is evoked at the gravesite is *Rachamim,* which means "compassion" and comes from the same Hebrew root as "womb." This is meant to remind us of the compassion we will eventually feel toward ourselves and the deceased, even though it is likely not accessible to us now. The anger and raw grief is still very much with us; we are still wrestling with finality. There's a wrenching and cathartic practice of ripping one's clothes at the gravesite to physically express one's broken heart and the feeling of being ripped away from a loved one.

The *Kaddish,* the mourner's prayer, also is first said at the gravesite. *Kaddish* is a powerful and complex meditation. It has a hypnotic rhythm that some have described as being a kind of rocking, like a lullaby. The entire prayer praises God: "*Yitgadal ve-yitkadash, Shmei rabbah*—May Thy Name be magnified and holy. . . ." But why would we praise God when we're memorializing the dead, and not mention death at all?

Israeli Nobel laureate S.Y. Agnon said that the prayer is not *to* God but *for* God; it's a way to reconstruct God, to rebuild reality after it's been torn asunder. God has been diminished by this death, and so needs to be magnified. It's a practice for building back a sense of meaning in the face of devastation. Ancient mystics taught that saying *Kaddish* also helps settle the dead or help them get where they next need to be. Translating the mystical into the psychological, it's a transition prayer for us to figure out how we're going to continue our relationship with the person in this new reality. Adult children of the deceased say *Kaddish* three times a day for eleven months. That's how devastating that loss is; parents are the only people who cannot be replaced. If you are the spouse or other close relative, you say *Kaddish* for thirty days. We say it so many times and for so long because reconstructing and remembering are practiced one day at a time.

At the gravesite, adult children and spouses of the deceased shovel dirt into the grave themselves. The sound of the dirt hitting the coffin is so raw and powerful: a thud that you will never forget. The finality is almost unbearable. I attended the funeral of the father of four adult daughters less than a year after the death of their mother. The eldest daughter threw the first shovel of dirt and then the four of them went into a kind of trance. They threw shovelful after shovelful into the grave; each taking a turn and then all doing it together in a kind of frenzy, crying out and sobbing. Many people had to turn away, so intimate and overwhelming was this scene.

During the week after the burial, the finality-reconstruction dance continues for the mourners. There is an intensive seven-day mourning retreat; an immersion course in the experience of loss and rebuilding life. It took God seven days to create the world, and every one of us is a world, one that never was before and never will be again. Mourning is a form of re-creation. These seven days are called *Shiva* (which literally means seven), and this ritual holds so many different truths together: The grief is profound and the remembering is sweet. During this time mourners stay home and family and friends visit them bearing both food and memories of the deceased.

It's almost as if you're a guest in your own home, because your house really isn't the same anymore. People are there to comfort you and feed you and there's no indulging in idle chatter. Visitors are not supposed to speak to the bereaved until he or she speaks to them first. After all, there's really nothing to say in the face of the void that death creates. Yet we are invited to tell stories about the dead, to help create the narrative of the person's life, to give them a life after life. These stories expand and deepen the memory of the person for the mourners as well. A friend of mine described how moving it was to hear former and current students of his mother, who'd been a professor, come up to him at the *Shiva* and tell him what an amazing teacher she'd been; how she made jokes, asked questions in a Socratic style, always kept them on their toes. He'd never seen her teach and now this, too, was one of his memories. He told me how he'd gotten to know his mother in some ways even better after she died.

Shiva is also a period in which to go inward. The external things of life fade into the background as virtually every aspect of ordinary behavior is transformed. Traditionally, mourners don't bathe or shave or change clothing every day; they don't use cosmetics or fix their hair; they don't do household tasks or any work. They're not to worry about social propriety or obligation or be held accountable for anything they say. There is a practice of covering up the mirrors in one's home. Seeing our image in this state can be distracting and upsetting. We are literally not our selves. A mourner sits on a low stool rather than chairs as an expression of how low they feel. A memorial candle burns for the whole week, a reminder that the light in each person lives on in another form, and it's up to us to find the place where it shines. The traditional parting greeting is "May you be comforted among other mourners." It is a way of saying that you are not alone—everyone on the planet is going through, has gone through, or will go through this very process.

When *Shiva* ends, we're expected to return to our regular lives, but mourning is far from over. There are two times we can die, and the second time is the most devastating: It's when we are forgotten. One way a person can be remembered is when loved ones do acts of loving kindness or service in their name. Acts of generosity and compassion literally make the memory of the person a blessing to the world. Yet remembering, like mourning, is a continuous, conscious practice, not a one-time act. We return to the gravesite every year on the anniversary of the person's death, and there's a tradition of placing rocks on the monument. Flowers are not part of the Jewish practice, as there's a feeling that they are ephemeral and themselves die. Therefore they don't speak to the memory that never goes away. Rocks speak to the weightiness of the person and the heaviness we feel when we miss them.

And there's literally a cycle of remembering. Four times a year on different holidays—Yom Kippur, Succot, Passover, and Shavuot—we say special memorial prayers called *yizkor*, which means "remember." When we summon up the memory, meditate, or visualize a person in different seasons, we see the person differently. As we grow and change, as the year unfolds, there are new memories as feelings surface and others soften. Some people try to remember their loved one in the spirit of the holiday being celebrated. At Passover we free ourselves from memories that enslave us; on Succot, the harvest festival, we focus on gratitude and the joy they brought us; at Shavuot, which celebrates the giving of the Torah, we remember the wisdom they gave us; on Yom Kippur, we think about what we'd like them to forgive us for or what we need to forgive them for. All year long we are enriching and expanding our memories, integrating the person into the rhythms of our lives, into our happy times and our sad ones.

Yom Kippur is in part a way to enact our own death in order to imbue our lives with meaning. The opening practice of Yom Kippur is freeing ourselves from all our promises and obligations: "They shall be null and void" for the next twenty-five hours. We imagine ourselves as no longer married, a parent, holding a job that we're responsible for. These parts of our selves die and we're left alone to contemplate what life would be like without its usual trappings and delights. Who are we without them? There's the sense that we are reassessing everything from our deathbed. What an opportunity! And the next evening we are, in a sense, born again. We accept our obligations back, hopefully at a higher or deeper level of appreciation and meaning. Or we recognize that we need to let go of obligations that have distorted or confined us.

It's no accident that one of the bestselling novels ever is Mitch Albom's *The Five People You Meet in Heaven*. It speaks so powerfully to our yearning for transcendence. The book imagines that heaven is about revisiting your life from a larger, more expansive perspective. Heaven means that we get to have a take on our life: It really did make sense; more sense than I knew. There's no ultimate happy ending—we can't make everything right—but the most painful events have a meaning we never could have understood at the time. There's also the message that all of us can have heaven right here. Heaven is those moments when we can hold it all together, even when it's almost too much to bear.

There is no way to know how we will be when it is time for us to die. Plato, on his deathbed, was asked by his students for one final piece of wisdom. He said, "Practice dying." A second-century mystic sage put it this way: "Repent one day before your death." Of course none of us can really know when our time will come, but when that time does come, will we be ready? It all depends on how we are living right here, right now in this very moment, which could be our last. Almost every day, we have the opportunities to embrace life more fully, to be free from pretense, to do the right thing for the right reasons. But we often put things off, thinking we still have time.

> To be ready to die, we have to be ready to live.

Whatever your theory of death, the ultimate test is, does it help you harness death for the service of life? To be ready to die we have to be ready to live—to live with such care and passion that we redeem life from the harshness and absurdity that death imposes. The question becomes less about death than about what kind of person we want to be so we can die that much more fully alive.

MESSIAH-İNG

IMAGINE THAT YOU'RE ABOUT TO BE BORN, AND YOU'RE given a choice about what kind of family you want to be part of. This is a pretty heavy decision for someone who's not even born yet, so it's boiled down to one very simple, almost trivial element. Do you want a family that allows you to believe in the tooth fairy or one that doesn't? "It all comes down to a measly tooth?" you ask. But when you think about it, it's actually not that easy to decide. There are three possible scenarios to choose from.

In the first, you're six years old and you put your first lost tooth under your pillow. When you wake up in the morning, the tooth is gone and there's a dollar there. It's delightful and magical. Wow, there's a fairy that wants my tooth so much that she comes at night and leaves me a gift. The same thing happens with every tooth until you're almost eight and one day you have a sinking feeling that it's all a charade. You go to your mother and tell her not to bother anymore. There is no tooth fairy. She looks disappointed, angry, and even a little afraid; she tells you you're wrong. It's a shame you don't believe in the tooth fairy anymore; now she won't come.

Second scenario. You have the same delightful experience until you're eight; then one day you wake up in the morning and the tooth is still there. You go to your mother and ask her why the tooth fairy didn't come. She says, "Oh, I forgot." With a knowing look and a touch of sadness she tells you you're really too old for that now; it's time to be a big boy. Then she hands you a dollar and says, "Now you get an allowance. You can keep the tooth."

Third scenario. The tooth goes under the pillow; the dollar's always there. It's really great—until one day it isn't. You're eight again, and you get that disappointed feeling of having been duped. You go to your mother and tell her you don't believe in the tooth fairy anymore. And she looks at you knowingly: A few tears are in her eyes; her little boy is growing up. She takes you to her bedroom and pulls a beautiful little box out of the back of her dresser drawer. When she opens it there's every tooth you ever lost. She smiles and touches your face and asks, "What do you think the tooth fairy does with the teeth?" A week later you lose another tooth, and there's a dollar under your pillow.

Whenever I lead people through this visualization I get the same response. Without skipping a beat, everyone chooses the third scenario. "Come on, it's so obvious," someone once said. Oh, really? We live in an age and culture in which our most educated elite sees as real only that which can be proven empirically; everything else is merely an illusion, nonsense, or an opiate for the masses. We may go along with some of that touchy-feely stuff for nostalgia's sake, but then it's time to get real. This is mom number two. At the same time there are a growing number of people in the world who fiercely defend their beliefs in the most literal way and who dismiss all doubters. You won't be included or rewarded if you don't believe. This is mom number one.

So, how many people like mom number three are there? How many of us honestly make the choice on a daily basis to hold two seemingly opposing truths together: tooth fairy and no tooth fairy; the empirical and the magical; the mystical and the pragmatic; the fantastic and the mundane; the idealistic and the realistic; the ordinary and the enchanted. More often than not we come down on one side or the other, sure that the other is hopelessly naïve, chillingly sophisticated, foolishly faithful, or smartly cynical. And yet we yearn for a more expansive view, for the beautiful little box that can contain the

vision and the reality; success and disappointment; the knowledge
and the dream.

On a far grander scale than the tooth fairy, all of us have yearnings, longings, hopes for a time in which suffering—racism, poverty,
disease, war—will be lessened or eliminated; a future in which every
individual is valued, even if we don't intellectually believe that that
time will ever come. The prophet Jeremiah
spoke of "a day when you will have a new
heart," when reason and emotion will teach
the same thing, enabling us always to know
what's right. There'll be no bad or good; no
guilt or merit. Isaiah imagined that someday
we "shall beat swords into plowshares and spears into pruning hooks.
Nation shall not take up sword against nation; they shall never again
know war." He imagined "The wolf shall lie down with the lamb. The
leopard with the kid."

**There isn't a culture or
tradition in the history
of the world that doesn't
have a dream of a world
of peace and goodness.**

There isn't a culture or tradition in the history of the world that
doesn't have such a dream. There's the Jewish end of days when peace
will reign; the Christian second coming when death shall be overcome;
a Marxist utopian vision of economic equality and justice; the American dream of democratic freedom, individual rights, and prosperity;
Samadhi, a state of personal enlightenment and transcendence; and the
scientific belief that reason and technology will perfect the world.
"Messianic" is the name for our greatest hopes for what the world can
be and hasn't yet become. It's no accident that messianic hopes have
tended to arise during dark times. Buddhism emerged out of a particularly chaotic time in Indian history. The Jewish prophetic dream was a
response to the destruction of the first Temple. The Christian tradition
arose during the first century when Rome was subjugating the people of
Israel, and there was tremendous political and social unrest. Commu-
nism took hold in countries where there was abject poverty. And both
the self-help movement and religious fundamentalisms are modern responses to the devaluing of the inner life and the spirit on the one hand,

and the dashed hopes of science, reason, and technology to transform the human condition on the other.

Whatever form it takes, the messianic longing—the yearning for transcendence, salvation, redemption, and transformation—is an integral part of the human experience and can lead to so much good. But with this yearning comes a gripping fear of the inevitable disappointment, disillusionment, and even despair that comes with such profound hope. And this fear can be dangerous—just look at the first two mothers.

They want more than anything else to shield their children from the dashed hopes, injustices, harshness, insecurity, and vulnerability that we all experience—anxieties captured so poignantly in the loss of a child's tooth. They are afraid they can't, and in their fear they hurt their children, however unwittingly. These mothers have precisely the same anxieties but respond in such different ways.

The first mother is holding on for dear life to the literalness of the tooth fairy: a version of an actual messiah. She really wants to protect and love her child. Wouldn't it be great if that pure magic could last forever? Yet in her response to her child's question and doubt, by telling him that if he doesn't believe there will be no more tooth fairy, she is actually denying him that very love, even threatening him with exclusion. She simply can't see that she *is* the tooth fairy. At her most extreme, this mother embodies the sentiments Bruce Springsteen sings about in his song "Devils and Dust," in which he asks whether having God on our side can turn our hearts black and actually kill the things we love.

The upside of the fundamentalist vision can be incredible hope, optimism, and joy for those who believe; just think of the exuberant singing in a Pentecostal church or in a West Bank settlement synagogue. The downside is that one often becomes harsh and severe, demonizing and in extreme cases even destroying nonbelievers. Here's the question for believers: Can we usher in a better world with beliefs that evoke such fierce anger and hurt so many people even if we think those people are wrong?

And then there's mother number two. She wants to love and protect her child just as fiercely. She is trying to spare him years of delusion and help him grow up and mature. In the process, she breaks her child's heart. Yes, the tooth fairy is a projection, and if we forget that, we become stalled, arrested, and uncompromising. But its enchanting, mystical qualities are enlivening. Just because the tooth fairy isn't real doesn't mean she isn't *real*. In this mother's rationalization, she simply can't see that she's the tooth fairy.

One of our holiest yearnings is to probe, to question, to deconstruct. Critical thinking advances our knowledge of how the world works—penicillin does work better than exorcisms. However, the danger of critical thinking is cynicism. We wind up living in a dis-enchanted world, in T. S. Eliot's wasteland. Here are the questions for cynics: Okay, the tooth fairy and the messiah are empirically senseless, even stupid, now what? Is life richer deconstructed? Yes, we have much more knowledge, but do we have more love?

One of our holiest yearnings is to probe, to question, to deconstruct.

As a society, we are trapped between two poles. On the one hand are the true believers, the naïve idealists who in defending the literalness of their traditions undermine their traditions' insights about love, awe, and compassion. And then there are the narrow realists, who in their desire to "know" deny the reality of anything science can't prove. In the process they desacrilize the world, diminishing meaning and depth.

One of the most profound realizations of my academic life occurred during the semester I studied the postmodernist philosopher Paul Ricoeur at Columbia University. When he first explained his idea of "second naïveté," it blew my mind. First naïveté is belief without reflection. We are so enmeshed that we don't see the cultural, historical, literary, social, and psychological forces and experiences out of which our belief arises. There is only one value system, one interpretation, one way that is meaningful and right.

Then there is the stage of critical distancing. We scrutinize and analyze the beliefs we've been taught since childhood: whether it's the parting of the sea or the resurrection. We lose the immediacy of the belief and turn away in what we experience as an act of maturity. Sometimes all hell breaks loose in our families, and we need to break away completely, leaving tradition and spirituality behind.

Then, over time, other disillusionments and disappointments may invite us to a higher level. This is second naïveté. We return to our so-called naïve ideas and experiences with a new kind of openness, seeking a deeper, more intuitive understanding of life. We appreciate similar, or maybe the same, stories, myths, and insights, but sung to a different melody. We reconnect to what we no longer believe in literally, integrating these visions and understandings into our inner life where they enchant and enrich our world.

Second naïveté is naïve because it revivifies our past beliefs rather than pushing them away, and it is second because it requires a high tolerance for contradiction and uncertainty. Second naïveté is an exquisite paradox. It combines the passion of first naïveté with the humility of critical thinking. Skepticism becomes revelatory, and we live "as if." Second naïveté is postdeconstruction: After we take reality apart, we put it back together on our own terms. We recover the outlines of the original inspiration. And in an act of what Catholic theologian Hans Kung calls "sacred retrieval," we reconstruct the yearning, the hope, the dream. Second naïveté is chosen hopefulness.

After all, fiction is not the enemy of reality; fiction informs and expands reality. Even new biological species begin as a kind of fiction, "a spontaneous variation," as Darwin called it, which corresponds to nothing previously found in the world. Innovative cultural and societal ideals begin as fiction as well, and they test and stretch us in new ways. How credible and provable was "all men are created equal" at the time it was first written? How real is it today? Theologian Reinhold Niebuhr wrote, "The truest visions of religion are illusions, which may be partially realized by being believed."

When we dwell in second naïveté, we feel the ongoing yearning for a perfect world while acknowledging the reality that our ideas of perfection are not only ever-changing but unattainable. Picture kids building a sand castle on the beach knowing full well the water will wash it away. They put their all into it and when the big wave comes they run away laughing. Fully and enthusiastically nested in first naïveté, the next day they're right back at it. Second naïveté is the experience of the child grown up. We don't leave sand castle building to our kids. We're right down in the sand with them, helping to build an elaborate, intricate castle that stretches our children's imaginations. When it's washed away, we laugh, too. It's a knowing laugh; even louder and more exuberant than the squeals of thirty years ago. We've absorbed the teaching that building beautiful worlds is about dreaming and creating and being washed away—only then setting out to build something even more amazing.

Second naïveté invites us to live as if the world could be transformed. It's idealistic realism or a realistic idealism. It is what the writer Thomas Moore calls the reenchantment of the world, and what I call being an enchanted skeptic. Second naïveté is the beautiful little box within which the ideal and the real continue to expand and illuminate. Second naïveté is mother number three. She lives her imagination, understanding that there is not a tooth fairy but we can always be "tooth-fairying."

The word for "hope" in Hebrew is *tikvah*, which comes from the same root as the word for "tension." It is the bow just before the arrow is released: poised, suspended, determined, but not there yet. Hope is often seen as pure, liberating, positive, optimistic. But *tikvah* emphasizes the yearning side of hope. *Tikvah* hope is taut, dynamic, and uncertain. Will the arrow hit the target? It's anyone's guess. *Tikvah* is a kind of holy anxiety.

To experience such hope, one must pull oneself into the future but stay fully present. You have to want so much that it hurts and be conscious enough to know that you will heal. *Tikvah* is a disciplined dream; a messy messianism; an incremental revolution. *Tikvah* reminds us that hope itself is a paradox.

The experience of giving birth to a child is the very embodiment of *tikvah.* There's so much risk, so much wonder, so much pain, so much love, so much anxiety, and so many dreams. Will the child be healthy? Will we be able to meet her needs? Who will she be? Nothing can be more messianic than that. This is, in part, why Christmas is such a moving and powerful holiday: The birth of a child is an expression of hope for a new world. And maybe that's why Jewish lore invites Elijah, the mythical prophet and harbinger of the Messiah, to every birth.

There's a practice during the Passover seder of leaving a specially designated glass full of wine in the middle of the table should Elijah come during this holiday so full of hope for freedom. Just after everyone at the table has told and reenacted the story of Exodus, a foreshadowing of final redemption, a child opens the front door for Elijah to usher him in. I remember the experience of this simple ritual being both frightening and magical: He might actually walk in the door and everything would be forever changed. But if I don't open the door, there's no way for him to come in. It's up to me. Of course, the wine doesn't get drunk by a visiting Elijah, and yet we sing songs of redemption. This practice, whimsical as it may seem, infuses dreams of transformation and radical patience. We need to develop a passion for actively waiting, not because we don't have the means to make the Messiah come but because we're always ushering him in the door.

Many people are struck when I tell them that the very people who invented or named the messianic yearning never accepted a single messianic figure, and yet they believed the messianic moment would come. Life is a mobius strip—cyclical and linear at the same time. There are both the repeating patterns of nature and the unfolding of a story. We are part of the constantly evolving, expanding universe, and we are conscious of our role in the universe. We can have an attuned relationship with the cosmos and know that we'll never fully be able to understand or envision all that is. We are here on this planet to strive for completion and perfection, but not to realize them. "We believe in the coming of the Messiah, not the arrival," wrote philosopher Herman Cohen.

The paradox of wanting it all and finding enough is captured so beautifully in jokes about the messianic yearning. Jokes, like Zen koans, hold together more than one truth. They play with contradictions and offer flashes of insight. When you juxtapose hope and reality, faith and skepticism, the effect can be quite funny.

In a small Russian town, the community council decides to pay a poor Jew a ruble a week to sit at the town's entrance and be the first to greet the Messiah when he arrives. The man's brother comes to see him and is puzzled as to why he took such a low-paying job. "It's true," the poor man admits. "The pay is low. But the work is steady."

A man visits a zoo. When he gets to the lion's cage he sees the literal fulfillment of Isaiah's prophecy—a lion and a lamb inside together. Amazed, he calls over an attendant. "How long have you had a lion and a lamb in a cage together?" "Over a year already," the attendant tells him. The man is breathless with awe. "How is this possible?" "It's easy," says the attendant. "Every morning we put in a new lamb."

And then there's Woody Allen's famous prediction: "The lamb and the lion will lie down together, but the lamb won't get much sleep."

If I were to boil these jokes down to one message, it's that lions don't become vegetarians and we'll always have to keep one eye open even when we're sleeping peacefully in that cage.

It may seem contradictory to live in the present and yearn for a transformed future. But isn't this true to our experience? So many of us practice the contemplative and meditative techniques of Eastern traditions, which are so effective at grounding us in the present. And many of us spend so much time thinking about the future, in part because our culture is rooted in monotheistic religions that emphasize progress and more linear visions of the world.

To experience hope, we must pull ourselves into the future, but stay fully in the present.

Living in the present prevents us from living a life deferred. And yearning for a new age keeps us from settling for less than what's possible. There is a power of now and a power of what can be. We'll never fully reconcile these leanings; but we can dance between them.

The messianic longing at its best pulls us into a better future while we remain present in the imperfect moment. There won't be a new garden of Eden, but we can create—however slowly and tediously, with however many false starts and missteps—Eden in our gardens. The messianic yearning is actually a call to love this world more deeply—whether our hopes can be realized or not.

The rabbis imagined that the only holiday that would remain in the messianic age would be Purim. The word "Purim" means "lot" or "luck"—the only holiday in a perfect world is about random luck? I imagine the rabbis sitting around a table doing shots of vodka. One said to the other, "Okay, let's say the Messiah comes. What holiday will we observe—will there be any holidays at all?" One rabbi says Yom Kippur will remain, but the first rabbi says, "What's to atone for in a perfect world?" The next says Passover, and the first says, "Redemption in a redeemed world?" Another says Sabbath: "Won't it be Sabbath every day?" By now they're getting pretty drunk. Suddenly the first rabbi's eyes light up and he shouts out, "Of course! Purim."

On Purim we tell the story of Esther, a kind of comic-book tale of larger-than-life characters, incredible intrigue, and wild twists and turns. Esther is the perfect heroine: a beautiful woman who is chosen by the king to be his wife. She is a Jew, but out of fear keeps her heritage a secret: The name "Esther" means "hidden." Her cousin Mordechai, who serves in the king's court, is open about being Jewish, but his relationship to Esther is not revealed so as to protect her.

Haman, the perfect bad guy, is the king's second in command, and out of hubris demands that those below him bow down to him in deference. When Mordechai refuses to flout his tradition and bow down to Haman, Haman plots to kill him and to annihilate the Jews. Haman orders that lots be cast to decide on a day for the destruction; the word "Purim" means lots. But the intrigue has only just begun. In a series of court and harem intrigues, in which Esther saves the day, the plot is revealed; Haman is hung; good defeats evil by the thread of a hair.

The Purim rituals are playful and raucous. Everyone yells and screams whenever Haman's name is mentioned; a way to drown out evil, which, of course, can never be drowned out. We eat a sweet pastry called hamantasch; a way to make even what is most bitter, sweet. And adults are supposed to get drunk so that they won't know the difference between Haman and Mordechai: between good and evil.

The holiday, hopeful and playful as it is, also has an edge. In the end Mordechai has Haman's job. Is this comforting or frightening? After all, this seems to be a rotating position. There is no end to the cycle. Good and evil will always exist. But don't stop hoping that they won't. Get drunk if you have to, but don't stop hoping.

Purim is about holding it all together—the anxiety, uncertainty, and the yearning for peace and love to prevail; for everything to work out when, really, everything is precarious and perilous. Purim is the only holiday that commemorates a story in which God doesn't appear. There's no apparent divine plan: Life is unpredictable, and danger is everywhere. The story teaches that good and evil are intertwined; Purim is a second naïveté story about the randomness of life and how if we all act consciously, take big risks in spite of it all, we will be "messiah-ing."

I once heard a wonderful story about the Messiah. Like the Purim story it teaches that when we can hold together the messianic yearning with the reality of the present, we'll have an explosive intuition that every one of us has the power to make the Messiah manifest in every moment.

Once upon a time, there was a magnificent monastery that had fallen on hard times. Only a few aging monks remained. One day, the abbot of the monastery met the local rabbi during a walk in the woods. The abbot told the rabbi about the monastery's troubles. The monks had tried everything to attract people but nothing had worked and now the end was coming. "There is only one thing I can tell you," said the rabbi, "and even of that I am not certain. I have on good authority that one of the remaining monks in your monastery may be the Messiah." Amazed and awed, the abbot returned to the monastery to share the rabbi's message. Unclear about what it all could mean, they all continued to go about their business. But during their daily chores, sitting in prayer, walking together through the abbey, the same thought kept arising in each of them. If the Messiah may be one of us, I wonder who it is.

It must be the abbot, they each thought at first—after all, he's our leader. But then they wondered whether it was John, the scholar, because surely the Messiah would have great knowledge. Then there was Thomas, the kindest and most compassionate of the monks. And finally, being human, each of them couldn't help but imagine, "Maybe it's me." In their uncertainty and wonder, they began to look at each other differently. And then they began to treat each other and themselves with more love and respect. Every day their appreciation of and affection for each other grew deeper. Soon a new aura pervaded the monastery. It was so enchanting and loving that people were drawn to visit in great numbers, and some even stayed on. Soon the monastery was thriving beyond the abbot's and the monks' wildest dreams.

The sages teach that if the Messiah comes when we are busy planting a sapling, we should continue our planting. Ignore the Messiah in favor of a small tree? Yes, because the planting of a tree is messianic work; a supreme act of hope about the future. We likely will not see the final result of this planting, the tree in full maturity, or even know if it will survive, yet we plant it anyway. Or maybe, if we're planting the tree, we don't need a messiah.

The planting of a tree is a supreme act of hope in the future.

Franz Kafka said, "The Messiah will come, not on the last day, but on the *very* last." What could this mean? The writer Leibel Fein, a teacher of mine, offers the following parable in explanation: Imagine that we're gathered in a performance hall, our minds hardly focused on the Messiah. Suddenly, he enters and announces himself. His presence is so compelling that all of us instantly recognize his authenticity. Incredibly, it really is the Messiah! Some of us burst into applause, cheering and giving him a standing ovation. Others weep, overcome by the wholly unexpected gift.

But very soon, a few of us begin to get uncomfortable, even angry, and we ask, "For God's sake, where have you been?" The Messiah has no answer. Where, indeed, was he during all the savagery, the tragedy, the annihilations? Ashamed, the Messiah leaves. This was the question he feared. He'd wanted to arrive unnoticed, at a time that this terrible question wouldn't be asked. How can there be such a time? Not on the last day, no. But on the day after the very last day. After the messianic era has already begun. On the day that his coming has been rendered irrelevant.

We have not yet reached that day, and it's never been more important to recognize that. We live in a time of such great possibility and such great danger. Mother number one and mother number two are at war with each other, each having become more convinced of her beliefs and convictions. Hamans are everywhere on the world stage. And tooth fairies and messiahs are being used and abused in an attempt to create a final truth. But mother number three, second naïveté, is also becoming manifest as she becomes more and more necessary. She embodies the faith that all three mothers, all of us, will be able to sit down at one table and share our yearnings, our fears, our hopes, and our plans to build a better world.

And who will be mother number four? She'll be the one who, decades ago, when she was eight years old, walked into her mother's bedroom one morning wearing a sweet and knowing smile. As she leaned over to kiss her mother and stroke her face, she said, "Thank you for the dollar, Mom. Thank you for being the tooth fairy. I love you." That will be the day after the final day.

REPAIRING THE WORLD

ISAAC LURIA WAS A SIXTEENTH-CENTURY MYSTIC WHO
had a wondrous vision about how the world came to be. Mystics are
always looking beneath things, uncovering and imagining hidden patterns and indiscernable realities. Their wisdom takes us to whole new
realms of understanding, extending the metaphors deeper into our psyches, giving us new questions and truths; inviting us to deconstruct and
reenvision our myths and imaginings. There have been countless mystical tellings of the Genesis creation story, and Luria's is among the most
influential; his thinking is an essential component of the radical wisdom tradition of the Kabbalah.

As he read and reread Genesis, imagining and reimagining the
world's beginnings, Luria wondered: How can an all-perfect, all-
encompassing God create something less than itself? The essential paradox of creation, Luria thought, is how the unity of the Divine gave rise
to the multiplicity of this world. How does Oneness make room for
otherness? In other words, how did God make room for life?

Luria imagined that God contracted, became smaller, in order to allow life to unfold. This alone is an amazing image. But Luria went further. He envisioned God as a series of vessels, luminous containers of all
that is. When God contracted, the vessels shattered from the incredible
energy and force, and shards were scattered throughout the universe.
Each of these fragments contained a spark of light, a grain of God.

Luria came up with this teaching after the devastating expulsion of

Jews from Spain. He taught that humankind could heal the Divine, restore God through contemplative practice such as study, prayer, and

**We all have the potential
to raise holy sparks.**

meditation, and through acts of loving kindness. If humankind can gather the shards of
good and evil, love and hate, destruction and
creativity, we can release the sacred sparks within them, dissolve all dualities, and repair all that is. We can make God whole again.

This Kabbalistic call to repair the world by making it whole is called
tikkun olam. Olam, "world," comes from the same root as the word for
"hidden." Luria taught that there is a parallel world to ours—the heavenly realm, invisible to the eye. Everything we do to heal the material
plane here on earth will heal the divine realm as well. Of course, high and
low, and heavenly and earthly, are metaphors for our own consciousness.

Luria recognized our yearning for a unified world and taught that,
in each moment of existence, we have the potential to raise holy sparks.
Other traditions similarly emphasize theologies of nonduality, monistic
systems of total unity. They remind us of our failure to see the unity
that has always existed, and still does. For example, our human view of
the universe is referred to in Sanskrit as *maya* or "illusion"—we are
trapped behind a series of veils that "distort" reality. But, in fact, there is
only oneness, and multiplicity is imaginary. This world appears to be
pluralistic only because our awareness is limited. Other systems teach
that wholeness awaits us only in the afterlife; polarities don't exist in
heaven. And in contemporary America, *tikkun olam* has taken on a secular meaning as well. The phrase is used to exhort us to mend the
disharmonies of the world through the pursuit of social justice.

These can be such beautiful visions. They awaken our own yearnings for wholeness and healing. They urge us to integrate what appears
fragmented, including our broken, wounded selves, so that we finally
can feel peace and oneness with all of who we are. And we also hope for
a world that is healed and united. We see our separateness from each
other as the cause of poverty, injustice, and suffering. Broken shards are
everywhere waiting for us to retrieve them and to put them back to-

gether again. But what if, in labeling our pain and yearnings as pathological and in need of repair, we prevent our own self-actualization?
What if, in lamenting the world's brokenness and working toward Oneness, we extinguish those sparks? Suppose in our drive to love the whole
we exile the parts?

What if the shattering, itself, is the point?

After all, those sparks were part of God's dream, the original design.
The Big Bang was a divine contraction, a sacred eruption. All-that-is exploded so that the universe in all its multiplicity and unknowingness
could exist. What if God doesn't want to be made One again? What if
the fantasy of the whole actually keeps us distanced from the blessing of
diversity, from more and more life?

Throughout the centuries efforts toward wholeness and Oneness
have actually caused far more suffering than healing. Utopian revolu-
tions, crusades of conversion, manifest destiny, and redemptive jihads—
we're so scared of difference that we fight and kill for sameness and
call it the pursuit of unity. We're so frightened by our inner diversity
and unknowableness that we forget that this is in fact what makes us
human.

Our current consciousness crusaders who preach a new age of personal enlightenment and self-discovery create the thickest veil of all.
Our many selves get labeled as fragments; our complexity, confusion;
our pain, neuroses; our uniqueness, loneliness; our dissonance, cacoph-
ony; our vulnerability, weakness. And our sparks get ignored in our
quest for infinite light. This is *tikkun hanefesh*, "repair of the self," of the
inner world. But this dream of self-realization actually can sometimes
dim the magnificent kaleidoscope of our many selves. After all, we are
finite creatures who cannot perceive the infinite sparks, let alone gather
them. And rather than strive to make our selves one thing, we might do
better to recognize how we are constantly discovering new selves, new
facets of who we are.

We are strangers in a strange land, as the biblical sages remind us.
Strangers in a new land. Strangers to ourselves. D. W. Winnicott called

this the incommunicado element, a matrix of emotional experience that can never be fully communicated, a self that's impossible to breach. When we confront our own strangeness, we are less likely to project strangeness onto others. When we embrace our own lack of wholeness, our own complexities, we are less likely to be oppressors, even passively.

I remember attending my very first demonstration as a teenager. My compatriots and I chained ourselves to the fence around the Russian embassy in silent protest, letting our signs speak for us. We were protesting the treatment of Jews in the Soviet Union. I felt high on our cause, such a strong sense of belonging to something larger than myself.

We are constantly discovering new selves, new facets of who we are.

Tears filled my eyes as I imagined my fellow Jews trying to escape and being turned back, being persecuted and ostracized by other Russians. But something in me shifted as I quietly watched the groundskeepers mowing and clipping in the early morning light, and the cleaning women arriving in old, beat-up cars, greeting each other in Russian. I felt my heart sinking, my rage soften. I thought, "Are these the people to whom my anger is directed? Are they evil? Are they hurting anyone? I don't even know them."

When we feel whole, often it's because we've ejected the other. Our worldview designates them as outsiders, people who must be eliminated. When there's no tolerance for sparks—the multiplicity within every People, every Nation, every Religion—the world may be more unified, but it's also a lot smaller. Dreams of unity and oneness are so dangerous because they can feel so right. They temporarily ease our anxieties and guilt about our judgments of others. When we preach the value of uniqueness, we often deceive ourselves by making the unique less frightening than it actually is.

When I was in college—and I imagine this hasn't changed much—there was much talk about "diversity," pride in how many ethnicities were being successfully recruited, especially by the white administrators. This was followed by the inevitable disappointment: Why was everyone sitting with his or her own group in the cafeteria? Why weren't people bonding? Where was the unity? What happened to the integrative dream? Of course, it was all so patronizing. The people who considered themselves the Ones were recruiting the Others to be part of the One. We appreciate your uniqueness. Now join Us, and make us feel good about being the Unifiers. Confirm for us who we already think we are. How different would the recruiting have been if those administrators saw their own inner diversity; if the white students perceived their own otherness and we remembered that we are all strangers. Maybe then there would have been a genuine openness and curiosity, a commonality of difference.

Martin Buber, in his influential book *I and Thou*, teaches that we each have our own integrity: you in your subjectivity and me in mine. Separateness and distinctiveness are crucial to the flourishing of any relationship. When we avoid objectifying or subsuming the other, we can truly be intimate. What if we said "I love you" out of a sense of awe of our lover's uniqueness? What if we had a genuine appreciation and celebration of our lover's uncanny differences, of the sparks which we only glimpse but never wholly understand or know? "I love you" would retain its mystery, its magic: It would have so much more meaning. Even periods of conflict become opportunities for still more revelation.

Most people doubt this is possible. I've heard many people say that human beings are hardwired to resist what feels different or alien. But haven't we all had the experience of embracing the other? Perhaps there is no such hardwiring and we just need better software. Our current software with its visions of oneness and unconditional love, as beautiful as they may seem, in fact really only intensifies our alienation. It's time to realize that repairing the world is not about gathering the sparks, but about dignifying each one.

There's no surrendering our differences. There's no absorbing embrace that removes distinctions. What's enlivening is not what is similar about us but what is different. What is life-affirming is the ever-expanding uniqueness of our selves and the uniqueness of others. What's important is that we share an interest in each other's strangeness; that we're one with our diversity.

It's time for a new generation of seekers to reinterpret Luria's kabbalistic vision, to embrace a messy messianism rather than a glorified, unified one. It's time to create a more evolved mystical teaching that challenges us to celebrate rather than fear the anarchy, mystery, and multiplicity of the spark-filled cosmos.

The deeper truth is that there is no cohesive self awaiting our discovery; no world waiting to be redeemed. There is no unity behind the curtain. The mystical realization that awaits us is not a leap into Oneness but a soaring into solidarity with and empathy for all the world's multiplicities.

These radical mystical ideas are present in all spiritual systems: They are sparks themselves, lost in the blinding light and seductive unity of the bonfire. If we look more closely at our own respective cultural and religious stories, we will find the sparks of this humbling insight and no longer feel a need to preach ultimate Oneness as the only truth. We need to shatter our myopia of wholeness and contract to make room for new light. Maybe then we'll be able to feel the depth and expansiveness of our vulnerability; our yearning to be loved for all of the many things we are and have yet to be.

In this light, we can read the story of the Tower of Babel not as an allegory about punishment or curse, but a teaching about blessing. What if the scattering of people and creation of so many languages was an act of liberation? The story tells us of a time when everyone in the world spoke a single language. At some point the people got the idea that to "make a name for themselves" they would build a city with a tower that reached to the heavens. When God took notice of their project he asked, "Is this how a unified people act? Now nothing will be beyond their reach." So God confounded their language, "making babble of the whole world" so that no one would understand each other. And God dispersed the people all over the earth.

The rabbis asked, "What was so bad about Babel? When a brick fell on someone's head, no one cared because they were building toward heaven." The height meant more than life itself. The people's obsession with making a name for themselves caused them to forget about the individual human being destroyed by those very efforts. Here's the thing about reaching for the heavens: In order to be all-one, an awful lot of people get hurt.

And so it was actually an act of love and mercy to disperse the people of Babel. The hope now was that, rather than destroying each other for the sake of being one, human beings could thrive, unfold, create breathtaking poetry in thousands of tongues, and spread light all over the earth. Rather than only One, there now would be an infinite number of ways to interpret and understand life.

One of the first nursery rhymes we recite to our children isn't so different from that biblical allegory. "Humpty Dumpty sat on a wall. Humpty Dumpty had a great fall. All the king's horses and all the king's men couldn't put Humpty together again." It's an edgy tale, even for grownups. From a young age, our deepest fear is that we're Humpty Dumpty, that we'll fall and shatter into so many pieces that no one will be able to put us back together again; that we'll be dispersed across the face of the earth and be alone in our brokenness. The story makes us wonder if we haven't already fallen and become irreparably splintered. The ditty makes light of that very real fear and helps soften it.

> **What's enlivening is not what is similar about us but what is different. There's no surrendering our differences.**

But what if we taught this story differently? Maybe Humpty jumped. Maybe he was stuck in his own Tower of Babel on top of that wall and wanted desperately to get down. Maybe the "great fall" was actually a deepening and expansion of his consciousness—a startling vision of his many selves. What if Humpty didn't want to be what the king wanted to him to be? He didn't want to be put back together again; to be an egg so full of the promise of life but giving birth to nothing. He didn't want to reach for the heavens; he wanted to be down on earth where the action is. What if what really happened is that he hatched?

After all, isn't that what happened to God when those vessels shattered? There's an edgy mystical teaching that captures the Kabbalisitic paradox of destruction and creation. It's a story about the ancient Temple in Jerusalem, which was the seat of the Divine One. In the Temple the presence of God was like holding a bottle of perfume under your nose: intense, powerful, subsuming. When the Temple was destroyed, devastating though it was, God's presence was actually liberated. The perfume spread around the world. The fragrance was less intense in any one place but so much more accessible, widespread, and, some say, even sweeter.

After the destruction of the Temple, the study table and the kitchen table become the new altars where, with the right intention, sparks of wisdom can be revealed. The bedroom becomes a sacred chamber, where *Shekinah* can manifest. Whenever a judge delivers a just decision, whenever anyone visits the sick, God is present. Acts of loving kindness would reconstruct our temples, and blessings would reenchant the world. Blessings release the light in every spark; every food we eat, every new thing we experience, every moment we're alive. There's a beautiful blessing that's said when you encounter a large crowd of people, "Praised are You who knows all of the secrets." Praised are You who created all this strangeness and distinctiveness. Praised are You for never putting it all back together.

There's a related but rarely cited vision of the messianic day in the book of Isaiah. "In that day, there shall be a highway from Egypt to Assyria. The Assyrians will join with the Egyptians; and the Egyptians with the Assyrians, for God will bless them, saying 'Blessed be My people Egypt, My handiwork Assyria, and My very own Israel.'" Isaiah proclaimed this when Egypt and Assyria were still archenemies of Israel; when Egypt was the biblical archetype of enslavers; and Assyria the destroyer of the northern kingdom. This vision translated to today might read: "Blessed be My people of Iran, My handiwork the people North Korea, and My very own people of America." Here, each nation in its own integrity (not its leadership) becomes beloved. Unlike so many other messianic stories, in this version, the "good guys" don't win the day and we don't become one people. Isaiah's scene is a profound affirmation of difference: three warring nations secure in their distinctiveness and connected in all their diversity with the capacity for being beloved.

IT MAY SEEM like a peculiar image, but when I look at a concrete sidewalk after it rains—all the broken pieces of glass and rock glistening—I get a visual hit of this more radical *tikkun olam*. The ordinary suddenly becomes glorious. The cement isn't as mundane or seamless as it might normally appear. Its luminousness shines forth from its diversity. Like that sidewalk, suddenly alight, we are not simply the sum of our parts. But we need to remind ourselves of that. We need to let the rain fall on us once in a while. Sometimes, we need to jump off that wall. We don't need to transcend, but to see as many sparks as possible, to sink into the messiness, to fall in love with multiplicity. We need to tune in to the conversation that is always going on among our many selves, and the dialogue, the contradictions, the harmony, and the dissonance that fills the world.

Sometimes it takes a tragedy to get us to this place. So it was for my friend Isabel. She grew up in a tough neighborhood and a broken home; she described herself as a survivor. She'd put herself through school and created the kind of family she'd always wanted—a husband who was kind and a daughter who would have everything Isabel didn't. She had a fiery, formidable personality; confrontational; no bullshit. And she also could be wild and provocative; yelling out in meetings at work

> We are more than simply the sum of our parts.

when she was bored or irritated, smoking like a fiend, and when she had to let loose, drinking until dawn. Except for those occasional binges, Isabel seemed to know exactly where she was going, and she was going there fast. Type A didn't even begin to describe Isabel. Her aggressive nature was matched only by her tremendous warmth. She was a loyal, loving friend.

The year she hit fifty, Isabel was diagnosed with a virulent form of bone cancer. We feared her reaction to a challenge she couldn't easily conquer. As one might expect, she was often angry and despairing and spoke of her terror of dying. As she said, referring to her chemotherapy, "I don't need to smoke now. I'm being smoked." But something had changed about her. She seemed to have arrived at a new dynamic equilibrium: Her intensity was somehow contained. She seemed so fully alive. I found myself talking to her about problems I was facing, not because she'd give me an answer but because she seemed so comfortable with the questions.

After months of tests and chemo, the doctors still couldn't locate the source of the cancer. At some point they determined that Isabel would be able to live with the cancer, but would never be cured. It would be a chronic disease that might eventually kill her. She'd be in chemo for the rest of her life. One week I'd see her and she had her hair back; the next time it would be gone. "Now I'm really a survivor," she once said with an abrupt laugh, "except I don't know of what. I don't know when I'll need a haircut and when a wig. And I don't know if the cancer will eat me alive."

I found myself thinking, aren't we all survivors? Isn't everything chronic? Isn't there some brokenness within us that can never be healed, no matter how we "treat" it? Can't being shattered release even more of our sparks? I wondered if, like Humpty, Isabel was being hatched. The way she lived now in her uncertainty seemed so much more honest. She was so vulnerable and yet so fierce; in so much pain and yet healing in such profound ways; so terrified, yet so wise.

Isabel's prognosis is now much improved, but I still think of her as being my rabbi of brokenness, my priestess of sparks. She taught me that no one is sum-up-able. Our parts, our fragments, are so much richer than any whole. One day she said to me, "I used to think I'd take the world by storm. Now the storm has got me." I responded with a quote I remembered from the first century sage Hillel, also a lover of fragments and contradictions. I told her, "Keep two pieces of paper in your pocket at all times. One says 'I am a speck of dust.' On the other,

'The world was created for me.'" Always the one to have the last word, Isabel said she didn't need a pocket; she wore it on her shiny, naked head for everyone to see.

Isabel perfectly embodied the wisdom of comedian Gilda Radner, who died from cancer and wrote one of my favorite insights about life. "I wanted to wrap this book up in a neat little package. Now I've learned the hard way that some poems don't rhyme. Some stories don't have a clear beginning, middle and end. I've learned that life is about not-knowing and having to change and I've discovered that life is filled with ambiguity. Delicious ambiguity."

Of all the biblical characters, Moses was a master of not-knowing. He was the passionate defender of ambiguity. He was a mythic priest of brokenness with all his stuttering and questioning; his unfulfilled yearning for the Promised Land; his leadership over an unruly people; his continual wrestling with God and with death. Indeed, Moses even names his first son "Stranger in a strange land" so both he and his son Gershom won't forget their origins—and so that we won't forget ours.

Moses was a preacher of uniqueness, a lover of sparks. He chose to listen rather than run from the burning bush and then left his peaceful "whole" life to free a people who were being oppressed for being different. And he fought for them even when they recklessly strayed from "the way."

In his humility, this patriarch of freedom, this leader of a people who would be a great nation knew that wholeness was a momentary illusion. Maybe that's why he had the audacity and courage to shatter the stone tablets when he came down from Sinai and witnessed the people worshipping the golden calf. Moses saw the dangers of the yearning for oneness. He knew the tablets of insight would only become another calf.

So rather than see divinity idolatrized, Moses threw the holy tablets to the ground, breaking them into so many pieces it was impossible to count. One might think that after he calmed down that he'd try to put them back together in some act of superhuman strength, like in the miracles in Egypt. Or maybe that he'd bemoan the loss of the divine word.

But in another amazing scene, Moses creates new tablets himself. These were earthly tablets; grounded insights. And he puts them into the Ark right next to the fragments from Sinai. The Ark then becomes the guiding light on the desert journey; our guiding light as we wander through the desert in wonder always on the way to the Promised Land.

I like to imagine what would happen if the Ark were actually discovered one hundred years from now. If it were to be found, what treasure of wisdom would be waiting? First, I picture the Ark in all its beauty and mystery traveling through that desert for those forty years; residing peacefully in the heart of the ancient Temple for centuries; somehow surviving the destruction of the Temple; lying buried for millennia.

Then, I imagine that, miraculously, one day we find it.

We're afraid to touch it at first. When we do we're both relieved and disappointed that it's not too hot to handle, as legend has it. The Ark is worn and fragile and yet still very beautiful. We can't wait to hold those tablets and sort through the fragments; maybe even keep some as souvenirs. We open the Ark. Our hands are shaking in anticipation of the truths we will find. And what do we see? Dust. Wait, where are the tablets? Where are the fragments?

Our distress soon turns to laughter as we take handfuls of dust and throw them up into the air. The dust flies in the wind, illuminated and glistening; then falls to the ground in a haze of light. We wonder aloud which dust was from the fragmented tablets and which was from the whole. Then we laugh even louder: Does it even make a difference?

It's all magic dust.

ACKNOWLEDGMENTS

AUTHORSHIP IS NEVER ORIGINAL. LIKE ALL CREATIVE enterprises, it is collaborative: dependent on the support, ideas, and influence of others past and present. I am profoundly grateful to the many people in my life who have contributed to making *Yearnings* a reality.

I am indebted to Linda Loewenthal, with whom I wrote this book. Linda is my muse. We shared hours and hours of intense conversation and more sandwiches and cups of coffee than I can count. Her excitement, perseverance, dedication, clarity of vision, sensitivity, and immense talent midwifed this book. Linda has done much more than capture my voice. She's a teacher of wisdom in her own right and I have learned much from her. I also want to thank Eric, Sam, and Ben for their support of Linda and their insight throughout the writing process.

I'm deeply grateful to David Black, my extraordinary literary agent, who has been an endless source of encouragement and confidence. From the moment we met, he overwhelmed me with his faith in people, his love for books, and his unmatched integrity. He was wise enough, throughout the writing of this book, to give me the freedom to find my voice and the firm guidance that ensured the book's completion. He is a confidant and friend.

Thank you to Hyperion for the way they got behind this book from the beginning. Hyperion president Bob Miller literally changed my life. He saw the possibility of a book before there was a word on a page. His unwavering interest and support have been invaluable. In a country polarized by religious and secular fundamentalisms, Bob took a chance on a first-time author because he had faith that a spiritual, thoughtful, and pluralist exploration of our yearnings using Jewish wisdom could be taken public. I am forever grateful. Thank you to Ellen Archer and her dedicated and innovative team for helping to bring *Yearnings* out into the world; to my editor, Bill Strachan, whose sensitive editorial comments and gentle touch were invaluable as I worked to improve the text; to Brenda Copeland for stepping in with passion, joy, and skill to help bring the book to fruition.

Jay Sanderson, the tireless president of JTN Productions, planted the first seeds of this book by producing and directing my thirteen-part public-television series, *Simple Wisdom*. The success of *Simple Wisdom* directly led to *Yearnings*, and it is Jay who has directed and produced the upcoming public-television special based on this book. Jay thinks big, believes in people, and is the most loyal of friends.

I owe a huge debt of gratitude to my colleagues at CLAL—The National Jewish Center for Learning and Leadership, a unique setting of creativity and imagination, where I am privileged to serve as president. Rabbi Brad Hirschfield has been my intellectual partner for the past decade. We finish each other's sentences, challenge each other's thinking, and celebrate each other's successes. Our relationship is proof that pluralism is not an intellectual abstraction, but a method of leading.

I am deeply appreciative to Donna Rosenthal, the executive vice chairman of CLAL. Donna has made CLAL a first-class non-profit operation, freeing me to think, teach, and write. She is a talented and formidable executive who cares deeply about people and is eternally optimistic. Her unwavering commitment to this book was as responsible for it becoming a reality as any other factor.

Special thanks to Janet R. Kirchheimer, my assistant. Besides being a published poet in her own right, a source of ideas, and a wonderful editor, she is the perfect assistant, who ensures my life runs smoothly. Thank you to the faculty at CLAL—Rabbi Tsvi Blanchard, one of the smartest people I know, who is always willing to help me think more clearly; to

Dr. Michael Gottsegen, Rabbi Steve Greenberg, and Dr. David Kraemer. I have learned much from all of them. Thank you to the administrative staff—Meredith Appell, Ruth Bregman, Dale Brown, Judy Epstein, Aliza Kaplan, Theresa Perruzza, Anna Rakhlin, and Cynthia Schupf.

Thank you to the past chairs of CLAL during the time I have been president—Radine Spier for the transition; Charles Bronfman for his generosity; Barbara Friedman for the sabbatical; Tom Katz for deep friendship; Fern Hurst for commitment. Each, in their own way, has contributed to making CLAL a secure place to fearlessly explore Jewish wisdom and the human spirit, and has ensured that I had the space and support to write this book.

This book could not have been written without the inspiration and support of teachers and friends. Unending gratitude to my teacher Rabbi Irving "Yitz" Greenberg, the founder and president emeritus of CLAL. Yitz has been the single most important teacher in my life since that day we met more than two decades ago and sat overlooking the Atlantic Ocean talking for eight hours straight about the "third era" in Jewish history. Yitz is an intellectual giant, a daring theologian, and an enchanting teacher. He is among the most religiously and intellectually sophisticated pluralists in the world and, not surprisingly, a teacher who celebrates his students' accomplishments even when he disagrees.

Thank you to Professor Joshua Halberstam, who read this book with such care and concern. Joshua provided the kind of sage counsel that could only come from someone deeply steeped in Jewish sources and general philosophy. Joshua is a true renaissance man and his wide-ranging intellect, sharp wit, and warm friendship helped me in more ways than I can express.

Thank you to Rabbi Joseph Telushkin. We have been blessed to have him and his family as our upstairs neighbors. Joseph read this book with his unique ethical genius and Jewish knowledge. His very constructive comments made *Yearnings* a more sensitive and inclusive book. He is the most dependable guide I know to doing the right thing.

I am most blessed to have wonderful friends. I can't imagine what my life would be like without Richie Pearlstone, who has taught me a love for life, mountain biking, and how to run a business; Gary Davis, who has been my mentor in the classical, spiritual understanding of that word; Al Engelberg for his moral passion, sharp mind, flawless counsel, and fierce loyalty. Dr. Marc Slutsky, my chaver in the rabbinic understanding, for helping me understand my dreams of Torah. I thank them for their inspiration, instruction, friendship, and generosity.

Ongoing conversations with J. J. Goldberg and Shifra Bronznick, Benyamin Cirlin, Michael Goldberg, David Gitlitz, Miriam Ben Hayim, Carmi and Shelley Fredman, Jonathan Jacoby, Rabbis Roly Matalon and Michael Paley, John Ruskay, Ken and Debra Tuchman. Each in their own way has enriched me intellectually, emotionally, and spiritually. Thank you to Barry and Mindy Gavrin, my oldest friends, who in the early years made sure I had dinner.

There is no *Yearnings* without my intense and loving family. My in-laws—Janice and Jules Kurzweil—break every in-law stereotype imaginable. They have been another ever-loving Mom and Dad, and I have learned much about love for children from them. They have profoundly enriched my life, and I love them dearly.

The stories in this book about my mother and father, Charlotte and Morton Kula, can only hint at their immeasurable influence on my life. They are among the most developed and evolved people I know. But their greatest contribution to my life has been my five brothers, Aaron, Mark, Barry, Elliot, and David, each of whom I love dearly. We live all around the country, and every brother speaks to every brother at least once a week. That says it all.

There is a saying—the last, the last is the most dear. Just as there are no words to adequately describe God, I have no words that can adequately express my love for my wife, Dana Kurzweil, my friend, partner, spouse, "lifer," and lover, and our beautiful and passionate children, Gabriella Leah Mirit and Talia Hadas. They have created a life of sweetness, stimulation, adventure, comfort and joy, laughter and dreams. They put up with my absences, listen to my ideas, and keep me grounded. So many of my yearnings revolve around them and it is they who have taught me I can want it all and always have enough.

I thank God for the privilege of being alive at this hour with all its conflicts and tensions and opportunities that call for courage, moral imagination, and deeper understanding of our yearnings for the infinite.

BIBLIOGRAPHY

Albacete, Lorenzo. *God at the Ritz: Attraction to Infinity*.
New York: Crossroads Publishing, 2002.

Berlin, Isaiah, and Henry Hardy, editors. *The Proper Study of Mankind*.
New York: Farrar, Straus, Giroux, 1997.

Bialik, Hayim Nahman, and Ravnitzky, Yehoshua Hana.
The Book of Legends. Translated by William Braude.
New York: Schocken Books, 1992.

Bloom, Harold. "Freud and Beyond," in *Ruin the Sacred Truths:
Poetry and Belief from the Bible to the Present*.
Cambridge: Harvard University Press, 1987.

Buber, Martin. *I and Thou*. Translated by Walter Kaufman.
New York: Free Press. 1971

Chopra, Deepak. *How to Know God*. New York: Harmony Books, 2000.

Csikszentmihalyi, Mihaly. *Flow: The Psychology of Optimal Experience*.
New York: HarperCollins, 1990.

Dalai Lama. *The Art of Happiness*. New York: Riverhead Books, 1998.

Dass, Ram. *Still Here*. New York: Riverhead Books, 2000.

During, Simon, editor. *The Cultural Studies Reader*.
New York: Routledge, 1993.

Dyer, Wayne W. *Wisdom of the Ages*. New York: HarperCollins, 1998.

Fish, Stanley. *The Trouble with Principle*.
Cambridge: Harvard University Press, 1999.

Fox, Mathew. *One River, Many Wells*. New York: Putnam Books, 2000.

Fox, Mathew. *Sins of the Spirit, Blessings of the Flesh*.
New York: Harmony Books, 1999.

Freud, Sigmund. *Civilization and Its Discontents*. Translated by James Strachey. New York: Norton, 1966 (orig. 1930).

Fromm, Erich. *You Shall Be As Gods*. New York: Holt, Rinehart and Winston, 1966.

Gallagher, Winifred. *Working on God*. New York: Random House, 1999.

Genesis Rabbah. Translated by H. Freedman. New York: Soncino Press, 1983.

Gergen, Kenneth J. *The Saturated Self*. New York: Basic Books, 1991.

Greenberg, Rabbi Irving. "Cloud of Smoke, Pillar of Fire," in *Auschwitz*, ed. Eva Fleischer. New York: Ktav, 1977.

Greenberg, Irving. *The Jewish Way*. New York: Summit Books, 1988.

Greene, Brian. *The Elegant Universe*. New York: Vintage Books, 1999.

Grimes, Ronald. *Readings in Ritual Studies*. New Jersey: Prentice Hall, 1996.

Halberstam, Joshua. *Everday Ethics*. New York: Penguin, 1993.

Hammerschlag, Carl. *The Theft of the Spirit*. New York: Fireside Publishing, 1992.

Heschel, Abraham Joshua. *Man Is Not Alone*. New York: Harper & Row, 1951.

Jabès, Edmond. *The Book of Questions*. Translated by R. Waldrop. Middletown, CT: Wesleyan University Press, 1978.

Jacobson, Simon. *60 Days: A Spiritual Guide to the High Holidays*. New York: Kiyum Press, 2003.

James, William. *The Varieties of Religious Experience*. New York: Macmillan Publishing, 1961.

Keen, Sam. *To a Dancing God*. San Francisco: HarperCollins, 1990.

Kraemer, David. *The Mind of the Talmud*. New York: Oxford University Press, 1990.

Kornfield, Jack. *A Path with Heart*. New York: Bantam Books, 1993.

Kushner, Harold. *When All You Ever Wanted Isn't Enough*. New York: Summit Books, 1986.

Lama Surya Das. *Letting Go of the Person You Used to Be*. New York: Broadway Books, 2003.

Lasch, Christopher. *The Culture of Narcissism*. New York: Norton, 1978.

Lew, Alan. *This Is Real and You Are Completely Unprepared.*
New York: Little, Brown, 2003.

Lifton, Robert Jay. *The Protean Self.* New York: Basic Books, 1993.

Loeb, Paul Rogat. *Soul of a Citizen.* New York: St. Martin's Press, 1999.

Miles, Jack. *God: A Biography.* New York: Knopf, 1995.

Needelman, Jacob. *A Little Book on Love.* New York: Dell, 1996.

Needelman, Jacob. *The Heart of Philosophy.* New York: Knopf, 1982.

Prager, Marcia. *The Path of Blessing.*
New York: Bell Tower, 1998.

Quinby, Lee. *Millennial Seduction.*
New York: Cornell University Press, 1999.

Ricoeur, Paul. *The Conflict of Interpretations.* Edited by Don Idhe.
Illinois: Northwestern University Press, 1974.

Safran, Jeremy. *Pscyhoanalysis and Buddhism.*
Boston: Wisdom Publications, 2003.

Santner, Eric. *On the Psychotheology of Everyday Life.*
Chicago: University of Chicago Press, 2001.

Santoni, Ronald, editor. *Religious Language and the Problem of Religious Knowledge.* Bloomington: Indiana University Press, 1968.

Schacther-Shalomi, Zalman. *Hello God, It's Me.*
New York: Riverhead Books, 2001.

Schacther-Shalomi, Zalman. *Wrapped in a Holy Flame.*
San Francisco: Jossey-Bass, 2003.

Sexson, Lynda. *Ordinarily Sacred.*
Charlottesville: University of Virginia Press, 1992.

Shapiro, Rami. *Hasidic Tales.*
Woodstock: Skylight Paths Publishing, 2004.

Talmud Bavli. Translated by Maurice Simon.
London: Soncino Press, 1984.

Tanakh: The Holy Scriptures.
New York: Jewish Publication Society of America, 1985.

Taylor, Mark C. *Erring: A Post Modern A/theology.*
Chicago: University of Chicago Press, 1984.

Teilhard de Chardin, Pierre. *On Happiness.* London: Harper&Row, 1973.

Wilber, Ken. *A Theory of Everything*. Boston: Shambhala, 2000.

Williamson, Marianne. *The Gift of Change*.
    San Francisco: HarperSanFrancisco, 2004.

Zornberg, Avivah Gottlieb. *Genesis: The Beginning of Desire*.
    New York: Jewish Publication Society of America, 1995.

Zornberg, Avivah Gottlieb. *The Particulars of Rapture*.
    New York: Doubleday, 2001.

Zweg, Connie. *The Holy Longing*. Boulder: Sentient Publications, 2004.

Steve Friedman and CLAL

RABBI IRWIN KULA is an eighth-generation rabbi, nationally known speaker and teacher, and the president of the National Jewish Center for Learning and Leadership. He is also the host of the public television broadcast called *The Wisdom of Our Yearnings*. Rabbi Kula lives with his wife and daughters in New York City.

LINDA LOEWENTHAL is a writer and literary agent who has published and promoted spiritual and religious books.